UNDERSTANDING AND DOING EARLY CHILDHOOD RESEARCH

Jo Josephidou & Polly Bolshaw

UNDERSTANDING AND DOING EARLY CHILDHOOD RESEARCH

3rd Floor
HYLO
103–105 Bunhill Row
London, EC1Y 8LZ
UK

2455 Teller Road
Thousand Oaks
California 91320

10th Floor, Emaar Capital Tower
2 MG Road, Sikanderpur, Sector 26
Gurugram, Haryana – 122002
India

8 Marina View Suite 43-053
Asia Square Tower 1
Singapore 018960

Editor: James Clark
Editorial assistant: Harry Dixon
Production editor: Sarah Cooke
Marketing manager: Lorna Patkai
Cover design: Sheila Tong
Typeset by: C&M Digitals (P) Ltd, Chennai, India
Printed in the UK by Bell and Bain Ltd
BB0363641

Library of Congress Control Number:
2025947189

British Library Cataloguing in Publication data

A catalogue record for this book is available from the British Library

ISBN 978-1-5296-9045-3
ISBN 978-1-5296-9046-0 (pbk)

CONTENTS

ABOUT THE AUTHORS

Jo Josephidou is Associate Head of School for Research and Knowledge Exchange in the School of ECYS (Education, Childhood, Youth and Sport) at The Open University. With a professional background as a primary school teacher (Early Years), her research interests include appropriate pedagogies for young children.

Polly Bolshaw is a Senior Lecturer in Early Years at Canterbury Christ Church University. Previously she worked as an Early Years Professional in a Sure Start Children's Centre. Research interests include the experiences of young children outdoors and research methods for undergraduate students. She is currently undertaking a Professional Doctorate at The Open University about babies' perspectives of the outdoors.

ACKNOWLEDGEMENTS

Thanks to everyone who enjoys discussing research with us as we continue our own personal research journeys.

PART I
UNDERSTANDING EARLY CHILDHOOD RESEARCH

PART I

UNDERSTANDING EARLY CHILDHOOD RESEARCH

1

WHAT IS RESEARCH IN EARLY CHILDHOOD AND WHY DOES IT MATTER?

CHAPTER OBJECTIVES

By the end of this chapter, you will:

- Understand what we mean by research in Early Childhood
- Recognise why Early Childhood Research matters
- Consider what topics you will explore as you read through this book.

INTRODUCTION

Welcome to *Understanding and Doing Early Childhood Research*. This book is designed to take you through the process of completing a research study in the field of Early Childhood. It will support you in understanding Early Childhood Research, developing your skills of how to plan your study, collect your data and analyse your findings before finally thinking about how to present and disseminate your research study.

Back in 2018 we published a book called *Introducing Research in Early Childhood* (Bolshaw and Josephidou, 2018), which supports those studying Early Childhood to understand what research in Early Childhood means, what it involves and how people conduct it. We then began thinking about how it would be useful for Early Childhood students to have a text that they themselves could follow to conduct their own research study. This became especially relevant as we carried out more research of our own (e.g. Kemp, Josephidou and Bolshaw, 2025) and became more mindful of ethical and power issues within Early Childhood Research and the need to foreground approaches that challenge issues of power and promote inclusivity in how Early Childhood Research is conducted.

This book is intended to respond to the need for Early Childhood students to have a guide to conduct their own piece of Early Childhood Research, drawing on some of the more innovative approaches to research, which challenge the power imbalances that can exist when research studies are planned, conducted and disseminated.

This first chapter of the book aims to put Early Childhood Research into context. It begins with a consideration of what research in Early Childhood is, how it should be conducted and who carries it out. It then considers some of the reasons why research in Early Childhood is important, drawing on ideas by Tisdall, Davis and Gallagher (2009). Finally, it introduces you to the structure of this book, outlining each of the sections in this book and showing you how you can use it to successfully complete your own research project.

WHAT IS RESEARCH IN EARLY CHILDHOOD?

Let's begin by thinking about what we mean by research in Early Childhood, explore some of the principles in how we think it should be conducted and consider who conducts Early Childhood Research.

What Do We Mean by Research?

You might talk about carrying out research as part of your everyday life: for instance, 'researching' on Google to find the best hotel to stay in on holiday, or when the last train is. In your university life you might talk about going to the library to 'research' a new topic that you've been introduced to in a lecture. When you use it in this sense, 'to research' means to find out something new that we didn't know before.

In an academic sense, we consider research in Early Childhood to be related to investigations, studies and experiments that contribute new information about young children, their lives, their families and their communities. In this sense it is about creating new knowledge, rather than learning knowledge that has already been acquired or provided by someone else. For example, let's say a reception class teacher wants to conduct research on what nursery educators think they need to do to help children make the transition to school. They carry out a study by interviewing nursery educators and analysing the conversations they have. This helps them come up with new knowledge, which researchers call 'findings', about how nursery educators support children to start school. This information might agree with what other researchers have found. Alternatively, it might contradict existing research-informed practice, and lead to changes in what teachers and nursery educators do.

In this book, we define research in Early Childhood as being about asking questions that we have about children and their lives and attempting to answer those questions by discovering new knowledge, opinions, perspectives and understandings. This fits with other definitions of research, such as by Fraser (2004, p. 16) who says conducting research is like discovery 'either because "no one has been there before" or because someone predicts what it is like there even though no one has been there'. Others note the importance of the role of enquiry within research, such as Lobe, Livingstone and Haddon (2007, p. 6) who explain 'research is designed to answer questions'. File et al. (2016, p. 2) echo this, suggesting that 'research revolves around questions, and typically in the search for more understanding, more questions arise'. Although these definitions are all slightly different, you can see the commonalities between them. Research is about generating knowledge and answers to questions – sometimes questions that have been asked before, and sometimes questions that haven't. With regards to young children, this might relate to questions about what children's experiences are, why they have those experiences and what we think the impact of those experiences might be.

How Should Research in Early Childhood Be Conducted?

In this book we are going to consider many ways that research in Early Childhood can be carried out. Some researchers choose to recruit participants to help them answer their research question, whereas others rely on secondary sources of data such as children's television programmes. Some researchers collect qualitative data while others generate data that is quantitative. Sometimes the findings of research studies are presented in reports and other times they are disseminated via podcasts, poster presentations or picture books. But however an Early Childhood Researcher goes about answering their research question, we believe there are three tenets that everyone should bear in mind:

- Early Childhood Research should be mindful of power imbalances and seek to minimise them.
- Early Childhood Research should maintain ethical compliance and uphold ethical values.
- Early Childhood Research should value young children's right to participation.

You will notice these three principles reflected across the rest of our chapters, particularly Chapter 2 (*Issues of power in Early Childhood Research*), Chapter 5 (*Ensuring we stay ethical*), Chapter 8 (*Centring the voice of the child*) and Chapter 9 (*Centring the voice of the very young child*).

Who Carries But Research in Early Childhood?

When we think about who conducts research in Early Childhood, we might think about an individual who carries out studies on a very small scale, or we might think of projects funded by large organisations who seek to carry out bigger pieces of research. But just because the scale of the study is different, that doesn't mean what the research focuses on necessarily is. For instance, currently an organisation called The Nuffield Foundation is funding a project about baby rooms in English nurseries, providing almost £280,000 for the research team to investigate what quality Early Childhood provision looks like for children aged 0–2 (The Nuffield Foundation, 2025). An initial report by the researchers suggests that from the existing literature, more research needs to be conducted about what quality in baby rooms looks like for different stakeholders, including by gathering perspectives from babies themselves (Sakr, Bonetti and Halls, 2025).

Gathering babies' perspectives is something that Kirby (2024, p. 21), a nursery practitioner and Early Childhood undergraduate student, attempted to do as part of a Year 2 university module. She used timed/tracked narrative observations to listen to babies' 'engagement, actions and movement within their indoor nursery setting' (2024, p. 21). One of her findings was that there seemed to be an area of the baby room that babies chose not to access; Kirby suggests that this means this space needs to change. We might argue that through noting where very young children choose to spend and choose not to spend their time, this gives some insight into what babies think quality provision in their baby room looks like. Both Kirby's (2024) small-scale research and Sakr, Bonetti and Hall's (2025) large-scale project highlight the need to gather very young children's perspectives about their experiences in their Early Childhood settings. We will consider in more detail how to do this in Chapter 9 (*Centring the voice of the very young child*).

What Kirby's (2024) study also tells us is that research in Early Childhood is carried out by people like you, who are studying it or working in the field. You might not have the funding or time to do a large-scale project, but that doesn't mean you can't complete a small-scale piece of research which seeks to find out new knowledge and answer questions about young children and their Early Childhood experiences. This book is designed to help you do that.

Activity 1.1 Understanding Research in Early Childhood

Starting something new is always a great time to do a self-audit about how much knowledge you already have about a subject. Spend 15 minutes noting down everything you already know about Early Childhood Research. You might want to ask yourself questions such as:

- How would I define research in Early Childhood?
- What Early Childhood Research am I already familiar with?
- What are my principles about how research in Early Childhood should be conducted?

Reflection

It's okay if you didn't know the answers to some of the questions that we posed. You might want to come back to these questions periodically as you work through this book so that you can see your knowledge about Early Childhood Research growing. If you are thinking about starting a research diary, as people like Roberts-Holmes, Levy and Harmey (2023) recommend, you might want to record your answer to these questions in there, too.

WHY DOES RESEARCH IN EARLY CHILDHOOD MATTER?

When thinking about why research in Early Childhood matters, we draw upon the work of Tisdall, Davis and Gallagher (2009) who give several reasons why it is important. Three of the ones that stand out to us the most are because 'research might open up new possibilities for children, and society more generally' (Tisdall, Davis and Gallagher, 2009, p. 4), 'it can question the ways in which we have always done or thought about things' (2009, p. 4) and it can be a way 'to ensure that children's voices and experiences are not only listened to but heard by other groups' (2009, p. 5). We will now think about each of these reasons in more detail.

Early Childhood Research Opens Up New Possibilities For Children

By doing research in Early Childhood, new possibilities may open up for children. Take, for instance, research that has been conducted to evaluate the short- and medium-term effects of Sure Start children's centres on children's health and educational outcomes (Carneiro et al., 2025). The study found, for example, that access to a Sure Start centre between the ages of birth to 5 improved the educational attainment for children at least until they completed their GCSEs at age 16. Greater Sure Start coverage led to a reduction in the number of children requiring hospitalisation. This research has been used to inform new policy, for instance England's Department for Education's (2025) strategy for supporting young children's development, which in part hopes to achieve this by creating up to 1000 new Best Start Family Hubs, which 'will draw on what we know works from Sure Start and similar programmes' (Department for Education, 2025, p. 18). These 1000 new family hubs will offer young children possibilities that support their, and their families', health, wellbeing, development and education.

Early Childhood Research Helps Us Ask Questions About the Way Things Are Done

Doing research in Early Childhood can help us question the way things are done and whether they can be done in a different way. For example, earlier we spoke about the project about quality in English baby rooms, which is called *Achieving high quality provision in the baby room of English nurseries*. As part of the project, the researchers have conducted an international literature review about the quality of baby room provision (Sakr, Bonetti and Halls, 2025) and have also carried out a survey of more than 300 baby room educators and nursery managers (Sakr and Bonetti, 2025). One of the things that they have found is that in England the average baby room size group is 13 children, and some baby rooms have up to 30 babies at any one time. This is despite the fact that the literature suggests that a group size of six to eight babies has been identified as good practice and 'the literature also shows a strong connection between lower group sizes and lower ratios when it comes to supporting high-quality practice in the baby room' (Sakr, Bonetti and Halls, 2005, p. 4). This is for several reasons, including that babies can struggle to form close relationships in large rooms and the noisier environment can mean it's harder to hear and thus develop language and communication skills. Through doing research about baby room quality and group size, questions can be asked about why there currently isn't a limit on how many babies can be in one baby room in England, and recommendations can be made that group size in baby rooms is regulated.

Early Childhood Research Offers Opportunities for Children to Have Their Voice Heard

Finally, doing research in Early Childhood can give children opportunities to have their voice heard. For instance, Drury, Blaisdell and Matheson (2025) have undertaken research that seeks to explore babies' right to be heard, as this is underpinned by Article 12 of the United Nations Convention on the Rights of the Child (UNCRC). As part of this they have worked with a Scottish arts and early years organisation called *Starcatchers* to explore how right-based approaches can be integrated into creative play sessions for babies. Through this they have developed a model of participation to cement how important relationships are – with caregivers, artists and others – in facilitating babies' right to be heard. Their model takes into account that 'one thing that sets this age group apart from others is that babies and young children are accompanied by a caregiver(s) to help them become an integral part both of their participation experience and of their "voice' at this stage' (Drury and Blaisdell, 2024, p. 7).

Activity 1.2   Exploring Why Early Childhood Research is Conducted

One of the best ways to prepare yourself for conducting your own piece of research is by becoming more familiar with how other researchers have approached theirs. Looking at research published within Early Childhood journals is a great starting point. Have a look online at a recent issue of an Early Childhood journal. You might want to consider one such as *Early Years: An International Research Journal* or *Early Child Development and Care*. Read through the abstracts of each article within one issue and attempt to identify why the research that has been conducted matters.

Reflection

Research should matter, and the perceived benefits of conducting research should outweigh any risks involved. Hopefully having a look at some abstracts of recent pieces of Early Childhood Research has helped you to identify why the research matters and what the implications for children might be. We had a look at recent issues of two Early Childhood journals; *An International Research Journal*; Table 1.1 shares our reflections on some of the articles.

Table 1.1   Exploring examples of why Early Childhood Research matters

Article	Why does this research matter?
Sak, A., Şahin-Sak, I. and Öneren-Şendil, C. (2025) 'Examining the relationship between four to six year olds' school readiness levels and their parents' tolerance of risky play', *Early Years: An International Research Journal*. DOI: https://doi.org/10.1080/0957514 6.2025.2516092.	This research matters because it suggests that Turkish parents need more awareness of the benefits of risky play.
Küpeli, K. and Bayındır, D. (2025) 'Preschool outdoor education environment quality predicts children's environmental attitude, awareness and affinity towards nature (biophilia)', *Early Years: An International Research Journal*. DOI: https://doi.org/ 10.1080/09575146.2024.2444886.	This research matters because it suggests that if outdoor areas in Early Childhood settings are improved, this increases young children's affinity towards nature.
Dýrfjörð, K. and Hreinsdóttir, A. M. (2025) 'Paving the way for slow pedagogy: leadership lessons from Icelandic preschools', *European Early Childhood Education Research Journal*. DOI: 10.1080/1350293X.2025.2523040.	This research matters because it highlights that if early years settings adopt a slow pedagogy approach then this can bring benefits for both children and educators.

WHAT DOES THIS BOOK AIM TO DO?

We intend that by reading this book, you will have all the information you need to go about conducting your own small-scale piece of research. This is the first chapter of **Part I: Understanding Early Childhood Research**; in which you'll also consider the importance of power issues in Chapter 2. Then you'll move on to **Part II: Doing Research in Early Childhood**, which will introduce you to how to go about designing your research, joining a research conversation and ensuring you stay ethical. After that, **Part III: Methods and Analysis** consists of chapters that focus on specific approaches to research, like autoethnography, creative approaches and centring children's voices, then particular data collection methods like observations, questionnaires, surveys and interviews and then finally guidance on how to analyse your data and form your argument. Finally, **Part IV: Telling the World About Your Early Childhood Research** explores how to disseminate your research through a presentation, poster and in other creative ways, before concluding the book. This book is going to stress that:

- You can carry out a successful research project which can have a meaningful impact however small.
- Your voice counts in research, however novice you may feel, however marginalised you consider yourself to be whether because of job title, education up to this point, ethnic group or socio-economic status.
- Never stop looking for issues of power in both your research activity and beyond in your practice with young children.

We know that some readers will want to read this book cover to cover, and others will want to dip in and out of it as their study progresses. But what we would like to encourage you to think about is how for each step of your research project, there is a chapter that will provide help and guidance, from deciding on an area of focus all the way up to thinking about how to disseminate your findings. Table 1.2 outlines which chapters will help you with which steps of your research project.

Table 1.2 Using this book to help you with each step of your research project

Step	Chapter
1 Decide on an area of focus	3
2 Read about this area	4
3 Decide on a potential research question	3
4 Read some more!	4
5 Decide on your methodology	3
6 Decide on your data collection methods and approach	6–12
7 Get ethical approval	2 and 5
8 Collect your data	6–12
9 Analyse your data	13
10 Write up findings	13
11 Analyse findings	14
12 Decide on your argument	14
13 Disseminate your findings	15–17

We will now introduce you to each of the four parts of this book in more detail.

Part I: Understanding Early Childhood Research

We've already begun Part I by thinking about what research in Early Childhood is and why it matters. Hopefully you are beginning to have some views on what you think the most important reasons are for doing Early Childhood Research and perhaps you are starting to think about whether there are research topics in particular that you are interested in.

There is only one other chapter in Part I, which is Chapter 2 that focuses on *Issues of power in Early Childhood Research*. In that chapter we will consider some of the frequent power issues that exist in research, identify some of the voices that have traditionally dominated Early Childhood Research and recognise how prominence has been given to Early Childhood Research conducted in the Global North and published in the English language. The chapter will argue that it is important to challenge power imbalances, because if certain voices are allowed to dominate, our understanding about young children will be impoverished.

Part II: Doing Research in Early Childhood

After we've built our understanding of Early Childhood Research, we will then move on to thinking about how to do it. The three chapters in Part II focus on three key areas you need to think about before commencing data collection – *Designing your research project* (Chapter 3), *Joining a research conversation* (Chapter 4) and *Ensuring we stay ethical* (Chapter 5).

In *Designing your research project* (Chapter 3) we will explore what is meant by research design, how researchers must consider their positionality and how they might go about choosing a research topic. We will also explore how to think about your methodology, refine your research question and overcome some common challenges that students may face when collecting data.

We will then move on to *Joining a research conversation* (Chapter 4). This chapter focuses on building your understanding of what we mean by 'literature' and 'research conversation' before considering what strategies can be used to find appropriate literature and then how and why you need to consider literature before and after data collection, as well as potentially using the literature for your data collection, if you are undertaking a literature review.

The final chapter in Part II is *Ensuring we stay ethical* (Chapter 5). In this chapter we explore the differences between ethical values and ethical compliance, and how it's important to consider your ethical values to address any power imbalances in your work. This chapter also considers ethics in analysis and how the concepts of validity and reliability relate to being ethical.

Part III: Methods and Analysis

The next section of the book, Part III, focuses on how, when you've designed your project, considered the literature and sought ethical approval, you will move on to collecting and analysing your data. Within this part we first consider some approaches to research, namely, *Taking an autoethnographic approach* (Chapter 6), *Creative approaches to research* (Chapter 7), *Centring the voice of the child* (Chapter 8) and *Centring the voice of the very young child* (Chapter 9). We then move on to discuss particular data collection methods, namely *Conducting observations* (Chapter 10), *Surveys and questionnaires*

(Chapter 11) and *Interviewing adults and children* (Chapter 12). The final chapters in Part III explore what you do with your data once it's been collected, through *Analysing your data* (Chapter 13) and *Forming your argument* (Chapter 14).

In *Taking an autoethnographic approach* (Chapter 6) we think about what autoethnographic approaches can look like and why they might be effective in Early Childhood Research. We think about how some of the challenges of this approach can be overcome and also identify how marginalised voices can benefit from an autoethnographic approach, because of how it can address power imbalances. Then, within *Creative approaches to research* (Chapter 7) we explore what is meant by creative approaches, how to use them and what the challenges in adopting them might be. We then move on to *Centring the voice of the child* (Chapter 8), in which we think about what we mean by the voice of the child and how to go about capturing it. We build upon this in *Centring the voice of the very young child* (Chapter 9), where we focus specifically on how to listen to the perspectives of children aged up to 2.

After this we begin to explore particular data collection methods, beginning with *Conducting observations* (Chapter 10). Within this chapter we consider why you might want to use observations as a research tool, how they are commonly employed in Early Childhood Research and how the limitations of observations can be minimised. Then in *Surveys and questionnaires* (Chapter 11) we look at what the key differences are between surveys and questionnaires, how they can be useful in Early Childhood Research for both adults and children and what their strengths and limitations are. Within *Interviewing adults and children* (Chapter 12) we explore the different kinds of interviews that are used in research, how they can be used as a data collection tool and the complexity of power dynamics within an interviewer/interviewee situation.

Finally, the chapters move on to consider what you will do with your data once you've collected it. In *Analysing your data* (Chapter 13) we explore how to transfer your raw data into findings and how to then analyse those findings. This chapter includes information on how findings can be presented, and how the way in which data are analysed may depend on whether it has a qualitative or quantitative nature. The last chapter in Part III is *Forming your argument* (Chapter 14) and it focuses on how, once you've analysed your data, you can begin to form your argument. It explores what is meant by an 'argument' and why it's important that you have one when you write up your research study.

Part IV: Telling the World About Your Early Childhood Research

Part IV, the final section of this book, focuses on the diverse ways that students may want to present and share their research. It considers *Disseminating your research through a presentation* (Chapter 15), *Using posters to share your research* (Chapter 16) and *Taking other opportunities for publication* (Chapter 17). The last chapter is our *Conclusion: What's next?* (Chapter 18).

In *Disseminating your research through a presentation* (Chapter 15) we will be looking at how oral presentations can be an effective way to share your research findings. We will explore what effective structures might look like, how slides or other visual aids can support a smooth delivery and how to undertake both group and individual presentations successfully. We then move on to thinking about *Using posters to share your research* (Chapter 16). This chapter considers how posters can disseminate research and how they can be one of the most inclusive ways to share your findings with a diverse range of audiences. Finally, in *Taking other opportunities for publication* (Chapter 17) we explore why it's important to think about disseminating your research to a wider audience, who your potential audiences may be and some of the more diverse ways that you might want to think about doing this.

We finish the book with our *Conclusion: What's next?* (Chapter 18) which draws together the main messages for the book and reiterates how you can use Table 1.2 as a tool to use this book to guide you through the research process.

Activity 1.3   Thinking About Your Research Journey

As we've said, this book has four main parts which will guide you through conducting your own piece of research. Consider the list below, which is designed to get you thinking about what you already know about these areas.
   What do you already know about…

- Understanding Early Childhood Research?
- Doing Early Childhood Research?
- Methods and analysis?
- Telling the world about your Early Childhood Research?

Reflection

As in Activity 1.1, it's okay if you aren't sure of the answers to some of the questions yet. The most important thing is that you are reading this book because it will help build your knowledge of what Early Childhood Research is, how to do it and how to disseminate it once it's completed.

Case Study 1.1   Thinking About Approaching the Dissertation

Efi has just started her Level 6 Early Childhood Studies degree and has begun to think about her dissertation. She understands that she has to conduct a piece of research that links to Early Childhood in some way. She thinks about what Tisdall, Davis and Gallagher (2009) say are important reasons for conducting research in Early Childhood and which seems the most important to her. She also thinks about what principles she holds about doing Early Childhood Research.

   She decides that the main reason that she thinks that research in Early Childhood is important is because it allows children to have their voice heard. As a mother,

(Continued)

she recognises that there are times when her own children's perspectives haven't been taken into account about matters that impact them. She recognises that this resonates with her guiding principle about Early Childhood Research, that it should value children's right to participation.

KEY POINTS FROM THE CHAPTER

- Research in Early Childhood is about creating new knowledge and answering questions about young children, their lives, their families and their communities.
- Research in Early Childhood matters because it can open up new possibilities for children, it can help us ask questions about the way things are done and it can offer opportunities for children to have their voice heard (Tisdall, Davis and Gallagher, 2009).
- Use this book to guide you through your own research project; Table 1.2 will help you identify which chapters will help at which stage of your journey.

FURTHER READING

1   The piece of research that we referred to by Early Childhood student Catherine Kirby (2024) was published in the Early Childhood Studies Degree Network (ECSDN) student journal. It's worth having a look at how she approached her research project, and also looking at other articles in the volume (or other volumes) for examples of other pieces of student research studies:

Kirby, C. (2024) 'Listening to young children and babies', *Early Childhood Studies Degree Network Journal*, Volume 2. Available at: www.ecsdn.org/_files/ugd/c871c5_ a5138422af4240ecaffa1c72680cc4ff.pdf (accessed: 30 July 2025).

2   We really love Tisdall, Davis and Gallagher's (2009) book about researching with children and young people, including their reasons for why researchers should do research with children:

Tisdall, K., Davis, J. and Gallagher, M. (2009) *Researching with Children and Young People: Research Design, Methods and Analysis*. London: Sage.

REFERENCES

Bolshaw, P. and Josephidou, J. (2018) *Introducing Research in Early Childhood*. London: Sage.

Carneiro, P., Cattan, S., Conti, G., Crawford, C., Farquharson, C. and Ridpath, N. (2025) *The short- and medium-term effects of Sure Start on children's outcomes*. Available at:

https://ifs.org.uk/sites/default/files/2025-05/IFS%20Report.%20The%20short-%20and%20medium-term%20effects%20of%20Sure%20Start%20on%20children%E2%80%99s%20outcomes.pdf (accessed: 31 July 2025).

Department for Education (2025) *Giving every child the best start in life.* Available at: https://assets.publishing.service.gov.uk/media/686bd62a10d550c668de3be7/Giving_every_child_the_best_start_in_life.pdf (accessed: 31 July 2025).

Drury, R. and Blaisdell, C. (2024) *Voice of the baby: A reflective guide for the arts.* Available at: https://starcatchers.org.uk/wp-content/uploads/2024/01/Voice-of-the-Baby-A-Reflective-Guide-for-the-Arts-June2024.pdf (accessed: 31 July 2025).

Drury, R., Blaisdell, C. and Matheson, R. (2025) 'Including baby's voice', *Nursery World*, 27 February. Available at: www.nurseryworld.co.uk/content/eye-supplement-research/eye-supplement-research-including-babys-voice/ (accessed: 31 July 2025).

Dýrfjörð, K. and Hreinsdóttir, A.M. (2025) 'Paving the way for slow pedagogy: leadership lessons from Icelandic preschools', *European Early Childhood Education Research Journal.* DOI: 10.1080/1350293X.2025.2523040.

File, N., Mueller, J.J., Basler Wisneski, D. and Stremmel, A.J. (2016) *Understanding Research in Early Childhood Education: Quantitative and Qualitative Methods.* Abingdon: Routledge.

Fraser, S. (2004) 'Situating empirical research', in S. Fraser, V. Lewis, S. Ding, M. Kellert and C. Robinson (eds), *Doing Research with Children and Young People.* London: Sage, pp. 15–16.

Kemp, N., Josephidou, J. and Bolshaw, P. (2025) '"Tiny humans outdoors": understanding the factors that mediate opportunities for babies and toddlers', *Children's Geographies.* DOI: https://doi.org/10.1080/14733285.2025.2479683 https://doi.org/10.1080/14733285.2025.2479683.

Kirby, C. (2024) 'Listening to young children and babies', *Early Childhood Studies Degree Network Journal*, Volume 2. Available at: www.ecsdn.org/_files/ugd/c871c5_a5138422af4240ecaffa1c72680cc4ff.pdf (accessed: 30 July 2025).

Küpeli, K. and Bayındır, D. (2025) 'Preschool outdoor education environment quality predicts children's environmental attitude, awareness and affinity towards nature (biophilia)', *Early Years: An International Research Journal.* DOI: https://doi.org/10.1080/09575146.2024.2444886.

Lobe, B., Livingstone, S. and Haddon, L. (2007) *Researching children's experiences online across countries: Issues and problems in methodology.* Available at: https://eprints.lse.ac.uk/2856/8/Livingstone_Researching_childrens_experiences_2007.pdf (accessed: 31 July 2025).

Roberts-Holmes, G., Levy, R. and Harmey, S. (2023) *Doing Your Early Years Research Project: A Step by Step Guide.* 5th Edition. London: Sage.

Sak, A., Şahin-Sak, I. and Öneren-Şendil, C. (2025) 'Examining the relationship between four to six year olds' school readiness levels and their parents' tolerance of risky play', *Early Years: An International Research Journal.* DOI: https://doi.org/10.1080/09575146.2025.2516092.

Sakr, M. and Bonetti, S. (2025) 'Babies thrive in smaller groups: it's time to regulate baby room group size', *Nursery World*, 19 June. Available at: www.nurseryworld.co.uk/content/opinion/babies-thrive-in-smaller-groups-it-s-time-to-regulate-baby-room-group-size/ (accessed: 31 July 2025).

Sakr, M., Bonetti, S. and Halls, K. (2025) *Quality in the baby room: Actionable findings from a global evidence review*. Available at: https://thebabyroom.blog/report-1/ (accessed: 31 July 2025).

The Nuffield Foundation (2025) *Achieving high-quality provision in the baby room of English nurseries*. Available at: www.nuffieldfoundation.org/project/achieving-high-quality-provision-in-the-baby-room-of-english-nurseries (accessed: 31 July 2025).

Tisdall, K., Davis, J. and Gallagher, M. (2009) *Researching with Children and Young People: Research Design, Methods and Analysis*. London: Sage.

2

ISSUES OF POWER IN EARLY CHILDHOOD RESEARCH

CHAPTER OBJECTIVES

By the end of this chapter, you will:

- Understand some of the frequent power issues that exist in research including those specific to Early Childhood
- Consider ways these power imbalances could be addressed
- Identify some of the voices which have traditionally dominated in Early Childhood Research and why this has happened
- Recognise the prominence given to Early Childhood Research conducted in the Global North and published in the English language.

INTRODUCTION

The aim of this chapter is to develop your understanding of the contextual influences on all research; these are influences that can impact greatly on power dynamics between all those involved. Research is not an activity that takes place in a vacuum; it is undertaken by certain people who engage with other people in certain locations. This means it is never value free. Because of this issue, certain voices have come to dominate in research generally and more specifically in Early Childhood Research. The context within which the researcher works (for example, the Global North), their first language (for, example, English), their age (for example, are they an adult or a child?), these are all factors which either lend power to the would-be researcher, or take it away. Many questions can be raised to help us understand how power imbalances impact on research; for example:

- Who is given the opportunity to carry out research? Is it a task open to all?
- What about the areas of focus? Why are some areas very popular as the subject of research while others are hardly considered?

- Which research is funded and who provides the funding?
- What about participants? Whose perspectives are sought? Who is considered to have something important to say?
- Once perspectives have been shared, would participants recognise the way they have been portrayed? What about if they don't agree with or understand the analysis of their perspectives?
- How are the findings disseminated? Does everyone have access to the findings or are they hidden behind journal paywalls that only the privileged can access?

All of these questions, which reveal key power issues, apply to most research. Early Childhood, however, in addition to these issues, has its own specific issues, including the fact that the younger the child involved, the more pronounced the power dynamic. This power imbalance also ironically includes the fact that the younger the child, the more likely they are to be excluded from research. As Guard (2023) recognises, drawing on others' work, 'research identifying babies, and those who work with babies … [is] … overlooked, forgotten, and marginalised in early years policy and practice (Goouch and Powell 2013a; Clark and Baylis 2012; Davis and Dunn 2018)' (p. 607).

WHO HOLDS THE POWER?

When examining the concept of power in Early Childhood Research it is important to examine who holds power.

Research on Children

Much of what we know about young children, and therefore which informs practice, is informed by research on children (Bolshaw and Josephidou, 2018, pp. 53–64). This is evident in both the historical works of seminal Early Childhood theorists such as Bandura (1925–2021), Piaget (1886–1980) and Laevers (1950–) and also recent evidence based on large-scale quantitative studies (see for example Josephidou et al., 2021). Featherstone (2016) sets out, for example, how the above-mentioned theorists' influence practice, as shown in Table 2.1.

Table 2.1 Three seminal theorists who have impacted on Early Childhood practice

Theorist	Research approach	Findings	Impact on practice
Bandura	Put children individually in an experiment room, accompanied by an adult who played either in a non-aggressive manner with some construction toys, or in an aggressive manner towards a Bobo doll (a weighted large inflatable doll) by	The intention of the experiment was to see if children were more likely to choose the aggressive toys and display violence in this room if they had observed the adult behaving aggressively, which indeed proved to be the case.	Behaviour management interventions

Theorist	Research approach	Findings	Impact on practice
	punching, kicking it and saying comments like 'Sock him in the nose ...' and 'Kick him ...'.		
Piaget	Conducted experiments in which he interviewed children to assess their understanding of number.	Children work through four sequential stages in their development, as their ways of processing information and understanding the world around them changes while they develop the ability to think.	Stages of development in curriculum guidance
Laevers	Created scales to assess a child's level of well-being and their level of involvement.	These scales have been used by researchers to comment on and make recommendations for practice. For example, Mackinder (2017) used the involvement scale to assess, through observation, how involved children were in forest school experiences, and DeClercq et al. (2011) used both scales to identify that there were big disparities in levels of wellbeing and involvement across Early Childhood Education and Care settings in a province of South Africa.	The process of learning

Yet if we consider some of the questions of power that we asked in our introduction, such as who is considered as having something important to say, we can see that all three of these seminal writers had the particular perspective of adult as expert. The examples of research on children cited in Table 2.1 have all been highly influential and therefore important pieces of work but they are only part of the jigsaw puzzle of how to support children in their holistic learning and development in Early Childhood; in terms of power dynamics they also lean heavily towards the expertise of the adult.

Problematic Participation

There is a growing recognition that children also have an expertise to share, such that research with children has come much more to the fore and there are some great examples of how children's voices can be louder in research. One of the reasons for this shift was the impact of the United Nations Convention on the Rights of the Child (United Nations, 1989) on policy and the fundamental rights that children are meant to enjoy and benefit from. For instance, Article 13 outlines the freedom children should hold both to express themselves and access information, while Article 12 sets out their right to express views and have them taken seriously. Recognition of these articles means it is possible to find many pieces of research in Early Childhood that have included the voice of the child. At the same time there are still problematic power dynamics so that participation can be tokenistic; for example, it is usually still adults who continue to set the research agenda, in fact often to support their own agendas (McMellon and Tisdall, 2020).

Which Children Can Participate?

However, excellent examples continue to emerge of children's seemingly authentic participation and how this participation can positively impact on their life experiences. For example, the Royal Hospital for Children in Glasgow included the child's voice to redesign aspects of their environment; this included such ideas as replacing 'the blood fridge, previously accessed by staff in full view of waiting families, … with a mini toy museum' (Brooks, 2024).

This clear example of inclusion of children's perspectives contrasts greatly with our previous description of children's hospitals in the past where Jean compares her great-granddaughter's hospital experiences with those she had experienced as a child in the 40s (Bolshaw and Josephidou, 2018, p. 62).

In the Glasgow example, there was a clear attempt to be inclusive as 'children from all over Scotland' were consulted 'with a range of conditions and backgrounds' (Brooks, 2024). This can be seen as an attempt to address power issues in children's participation in research, however when looking critically at such research we still need to ask which children are being given a platform to make their views known; i.e. which ethnic groups are being represented, which geographical locations are being drawn upon, what was the age range of the children, how could they be categorised in terms of class, gender etc?

McMellon and Tisdall (2020) carried out a review of the participation literature and found that: 'contextual matters, such as socio-economic, political, cultural or organisational factors, … can dramatically impact on children and young people's participation' (p. 161).

They cite Theobold et al. (2011) who suggest that 'particular groups of children and young people, … may risk being excluded … such as disabled children and very young children' (Theobold et al., 2011). McMellon and Tisdall also discuss ideas developed by Lundy around considerations of how to facilitate young children's participation; we have summarised this model in the following list:

- **Space**: Children must be given safe, inclusive opportunities to form and express their view.
- **Voice**: Children must be facilitated to express their view.
- **Audience**: The view must be listened to.
- **Influence**: The view must be acted upon, as appropriate.

It is interesting to consider what Lundy's ideas would look like for very young children, so this is what we will do now in Activity 2.1.

Activity 2.1 Facilitating Babies' Participation in Research

Benoit, a student and practitioner, was interested in pursuing their research interest in babies' engagement with nature. They realised there was very little work which encouraged active participation from babies in research so that perspectives of very young children were not captured. They read the paper by McMellon and Tisdall (2020) and were interested in the model they describe developed by Lundy; they considered how they could use this model of Space, Voice, Audience and Influence to facilitate very young children's participation in this area of research. They had to think long and hard about how they could address these four ideas. What kind of advice would you give Benoit?

Reflection

When Benoit reflected on this activity, they considered what they would need to do in terms of:

Space: I know there are some settings which have free flow between outdoors and indoors for babies even on rainy days. It would be great if I could carry out some observations at such a setting, as the children would be freely choosing to go outside rather than being taken out by an adult.

Voice: I need to consider all the different ways that very young children can communicate their views, including looking, pointing, babbling, crying, moving towards or away from, interacting with others or objects.

Audience: I need to ensure I don't prioritise one way of communicating views over others; for example, I must ensure that I don't focus on the older children because this fits with my adult way of knowing.

Influence: If I can capture very young children's preferences and perspectives of being outdoors then I can use what I learn to make recommendations as to how the outdoors could be enhanced.

WHOSE VOICE COUNTS?

The previous section touched on power issues in Early Childhood Research and in this section we are going to consider one way of ensuring that such power imbalances can be addressed; for example, we will reflect on how more diverse voices can be invited to research conversations about the experiences of young children. This could mean more children, more even younger children, or adults from more marginalised groups.

Inviting More Voices to the Early Childhood Research Conversation

If we consider the case of very young children, Salamon and Palaiologou (2022) suggest that: 'When we seek to listen to infants' and toddlers' voices this becomes even more problematic, because participation is often seen as the verbal ability to articulate one's views about the matters of participation that concern them so adults can respond and act on them' (p. 49). As a researcher, we can either see this as a problem and choose not to invite babies and toddlers to participate in research or we can look for new ways that they can be included in research conversations if we truly believe that they have something important to tell us. Yes, we are not claiming at all that this is a si mple task, that would be naïve, however Salamon and Palaiologou cite Mazzei (2009) who encourages us to 'seek the messy, opaque, polyphonic; a voice that exceeds easy knowing and quick understanding' (p. 49). Polyphonic is a musical term which describes a piece of music that has more than two lines of melody. It is a lovely metaphor to describe the holistic manner in which a young child may display their knowledge and understanding in numerous ways while engaging in one simple activity. Our role as an adult researcher is to ensure we can listen to these different melodies. This is a research aspiration that does not just relate to young children but to all voices who are entitled to share their perspectives but may be seldom asked. As McMellon and Tisdall (2020) assert 'We need to expand who counts' (p. 172) in research concerning children.

Indigenous Voices

One such example of silenced voices is the case of indigenous voices. Before we proceed any further, it would be good to see how this term indigenous can be defined. The United Nations uses the definition:

> Indigenous Peoples are inheritors and practitioners of unique cultures and ways of relating to people and the environment. They have retained social, cultural, economic and political characteristics that are distinct from those of the dominant societies in which they live. Despite their cultural differences, Indigenous Peoples from around the world share common problems related to the protection of their rights as distinct peoples. (United Nations, n.d.)

It has always been problematic that indigenous people have had research done 'on' them rather than 'with' them and that also they have been subject to policy informed by such research so that it is inappropriate for their needs and their everyday lived experiences. We can see parallels here with the research done 'on' children that we have already discussed.

Take, for instance, research carried out by Taylor (2011) in which she looked at how ready Aboriginal children in Western Australia were to start school. In Australia, at the time Taylor was writing around 75% of schools had Indigenous children as pupils, although in half of these schools Indigenous pupils made up less than 5% of overall pupil numbers. Since 2013 pre-primary education has been compulsory in Western Australia for children in the academic year in which they turn 5 years old. When they first start pre-primary, children are assessed in literacy and numeracy. However, Taylor suggests that the on-entry assessment merely assesses 'that which particular cultures, socio-economic circumstances and individual families have or have not instilled and reinforced' (2011, p. 145). She continues to explain that what is considered as 'normal' for pre-primary children to be able to achieve and do in terms of literacy and numeracy by the Western Australia Department of Education comes from an ethnocentric non-Indigenous belief, so when Indigenous pupils are evaluated in the on-entry assessments, they are seen as 'problems' and 'deficits'. In terms of ethnocentrism, the Western Australia Department for Education are judging the Indigenous students on the standard of the non-Indigenous culture. A paper written 12 years later (Dadi et al., 2023) recognises that ethnocentric measures are still being used to assess children for school readiness. We can also see this in the English context where the document Development Matters discusses how between the ages of 0 and 3 children will be learning how to use a knife and fork (DfE, 2023, p. 64). Or how the widely used Ages & Stages health visitor questionnaire that parents have to complete for their child's 33-month check asks, 'Does your child use a spoon to feed herself with little spilling?' and 'Does your child put on a coat, jacket or shirt by herself?' (ASQ-3, n.d.).

However, there are good examples of not just how indigenous voices are being promoted in Early Childhood Research but also in how their inclusion benefits our understanding of all children. Take for example the work of Maria Cooper, an academic in the context of New Zealand, who writes about Pasifika Indigenous knowledge in Early Childhood practice (see for example, Cooper and Matapo, 2021) or Malone and Moore (2019) who draw on indigenous ways to understand how two very young children engage with their environment, including how best to understand the child's way of knowing.

To sum up this section, ethnocentrism has often led to issues of power imbalances in Early Childhood Research. Including more diverse voices could have a beneficial impact on children who may be from more marginalised communities such as children from indigenous groups. However, there is a case to be made that such diversification in who is allowed to research, choice of methodologies and conceptual frameworks can support a better understanding of all children within their own specific contexts and therefore impact positively on practice. In the next section we will consider how children's voices can be supported to become stronger in research as part of this diversification to counteract issues of power.

Children's Voices

Let's now specifically focus on young children and how their voices can be foregrounded in research, remembering that when we use the term 'voice' we are not specifically meaning verbal communications but rather ways young children choose to convey meaning whether that be "behaviour, actions, pauses in action, silences, body language, glances, movement and artistic expression" (Wall et al., 2019, p. 268) to draw attention to their presence in a particular time and space' (Guard, 2023, p. 608).

One way to do this is to recognise that children are indeed 'experts in their own lives' and if we allow them to be, we can learn from them. Although of course, this does not mean they are experts in *all* children's lives but they can help us to understand their own. For example, Huser (2015) sought to support children to understand and reflect on their play behaviours while also being 'conscious participants in the research process' (p. 35). Huser argues that 'Children as "natural users" of play are experts on this phenomenon. They therefore should be heard on how they experience and perceive play' (p. 36). Huser believed that they had mitigated against power imbalances in this research as:

> [the] children were in control. After asking if I was allowed to watch them play or enter their play room, one child indirectly offered me to play with them by saying: 'That is your car!' Philip said on the first day: 'I would like you to watch us.' But after a while he changed his mind: 'You have to play with us now, otherwise it is getting boring.' (p. 43)

Elsewhere, they emphasise this point by explaining how they obtained ethical approval from the children:

> When I introduced myself to the target children in a special occasion, I confronted them with the letters I had given to their parents, explaining that I had asked all their parents for permission to do a study with them. One child immediately said: 'I did not receive a letter from you!' Some others agreed. So, we decided that the children would receive a letter, which they could sign like their parents did. One boy mentioned that he could not write his name yet, so new ideas came from the children, such as drawing pictures of themselves, taking a photograph or all three together. The children themselves had asserted their rights. (p. 44)

Another paper useful in understanding how children's voices can be made stronger in research is that by Ibrahim et al. (2022). The children involved in this research had severe speech and physical impairments and so it was recognised that such research was 'highly challenging' (p. 63), but they were adamant that they wanted to 'consider new child-centred perspectives for conceptualising new communication technologies' (p. 63). As the research progressed, the authors recognised that not only were they managing to draw on the children's expertise of their lived experiences, but that they were also empowering the children, a group of children who were 'rarely involved in research' (p. 64). The researchers worked with a small group of children aged between 6 and 9. They took into consideration the children's individual 'communication styles and assistive equipment' (p. 70) so that methods were used which 'would allow for children to participate in ways that were familiar and natural to them' (p. 71), including the use of

AAC (augmentative and alternative communication) devices. They also observed how the children interacted with their peers outside the classroom when they were not using such devices. In addition, the researchers used various creative methods which would already be familiar to the children and which they felt confident to use.

You will remember from Activity 2.1 Lundy's idea of Audience being that children's voices must be listened to if power imbalances are to be addressed in Early Childhood Research. This was a consideration of Ceballos and Susinos (2022) when they considered how they could make sure children's voices counted more by asking themselves if, as researchers, they were authentically representing the children's views. The children they engaged with were under the age of 3 and they wanted to understand their views on how educational experiences could be improved. They understood that one of the ways they could do this would be to seek research methods that spoke to individual children rather than having a one-size-fits-all approach. They also recognised that they needed to reflect continually on their own assumptions about what the children wanted them to know. They used the term 'empathetic imagination' to describe how they chose to analyse and interpret the data of 'actions, gestures, babbling and actual words' that they collected.

This section has looked specifically at power issues in including children's voices in research. As you read through the book you will learn much more about how you can listen to children through research but here we emphasise the importance of children's voices – how it is important that we allow them to be the expert in their own life (although not speak for all children), ways that we can support children to have a stronger voice in research and how being involved in research can be empowering for them.

Activity 2.2   Looking for the Power Imbalances

As you reflect on what you have learnt about power issues in this section of the chapter and how they relate to children's voices, think about how, as a novice researcher, you can be an ally and support children in having a louder voice in research. Table 2.2 describes three potential undergraduate projects but have the student researchers thought about power issues? You can see a snapshot of their ideas but how could you encourage them to address power imbalances?

Table 2.2   Addressing power imbalances

Research focus	Age of children	Methods chosen
Student A works in a reception class. They want to carry out some action research in the reading corner to find out who is or isn't using it, how it is being used and ways it could be enhanced.	4–5 years	They decide to undertake two different types of observations to include both narrative, qualitative accounts where they record what is happening in this area of the classroom for 60 mins each day over one week with the time varying each day.

(Continued)

Table 2.2 (Continued)

Research focus	Age of children	Methods chosen
		As part of this they will also audio record any children's discussions that are happening in the book corner. They also decide to time track who is using the book corner at 15-minute intervals.
Student B is a childminder. She has various siblings in her care and is interested to understand how having a sibling impacts, or not, on a child's development.	3 years old	She decides to ask the parents if they will complete an online questionnaire. She will also ask her childminder network if they will send the link to the parents that they work with. In addition to this, she wants to interview informally the parents of the children that she cares for.
Student C has a young baby and is interested to find out about babies' gendered play choices	12–18 months	He asks if he can carry out some observations of babies in his local baby room. In addition, he would like to interview practitioners and parents.

Reflection

Did you see the potential in these three scenarios to address power imbalances and what advice would you give these three students? Perhaps you encouraged Student A to also ask the children about their views on the book corner – after all they are the ones using it so they must have some expertise they can share. Student B could also ask children but in addition to this will need to be careful about making cultural assumptions informed by her own background. She should ensure she interviews a diverse range of parents if she can and also draw on a diverse range of literature to inform her understanding of siblings. Student C will also need to reflect on his own assumptions as he interprets and analyses the babies' interactions with their environment.

THE GLOBAL NORTH AND ENGLISH LANGUAGE

In the previous section we considered 'Whose voice counts in research' and we are going to continue this discussion a little further here by thinking about the world map and which geographical locations are deemed to have something important to say about Early Childhood.

The Domineering Global North

McMellon and Tisdall (2020), in their review of the children's participation literature, remind us that although most children live in the Global South, it is the Global North that dominates considerations of how and why children are studied. This issue has also been long discussed by Penn (2008, 2018) who reflects in her writing on the fact that European or North American childhoods are generally seen as the lens through which all childhoods should be viewed. This is a great mistake on many fronts, not least because even within one particular geographical location there will be ever-shifting understandings and assumptions about what children need and how they behave. This leads Penn (2018) to advise that, in terms of what is appropriate and useful in Early Childhood Research, 'rather than understanding the generalities, it may be more useful to understand the particularities' (p. 45), i.e. the context-specific findings that add to our understanding about diverse children's lives. She supports this perspective by drawing on Bruner's (2000) argument that 'childrearing practices and beliefs reflect local conceptions of how the world is and how the child should be readied for living it' (p. xi).

Gaps in Our Early Childhood Knowledge

Hand in hand with this geographical dominance is a linguistic dominance whereby English language has become research's first language. Because of this, we are losing a great deal in terms of developing our understanding of ways of working with and caring for young children. Teszenyi et al. (2022) raised important points pertaining to this issue when they edited a special edition of the *Journal of Childhood, Education and Society*, which focused on socialist childhoods. As they worked

> with authors, whose mother tongue was not English, the linguistic and conceptual difficulties in crossing language boundaries sensitised us to the risks of losing meaning and/or understanding. Hence, we found ourselves in a precarious position again as we attempted to contribute to re-dressing the imbalance in knowledge production and dissemination hierarchies between the East and the West (Collyer, 2018; Demeter, 2019). Giving many of the authors the opportunity to write with authority and with authentic voices about a subject they hold an insider view of, disrupts the historical and epistemological Western paradigms and questions the long-held belief that those on the periphery of global knowledge production can only create local knowledge or voice local 'truths' (Frank and Meyer, 2007; Mignolo, 2009).

They recognised that 'Expression in some of the papers may be somewhat awkward or lacking fluency' (p. 213) and called for 'linguistic tolerance towards the authors' (p. 213).

Ways Forward

So how can we move forward in terms of supporting a more diverse range of voices to contribute to discussions about Early Childhood Education and Care (ECEC)? How can we ensure that more voices are invited to the discussion to address power imbalances that are not only detrimental to experiences of children in the Global South but also leave researchers and children in the Global North impoverished, with great gaps in their understanding about children's ways of 'knowing and being' (Cooper and Matapo, 2021, p. 26)? In their review of the children's participation literature, McMellon and Tisdall (2020) discovered that 'there is much that the Global North can learn from the Global South about viewing children and young people as important social contributors' (p. 170). They offer one example from Butler (2008) who 'describes how children and young people in Brazil ... utilise their own preferred means of communication (hiphop music, online networks) to share their views and campaign for change' (p. 170), echoing Ceballos and Susinos' (2022) advice to avoid a one-size-fits-all approach. They continue by recommending that the researcher adopts a disposition of wanting to learn from those in other geographical and cultural contexts, in particular those from the Global South.

Case Study 2.1   Adult/Child Power Dynamics

Ben wanted to find out what children in Year 2 (aged 6 to 7 years) felt about playtime. He took lots of pictures of the playground and then asked groups of children to talk about them. However, he became a little frustrated as he felt that the children were repeating comments that adults had made, revealing their understanding of adult/child power dynamics. For example, when they talked about the climbing frame, they discussed the rules and why they knew they were important, but he couldn't seem to find the right questions to get them to talk about what they thought of the rules. After discussing with his student peers, he decided to ask the children about the best ways to find out their thoughts on playtime. They came up with some creative ideas including make a large class collage which led to a great deal of discussion that he was able to capture and analyse.

KEY POINTS FROM THE CHAPTER

- All research includes documented power issues and imbalances; there are some that are particular to Early Childhood given the age of children involved.
- Much of what we know about children, and which informs practice, derives from research on children.
- The younger the child involved in research, the more pronounced the power dynamic.
- It is important as a researcher to look for ways to minimise and mitigate against these power imbalances.

- If certain voices are allowed to dominate in Early Childhood Research, we are impoverished in our understanding about children.

FURTHER READING

1   This report reflects on a key message of this chapter, that much of the research that impacts on children's life has no recognition that they have an important voice to contribute to the debate.

   Josephidou, J., Rodriguez-Leon, L., Bennett, S., Bolshaw, P., Musgrave, J. and Rix, J. (2021) *Where measurement stops: A review of systematic reviews exploring ECEC workforce qualifications and training, the quality of provision and outcomes for children and families.* TACTYC. Available from: https://oro.open.ac.uk/81980/ (accessed: 30 June 2025).

2   This special issue of the *Journal of Childhood, Education and Society* brings together a range of voices not necessarily always heard in research as it collates articles which focus on socialist childhoods.

   Journal of Childhood, Education and Society (2022) 3(3). Available at: https://www. j-ces.com/index.php/jces/issue/view/8/21 (accessed: 30 June 2025).

3   This short report from Caroline Guard's PhD work entitled 'Hearing the voices of babies in baby-educator interactions in Early Childhood Settings' gives food for thought for those looking to address the lack of babies' voices in research:

   Guard, C. (2023) *Hearing the voices of babies in baby-educator interactions in Early Childhood Settings.* Available at: www.froebel.org.uk/uploads/documents/ FT-Hearing-Infant-Voices-summary-report.pdf (accessed: 30 June 2025).

REFERENCES

ASQ-3 (n.d.) Ages and Stages questionnaires. Paul H. Brookes Publishing Co., Inc. (33 month questionnaire accessed at www.socfc.org/SOHS/Disabilities%20Mental%20Health/ASQ/ ASQ%203%2033%20Months.pdf (23 May 2025.)

Bolshaw, P. and Josephidou, J. (2018) *Introducing Research in Early Childhood.* London: Sage.

Brooks, L. (2024) '*A space with a soul': Children's ideas help transform Glasgow hospital unit.* Available from: www.theguardian.com/uk-news/2024/jan/03/childrens-ideas-help- transform-glasgow-hospital-unit-murals (accessed: 30 June 2025).

Bruner, J. (2000) Foreword, in J. DeLoache and A. Gottleib (eds) *A World of Babies: Imagined Childcare Guides for Seven Societies.* Cambridge: Cambridge University Press, p.xi.

Butler, U.M. (2008) 'Children's participation in Brazil – a brief genealogy and recent innovations', *The International Journal of Children's Rights, 16*(3), pp. 301–34. DOI: 10.116 3/157181808X311150.

Ceballos, N. and Susinos, T. (2022) 'Do my words convey what children are saying? Researching school life with very young children: dilemmas for "authentic listening"', *European Early Childhood Education Research Journal*, 30(1), pp. 81–95. DOI: https://doi.org/10.1080/1350293X.2022.2026435.

Cooper, M. and Matapo, J. (2021) 'Mobilising tofā sa'ili for ECE leadership: a talanoa confronting dominant conceptualisations from a Pasifika perspective', *Contemporary Issues in Education*, 41(2), pp. 26–32. DOI: https://doi. org/10.46786/ac21.2955.

Dadi, A.F., He V., Nutton G., Su J.Y. and Guthridge, S. (2023) 'Predicting child development and school readiness, at age 5, for Aboriginal and non-Aboriginal children in Australia's Northern Territory', *PLoS ONE, 18*(12), pp. 1–23.

DeClerq, B., Ebrahim, H., Koen, M., Martin, C., van Zyl, E., Daries, G., Oliver, M., Venter, R., Ramabenyane, M. and Sibeko, L. (2011) 'Levels of well-being and involvement of young children in centre-based provision in the Free State Province of South Africa', *South African Journal of Childhood Education*, 1(2), pp. 64–80.

Featherstone, S. (2016) *An Anthology of Educational Thinkers: Putting Theory into Practice in the Early Years*. London: Bloomsbury.

Guard, G. (2023) "It's the little bits that you have enabled me to see". Reconceptualising the voices of babies using the video interaction dialogue model with early years educators', *Early Years*, 43(3), pp. 606–25. DOI: 10.1080/09575146.2023.2190498.

Huser, C. (2015) 'Children's voices on play in a mosaic approach study: children as conscious participants in a case study', *Boğaziçi Üniversitesi Eğitim Dergisi*, 26(1), pp. 35–48.

Ibrahim, S., Vasalou, A., Benton, L. and Clarke, M. (2022) 'A methodological reflection on investigating children's voice in qualitative research involving children with severe speech and physical impairments', *Disability & Society*, 37(1), pp. 63–88. DOI: https://doi.org/10.1080/09687599.2021.1933389.

Josephidou, J., Rodriguez-Leon, L., Bennett, S., Bolshaw, P., Musgrave, J. and Rix, J. (2021) *Where measurement stops: A review of systematic reviews exploring ECEC workforce qualifications and training, the quality of provision and outcomes for children and families*. TACTYC. Available at: https://oro.open.ac.uk/81980/ (accessed: 30 June 2025).

Mackinder, M. (2017) 'Footprints in the woods: "tracking" a nursery child through a Forst School session', *Education 3-13*, 45(2), pp. 176–90.

Malone, K. and Moore, S. J. (2019) 'Sensing ecologically through kin and stones', *International Journal of Early Childhood Environmental Education*, 7(1), pp. 8–25.

Mazzei, L. A. (2009) 'An impossibly full voice', in A. Y. Jackson and L. A. Mazzei (eds), *Voice in Qualitative Inquiry: Challenging Conventional, Interpretive, and Critical Conceptions in Qualitative Research*. Abingdon: Routledge, pp. 45–62.

McMellon, C. and Tisdall, K. (2020) 'Children and young people's participation rights: looking backwards and moving forwards', *International Journal of Children's Rights*, 28, pp. 157–82.

Penn, H. (2008) *Understanding Early Childhood*. London: Sage.

Penn, H. (2018) *Be Realistic: Demand the Impossible*. London: Routledge.

Salamon, A. and Palaiologou, I. (2022) '"Infants" and toddlers' rights in Early Childhood settings', in F. Press and S. Cheeseman (eds), *(Re)conceptualising Children's Rights in Infant-Toddler Care and Education. Policy and Pedagogy with Under-Three-Year Olds: Cross-disciplinary Insights and Innovations*. Springer, pp. 45–58. DOI: https://doi. org/10.1007/978-3-031-05218-7_5.

Taylor, A. (2011) 'Coming, ready or not: Aboriginal children's transition to school in urban Australia and the policy push', *International Journal of Early Years Education*, *19*(2), pp. 145–61.

Teszenyi, E., Varga Nagy, A. and Pálfi, S. (2022) 'Re-imagining socialist childhoods: changing narratives of spatial and temporal (dis)orientations', *Journal of Childhood, Education & Society*, *3*(3), pp. 212–17.

Theobald M., Danby S. and Ailwood J. (2011) 'Child participation in the Early Years: challenges for education', *Australasian Journal of Early Childhood*, *36*(3), pp. 19–26.

United Nations (no date) *Indigenous Peoples at the United Nations*. Available at: https:// social.desa.un.org/issues/indigenous-peoples/indigenous-peoples-at-the-united-nations (accessed: 17 October 2025).

United Nations (1989) United Nations Convention on the Rights of the Child. Available at: www.unicef.org.uk/wp-content/uploads/2016/08/unicef-convention-rights-child-uncrc.pdf (accessed: 16 December 2025).

Wall, K., Cassidy, C., Robinson, C., Hall, E., Beaton, M., Kanyal, M. and Mitra, D. (2019) 'Look who's talking: factors for considering the facilitation of very young children's voices', *Journal of Early Childhood Research*, *17*(4), pp. 263–78.

PART II
DOING RESEARCH IN EARLY CHILDHOOD

3

DESIGNING YOUR RESEARCH PROJECT

CHAPTER OBJECTIVES

By the end of this chapter, you will:

- Understand what the stages are in conducting a piece of research
- Be able to identify some of the difficulties that students can face when carrying out their own studies
- Recognise what strategies may be useful in overcoming common challenges when collecting data.

INTRODUCTION

It can be difficult to know where to start with designing your research project. This chapter intends to think about what we mean by research design. It will focus on how students can go about collecting data, choosing a research question, and choosing a method. It will consider the difficulties that students can face in collecting empirical data for their undergraduate dissertations including those that exist on ethical grounds, because of the sensitive nature of the research topic (areas such as race, gender, sexuality or first language). This chapter also discusses convenience sampling, a strategy often used by dissertation students, and how this approach to collecting empirical data has its own limitations in terms of reliability and validity. It goes on to consider how these difficulties in collecting empirical data may be overcome by instead taking one of the different approaches outlined in Part III (*Methods and Analysis*).

BEGINNING TO DESIGN YOUR PIECE OF RESEARCH

To begin to design your piece of research, you need an understanding of what research design actually is. You also need to think about how your position has an impact on how you design your research, and how to choose a research project. Those are the areas that this first section of the chapter will consider.

What Is Research Design?

From Chapter 1 (*What is research in Early Childhood and why does it matter?*) and Chapter 2 (*Issues of power in Early Childhood Research*) you will have developed your understanding of how others do research, and what's important to consider when undertaking a piece of research. Now it's time to move on to think about yourself as a researcher. The first step in doing your own research is designing a potential project. As you know, research often comes about as a result of someone wanting to find out the answer to something (a research question) or wanting to know more about a particular area (a research topic). But deciding how best to go about answering that question or discovering more about a particular topic is part of the skill in designing your research project.

Beginning in this chapter and then continuing in the subsequent chapters, we will think about all the components and processes that need to be considered when you are designing your piece of research. We can think about a research project in terms of a housebuilding project, with the researcher as the architect.

Different architects design houses in different ways – the number of bedrooms may change, the placing of the stairs may be unique. But some things stay the same – the building must have strong foundations (which may be dependent on the type of soil) and a similar structure in terms of walls, windows and doors. The same is true of research projects. Between research projects there will be elements that are different – like how many methods are used – but the foundations of research projects – for instance a strong literature review and considerations of ethics – stay the same. And what's good if you are designing a research project for the first time is that, generally, all research projects follow a similar structure. Just like, when we imagine a house, we have a rough idea of what it's going to contain and where different rooms and features will be, research projects typically all contain the same elements and typically follow the same structure, as you will notice when reading academic journal articles which, in the discipline of Early Childhood, are the write-ups of pieces of research. For instance, have a look at the headings used in the journal articles outlined in Table 3.1.

Table 3.1 Examples of headings used in Early Childhood Research articles

Article Title	Making the invisible visible: the pedagogical affordances of outdoor learning in a nursery and primary school	'Switch that off!': the influence of digital parenting and mediation practices on young children's engagement with digital technologies in the home	Ghanaian kindergarten teachers' curriculum knowledge and perspectives on play-based learning: does teacher qualification matter?

Author	Papadopoulou and Vincent (2025)	Wilson, Murcia and Leaver (2025)	Dzamesi, Avornyo and Amissah-Essel (2025)
Headings	• Abstract • Introduction • Literature review • Methodology • Data analysis • Discussion	• Abstract • Introduction • Theoretical framework • Methodology • Findings • Discussion • Future directions • Limitations • Conclusion	• Abstract • Introduction • Review of the relevant literature • Early Childhood education and training in Ghana • The present study • Findings • Discussion • Limitations and areas for further research

Can you see how these articles have slightly different subheadings, but the general architecture is the same? It's the content in the middle that you need to consider when designing your research project – your literature review and your methodology. The later chapters in this book focus on these elements in more detail; this chapter is to help you to see the 'bigger picture'.

Identifying Your Position

Before a researcher begins to think about a literature review or a project's methodology, they need to explore and be aware of their own *positionality*. On a basic level, you can think about it as linking to where you position yourself in relation to things that people hold true. This is quite a tricky concept to get your head around, as we don't often question what we take for granted in terms of what the 'truth' is. But being aware of our 'truths' is very important. For instance, some people say their personality traits are as a result of their star sign – 'of course I'm stubborn, I'm a Capricorn!' In fact, a YouGov survey in 2021 found that 22% of women and 9% of men believed that one's star sign influences personality and how compatible they are with others (Nolsoe, 2022). Others may find that strange, because their 'truth' about what determines their personality is different. Others may not give much credence to their star sign but may believe in superstitions that others don't – for instance believing that when the 13th of a month is a Friday it's unlucky. In fact, the travel search engine (Kayak, 2016) found that flights can be up to 14% cheaper on a Friday 13th compared to equivalent flights the rest of the month, because demand is lower due to passengers wanting to avoid that date.

Whether you believe in horoscopes or superstitions or not, what they illustrate is that we all hold different things as 'truths'. And that extends beyond whether breaking a mirror gives seven years' bad luck to what we believe about children and families. This is called our *ontology*. Tisdall, Davis and Gallagher (2009, p. 66) describe one's ontology, in relation to young children, as 'a theory about the nature of being, of what is'. Ontology relates to what you believe to be true. Tisdall, Davis and Gallagher (2009) continue that for those doing research in relation to children 'the most obvious ontological questions are: What is a child? What is childhood?' It's worth pondering that for a minute. How would you describe children? Innocent? Vulnerable? Well-informed? Powerful? Naïve? Empty vessels? Full of potential? Unique? Diverse? Now think about how others around you might describe them – perhaps people around you like your parents, grandparents or older family members. Do you think your ontologies about children would be the same? What about any children you know – how would they describe children?

It's important to recognise that everyone has different *ontologies* about children, because your ontology informs your *epistemology*. Tisdall, Davis and Gallagher (2009) describe epistemology as 'a theory about the nature of knowledge and how it can be acquired' (p. 66). They go on to say that in contexts like ours, we might ask ourselves questions such as 'What can we know about children and childhood? How can we acquire this knowledge?' Different people have different ideas about how to define ontology and epistemology; they are difficult concepts to grasp. Table 3.2 explains some ways of looking at the terms.

Table 3.2 Exploring ontology and epistemology

Term	Focus	Meaning
Ontology	Thinking about truth	What is
Epistemology	Thinking about knowledge	How we find out about it

Different people have different ideas about what it's possible to know, what's the 'best' kind of knowledge to have and what are the best ways to generate that knowledge. For instance, some people might think that the 'best knowledge' about children is generated by having a large sample size (i.e., lots of participants), because then you've got a greater range of voices and perspectives. Others might counter that the 'best knowledge' about children needs to have children as active participants, because it is them themselves that know what it's like to be a child. Others might suggest that the 'best knowledge' about children is information that is measurable and objective, whereas others may argue that this isn't as important as subjective information such as children's feelings or opinions on a particular topic.

Your ontology will inform your epistemology; what you believe is true about children will inform what you think is the best way to get knowledge about them. So, if you think what is true about children (i.e., your ontology) is that they are well-informed, then that might lead to an approach to the best way to get knowledge about them (i.e., your epistemology) that it's best to ask the children themselves. Conversely, if your ontology is that children are vulnerable, or empty vessels, your belief about the best way to get knowledge about them may be to ask other people close to them.

Just as your ontology informs your epistemology, your epistemology informs your *methodology*. We'll talk about this in more detail later in this chapter, but for now it's important to remember that it's your methodology that incorporates all the processes and procedures that you put in place to collect data, analyse findings and disseminate your study. But before we think about methodology, let's think about how to choose a research topic.

Choosing a Research Topic

The first thing to do when planning a piece of research is to choose a research topic. It can be difficult to choose a topic – it may seem like a big decision that you don't want to get 'wrong'. Asking yourself some questions can help you decide what would make a suitable and engaging research topic.

Activity 3.1 Choosing a Research Topic

Have a look at the following list of questions about choosing a research topic. Spend some time answering them to think about what potential research topics might appeal to you.

- What are you interested in in relation to Early Childhood?
- In the modules you've studied so far, what subjects have you enjoyed studying the most?
- What do you think we need to know more about concerning young children?
- What are the unanswered questions about childhood?
- What do you think children want to tell us?

Reflection

Asking yourself those questions can give you an opportunity to think carefully about what would make a good research topic for you. Sometimes you might be surprised that what appeals to you as a potential topic doesn't sound attractive to your peers, or vice versa. Don't forget that this is down to your positionality – because everyone has their own unique viewpoint on the world. In relation to the world of Early Childhood, this is often because students' views about children are shaped by their own childhoods.

Some students tie themselves in knots trying to think about what research topic would be 'perfect'. But, for many of us with particular ontologies, the 'perfect research topic' doesn't exist. Choose one that engages and interests you, that makes you want to find out more. If you are already working in Early Childhood, draw on the work of Mason (2001) and his Discipline of Noticing – what have you noticed? Or, if you have the opportunity, head to the library and browse the books in your discipline and see which ones make you want to pick them up – what topic are they about? Sometimes your library catalogue may have the function to electronically browse bookshelves, too. What will make a successful research project isn't one with a topic that is 'perfect' but rather one that inspires you to want to find out more.

THINKING ABOUT YOUR METHODOLOGY

After you've chosen your research topic, you can begin to give real thought to your methodology. This is where we notice students often get a couple of things confused. They sometimes use the term 'methodology' and 'methods' interchangeably when in fact they are different things. Methodology incorporates all the processes and procedures that the researcher undertakes to conduct their research, whereas method refers to the specific type of data collection that the research utilises. Some common examples of methods and methodologies are included in Table 3.3.

Table 3.3 Common methods and methodologies used in Early Childhood Research

Methodologies	Methods
Case study	Observations
Ethnography	Interviews
Autoethnography	Focus groups
Qualitative	Questionnaires
Quantitative	Surveys
Mixed methods	Literature review (systematic or narrative)

Before You Collect Your Data

When you've chosen your research topic, that's where the fun begins. Then you can begin to explore the literature that exists around your topic. Because you've chosen a topic that appeals to you, this is something you should find interesting. You'll learn more about how to conduct your literature review in Chapter 4 (*Joining a research conversation*) but in essence, reading your literature should help you in two respects. Firstly, you want to know what is already known in relation to your research topic, because there's no point in answering questions that have already been answered if your aim is to generate new knowledge. Secondly, reading the literature around your research topic will allow you to identify what types of methodology are used to answer research questions that are similar to your own. Those working at PhD level and beyond will consider the literature related to their research topic, identify what isn't yet known and what *gap in the literature* exists and base their research studies around that. At undergraduate and postgraduate level, reading the literature will allow you to identify what questions appeal to you and you might want to attempt to answer in relation to your particular context.

By the time you've finished considering the literature surrounding your topic, you should have a good grasp of what yet needs to be found out and what in particular sufficiently interests you that you want to conduct a study to find out more.

Coming up with a research question to base your research project around is the next step. Clough and Nutbrown (2012) have come up with two tests to help you devise your research question – the Russian Doll Test and the Goldilocks Test. Are you familiar with Russian dolls? They are sometimes known as Matryoshka dolls or nesting dolls. The principle is that a set of them has a carved, wooden, hollow doll in two pieces, a top and a bottom. When you open and separate them, you'll find a smaller doll inside, again in two pieces. Inside that is another one, and so on. Clough and Nutbrown suggest that thinking about your research question like this is a clever way to narrow down the specifics of exactly what your research question should ask. A similar principle is a funnel, which starts broad and gradually narrows down. In a similar way, your research question may start broad and gradually be refined until it's fit for purpose. What counts as 'fit for purpose' will depend on factors like how much time, money and expertise you have. What is doable for one student may not be for another, but either way, we'd hope they end up with a research question that shares some similar features to that of a SMART objective in terms of being specific, measurable, achievable, relevant and time-bound (though we acknowledge that whether the answer to your research question is measurable may depend on your ontology and epistemology!). The following list gives an example of what the Russian Doll Test might look like in practice:

- Attempt 1: What are teachers' perspectives on working with parents to support children's development?
- Peer feedback: Do you mean all teachers?
- Attempt 2: What are *reception* teachers' perspectives on working with parents to support children's development?
- Peer feedback: Do you mean all children?
- Attempt 3: What are reception teachers' perspectives on working with parents to support *four- and five-year-old* children's development?
- Peer feedback: 'Development' is quite broad. What type of development in particular are you interested in?
- Attempt 4: What are reception teachers' perspectives on working with parents to support four- and five-year-old children's *social and emotional* development?
- Peer feedback: This is getting much more focused! Do you mean all reception teachers, or just ones working in a particular area?
- Attempt 5: What are reception teachers' *in the West Midlands* perspectives on working with parents to support four- and five-year-old children's social and emotional development?
- Peer feedback: This is great!

By the time you have finished refining your research question, it should be a question you are confident that you will be able to answer. It can be good to work with a peer to help you whittle down your question as they may be able to see it and envisage what isn't specific enough in a different light. We will think about the Goldilocks Test a little bit later on, in the *Common Challenge 1* section.

Activity 3.2   Using the Russian Doll Test

As we said earlier, one of the first steps for you after you've chosen your research topic is to read some literature and use your readings to devise a research question. Use the Russian Doll Test (Clough and Nutbrown, 2012) to complete the following list and refine the following research question: 'What do adults think about children's media use?'

- Attempt 1: What do adults think about children's media use?
- Peer feedback:
- Attempt 2:
- Peer feedback:
- Attempt 3:
- Peer feedback:
- Attempt 4:
- Peer feedback:
- Attempt 5:
- Peer feedback:

Reflection

There are many ways that you could have developed the question What do adults think about children's media use? Here is an example of the approach you could have taken.

- Attempt 1: What do adults think about children's media use?
- Peer feedback: 'Adults' is quite broad. Do you mean all adults, or just some in particular?
- Attempt 2: What are *parents'* views on children's media use?
- Peer feedback: Do you mean all media use? Remember that includes things like listening to the radio and reading magazines.
- Attempt 3: What are parents' views on children's *digital* media use?
- Peer feedback: You might find it tricky to consider children of all ages – what about choosing a particular age range?
- Attempt 4: What are parents' views on *toddlers'* digital media use?
- Peer feedback: This is getting close! Are you going to ask parents worldwide, or just those that live in a particular area?
- Attempt 5: What are parents' views on toddlers' digital media use *in a rural area of Wales*?
- Peer feedback: This looks great!

The other key thing that you need to do before you collect your data is gain ethical approval to conduct your study. This may involve completing forms such as an 'ethics application' which sets out what you plan to do, what you think the risks and hazards are of conducting your study, how you plan to ensure your participants' wellbeing and keep their data and personal information safe. This may also involve providing sample copies of documents like consent forms and participant information sheets. We will talk more about this in Chapter 5 (*Ensuring we stay ethical*).

While Collecting Data

Once you've gained ethical approval, that's when you can start to think about collecting your data. There are lots of different ways to collect empirical data, which are built upon in later chapters of the book in Part III, such as observations, interviews and questionnaires. We sometimes come across students who decide first and foremost that there's a particular method they want to use and then work backwards to fit a research question around that. We're going to advise against this – you should have identified a suitable research question following a consideration of the relevant literature, and **then** decide which methods and methodology could help you answer that question and whether you think it would be beneficial or feasible to use more than one method. Table 3.4 outlines some common methods used in Early Childhood Research.

Table 3.4   Common methods used in Early Childhood Research

Common data collection method	Example research question
Interviews	What are parents of under 5s' perspectives about the school starting age in a rural area of North Wales?
Observations	In what ways do children aged 3–4 use mathematical language while engaging in sand and water play in a childminding setting in the South East of England?
Questionnaires	To what extent do Early Childhood practitioners feel they would benefit from ASD training in Manchester, England?
Surveys	What are parents' views on their young children (0–5)s' use of digital technologies at their Early Childhood settings in a rural area of Scotland?
Focus groups	What are the perspectives of Early Childhood Studies students in Northern Ireland about the benefits of undertaking placements?
Children's photographs	What can preschool children's photographs tell us about their favourite outdoor spaces?
Children's drawings	What are reception-aged children's perspectives on why they go to school?
Children's maps	What are Key Stage 1 children's understandings of the features of their local area?

After You've Collected Your Data

When you've collected your data, you might feel like your study changes direction because instead of you predominantly looking outward to other sources of literature and pieces of research, you now begin to look inward at what your own data is telling you. Firstly, you need to make sense of it to work out what you've found, which will become the *Findings* section of your study. Your findings section is a relatively straightforward, descriptive section when you focus on describing what your data tells you. It's often one of the sections of a study that students like writing the most, as it's their chance to tell the reader exactly what they've found through conducting their data collection. The next section of a research study is your *analysis*. This is where you tell the reader (a) what is significant about what you've found, (b) how your findings link to that of wider literature and (c) how your findings help you to answer your research question. We will think more about analysing your findings in Chapter 13 (*Analysing your data*).

What you also need to plan for when designing your study is how you are going to *disseminate* your research. Disseminate literally means 'to spread out'. In relation to research, it means how you plan to share your study so that more people find out about what you've done and may be impacted by it. There are a variety of ways in which you can, or might have to, do this, and these are considered in Chapter 15 (*Disseminating your research through a presentation*), Chapter 16 (*Using posters to share your research*) and Chapter 17 (*Taking other opportunities for publication*). It's really key that you think about dissemination in your initial planning stages, as if you have this in mind while undertaking your project, you can be naturally thinking about how what you are doing translates to your method of dissemination (whether that's a traditional research report, oral, poster or digital presentation, blog, vlog or similar) as you progress through the stages of your study.

OVERCOMING COMMON CHALLENGES WHEN COLLECTING DATA

Sometimes students face challenges when undertaking their research project, particularly when their research design is focused on collecting primary data. Primary data is information that is collected by the researcher themselves. This is in contrast to secondary data, which is data that has been collected by somebody else. In this section we will be thinking about some of the challenges that students face when collecting primary data, and then we will consider some of the ways around those challenges.

Common Challenge 1: Your Research Question

One of the challenges that students face is that sometimes the research question that they are interested in is inappropriate or unsuitable for undergraduate students to answer using primary data. Often this happens because students want to explore a research topic that is too ethically sensitive. For instance, students may want to ask participants questions that are a high risk of causing them emotional harm. Can you think of any examples of what these topics might be? For example, asking participants questions about the impact of an event such as parental divorce or separation on children might cause them to be upset if they themselves experienced this as a child, or if they themselves are parents in this situation. Similarly, asking participants about the impact of sexual, physical or emotional abuse or neglect on a child might be traumatic for participants if they themselves have experienced it. That's why students may find it's not possible to gain ethical approval to carry out their study at undergraduate level for certain sensitive subjects. That means there are some topics that are left to more experienced researchers, maybe those who have already completed their undergraduate degrees, Masters degrees or even PhDs. That could be you one day!

Earlier in this chapter we spoke about how Clough and Nutbrown (2012) have a test called the Russian Doll Test to help students refine their research questions. They have another test for research questions too, called the Goldilocks Test, which we can apply to thinking about research topics instead. If you think back to the traditional tale, Goldilocks' grievances at the bears' cottage centre around how the porridge is too hot and too cold and the chairs are too big and too small, until she finds ones that are 'just right'. Clough and Nutbrown suggest the same can be true in research. It's important that when students consider their potential research questions that they avoid ones that are 'too hot', that is to say, questions that are too ethically sensitive or contentious for undergraduate researchers to explore. They also explain that researchers must avoid ones that are 'too big', for instance topics or questions that are too broad for students to answer in a meaningful, in-depth way, often because of budget or time constraints. And simultaneously, they heed against asking questions that are 'too small', which wouldn't give enough opportunity to demonstrate your ability and skills in devising and conducting a small-scale research project. While we note that Clough and Nutbrown have developed the Goldilocks Test for research questions, the principles hold true for students considering whether they've got a suitable research topic.

Common Challenge 2: Finding Your Participants

The second common challenge that undergraduate students often face is with regard to their participants – whether that's accessing them or sampling them. Sometimes students find it difficult to recruit participants to take part in their studies, or even know where to start with approaching potential participants. Some students overcome this problem by asking their fellow classmates to be their participants but, as we spoke about earlier, we recommend that students work out what methodology will answer their research question and not devise a research question based upon their potential methodology, so recruiting fellow students as participants isn't going to work in all scenarios. This means that some students may need to think of more innovative methods to approach some research questions.

The other challenge about participants that students can face is the sampling technique that they use. Think about the word 'sample' for a moment. If you sample a cake, you try a small bit of it. If you pick up a paint sample tester pot at the DIY shop, you have a small amount of paint to try out. In both instances, the sample is designed to be illustrative of the object as a whole – the cake sample and paint sample should not differ dramatically to the whole cake or a huge tin of paint. The same is true for research. In research, your sample are your participants, and sampling is the process of identifying how you are going to choose from potential research participants. Denscombe (2014) outlines that there are two different approaches to sampling – researchers may use a *representative sample* or an *exploratory sample*. A representative sample is often used in large-scale research and it's intended that the sample of participants will be representative of the wider research population. Conversely exploratory samples are those that aren't a representative cross-section of the wider population as a whole, but instead may include 'interesting, extreme and unusual examples that can illuminate the thing being studied' (Denscombe, 2014, p. 63).

Denscombe goes on to talk about particular sampling techniques. We find that many students utilise convenience sampling, which (as the name suggests) is choosing your sample of participants based on what's convenient. Denscombe describes this as a 'first to hand' approach, as researchers '[use] convenience as the main basis for selecting the sample'. This brings about the advantages that sampling becomes much easier, cheaper and quicker to achieve. However, there are many disadvantages to this type of sampling technique. Denscombe argues that 'choosing things on the basis of convenience runs counter to the rigour of scientific research. It suggests a lazy approach to the work', continuing that 'the practice of convenience sampling is hard to equate with good research' (p. 77).

A Solution: Taking a Different Approach

If you are already thinking that these challenges might relate to you, or there are others that are in the way, don't worry. In this book we acknowledge that there are lots of different, innovative ways for students to overcome some of those common challenges by approaching their research and their data collection in a variety of diverse ways. For instance, Chapter 4 (*Joining a research conversation*) looks at how students can conduct an undergraduate research study by undertaking a systematic or narrative literature review. Meanwhile, Chapter 6 (*Taking an autoethnographic approach*) looks at how a researcher can take their own personal experiences as the basis for answering their research question and Chapter 7 (*Creative approaches to research*) looks at how sources such as photographs from newspapers, films, print and television advertisements, blog posts and children's literature can be used as data to generate knowledge about children, their lives and their childhoods.

The steps you follow to design your research will look similar whether you choose to take a more innovative approach or not, which reflects the fact that – just as we said earlier in this chapter – generally write-ups of research studies all have a similar format.

With this in mind, using a checklist like the one in Table 3.5 can be useful to help you stay on track as you plan your project.

Table 3.5 Designing your research checklist

Have you...	Yes/No
Chosen a topic that is interesting to you?	Yes/No
Had a look at the relevant literature that relates to your topic?	Yes/No
Identified what your research question could be?	Yes/No
Thought about what methods would be appropriate to answer your research question?	Yes/No
Considered who your participants will be?	Yes/No
Reflected on how you will ensure ethical compliance and maintain ethical values?	Yes/No
Explored how you will analyse your data?	Yes/No
Decided how you will disseminate your findings?	Yes/No

Case Study 3.1 Beginning to Think About a Research Study

To begin, Ash feels quite daunted about thinking about their research project, which they have to undertake as part of their Level 6 university studies. They begin by making a list of the topics that they've enjoyed studying and learning about at university so far and decide that one that really stands out to them is about young children who speak English as an additional language. They use their online library catalogue to find out more about the experiences of EAL children in Early Childhood settings and decide that they'd like their research question to focus on the perspectives of Early Childhood practitioners on supporting children who speak English as an additional language. Ash knows their next step is to refine and revise their research question by using a technique such as the Goldilocks Test, and then to begin to think about what might be an appropriate method to collect data to answer their research question and how to gain ethical approval to be able to conduct their study.

KEY POINTS FROM THE CHAPTER

- You need to have worked out and designed how you are going to carry out your research project before you begin it – it may feel daunting at first but planning it all out in advance will make it a lot easier as you go on.
- People will approach their research studies in different ways because everyone sees the world differently. Researchers have their own positionality, which will impact on how they view children and childhoods.

- When thinking about your methodology, you can consider it in three parts – (1) the things you need to sort before you collect your data, (2) the steps involved when collecting your data and (3) what happens after you've collected your data.
- There are some common challenges that undergraduate researchers sometimes face when collecting data. That's okay, because research is supposed to be 'messy'. Using one of more innovative ways outlined later in this book may be a way to overcome these challenges.
- Using a 'Designing your research checklist' can help you keep track of all the steps involved in planning your study.

FURTHER READING

1 In Chapter 1 (*What is research in Early Childhood and why does it matter?*) we recommended you read a book by Tisdall, Davis and Gallagher (2009). We are going to recommend it again here, specifically Chapter 3, called 'Data collection and analysis'. The chapter is brilliant for explaining ontology, epistemology and methodology and giving examples that are specific to research with children:

Tisdall, K., Davis, J. and Gallagher, M. (2009) *Researching with Children and Young People: Research Design, Methods and Analysis.* London: Sage.

2 Clough and Nutbrown (2012) have a lovely chapter called 'What is methodology?' (Chapter 2) which is where you can find more information about their Goldilocks and Russian Doll Tests:

Clough, P. and Nutbrown, C. (2012) *A Student's Guide to Methodology: Justifying Enquiry.* London: Sage.

REFERENCES

Clough, P. and Nutbrown, C. (2012) *A Student's Guide to Methodology: Justifying Enquiry.* London: Sage.

Denscombe, M. (2014) *The Good Research Guide: For Small-Scale Social Research Projects.* Maidenhead: Open University Press.

Dzamesi, F. E., Avornyo, E. A. and Amissah-Essel, S. (2025) 'Ghanaian kindergarten teachers' curriculum knowledge and perspectives on play-based learning: does teacher qualification matter?', *Early Years*, DOI: 10.1080/09575146.2025.2525966.

Kayak (2016) *Friday the 13th Savings.* Available at: www.kayak.co.uk/news/friday-the-13th-flight-savings/ (accessed: 31 July 2025).

Mason, J. (2001) *Researching Your Own Practice: The Discipline of Noticing.* London: Routledge.

Nolsoe, E. (2022) *Positive vibrations, chakras and star signs – what spiritual beliefs do Britons hold?* Available at: https://yougov.co.uk/society/articles/40379-positive-vibrations-chakras-and-star-signs-what-sp (accessed: 8 March 2024).

Papadopoulou, M. and Vincent, K. (2025) 'Making the invisible visible: the pedagogical affordances of outdoor learning in a nursery and a primary school', *Education 3–13: International Journal of Primary, Elementary and Early Years Education*. DOI: https://doi.org/10.1080/03004279.2025.2469724.

Tisdall, K., Davis, J. and Gallagher, M. (2009) *Researching with Children and Young People: Research Design, Methods and Analysis*. London: Sage.

Wilson, S., Murcia, K. and Leaver, T. (2025) '"Switch that off!": the influence of digital parenting and mediation practices on young children's engagement with digital technologies in the home', *Early Child Development and Care*. DOI: 10.1080/03004430.2025.2518300.

4

JOINING A RESEARCH CONVERSATION

CHAPTER OBJECTIVES

By the end of this chapter, you will:

- Understand what it means to 'join a research conversation'
- Recognise some strategies to identify relevant and useful literature
- Understand the differences between narrative and systematic literature reviews.

INTRODUCTION

Have you heard of the idea that when you carry out a study you are actually joining a research conversation about your topic? This chapter will explore the importance of considering the literature as a first step to joining a research conversation. We'll begin by thinking about what we really mean by the term 'literature' and 'research conversation'. We will then consider how we can ensure we are using appropriate sources of literature, through assessing what we read by looking for markers of quality. We will then explore how literature is used both to inform a researcher's knowledge of the topic but can also be used as data itself when conducting literature reviews as the study, for instance through taking a narrative or systematic approach.

BEGINNING TO THINK ABOUT LITERATURE

To begin to think about literature, we need to identify what we mean by the term 'literature', what we mean by 'research conversation' and then consider how we can make sure we are using the most appropriate sources of literature.

What Do We Mean by Literature?

To start off, let's think about what we actually mean by the term 'literature'. In an academic sense, when we say literature, we just mean 'things that are written down'.

Literature can encompass a lot of different types of reading material, which are sometimes called 'texts'. Take a moment to have a think about the types of reading material you might have come across recently. Perhaps you've read a news article on your phone? Got a novel on your bedside table? Flicked through a magazine at the hairdressers? Searched your university library catalogue for a journal article related to something you are studying at the moment? You'll be able to identify that there are differences to each of these types of literature; people read lots of different types of sources as part of their everyday lives because different types of text are used for different purposes.

Different types of texts are also read by different audiences. Some might be described as popular while others might be described as scholarly. There are distinctions between those two types of literature both in terms of who is writing them and who is reading them. Popular sources are more likely to be written, and read, by a general member of the population. Scholarly sources are more likely to be written, and read, by those who are scholars or specialists (or those seeking to become them) in a particular field. Some of the most scholarly sources of information are articles in peer-reviewed journals and academic books. Some of the most popular are blogs from a lay person, tweets and newspaper articles. Yet we need to be mindful about where sources of information are published; as we spoke about in Chapter 2 (*Issues of power in Early Childhood Research*), we know that prominence has been given to Early Childhood Research published in the Global North and published in the English language. So it may be that voices who have been marginalised have sought to publish their work via means that have fewer gatekeepers that are by default more popular, such as in personal blogs or podcasts.

Despite this, it's still worth thinking about where your information is coming from. Hopefully a fair bit of it is comprised of articles in peer-reviewed journals and academic books because those types of literature are most likely written by those with authority in your field. You might also want to add research reports written by other organisations who sit within your discipline; in Early Childhood this might be reports written by bodies such as TACTYC (Together and Committed to Young Children) and BERA (the British Educational Research Association), or charities such as Save the Children, UNICEF and the Children's Society. However, we can't say for certain that publications that sit at the top of the hierarchy will automatically be worthy of including in your academic work, and we can't automatically discount that more popular sources won't. Later on we will consider how other strategies, such as identifying markers of quality, can help us decide what literature to read and refer to. The most important thing to remember is if you are joining a research conversation, you are building on research that has already taken place, and that will determine whether the sources you read are on the more popular or scholarly side.

Sometimes students feel like they don't have time to read the literature – they feel like they need to start planning, writing or conducting their research straight away. It is really important students do devote time to doing this because it'll make it easier to achieve their goal of conducting a successful research project in the long run. It helps guide your thinking and allows you to make well-informed, in-depth points, due to what you've read. It means your reader is able to trust what you are saying, because by referring to literature through including a citation, you are providing evidence to back up your points. And more than that, reading literature allows you to join a research conversation.

What Do We Mean by 'Research Conversation'?

You might be wondering what we mean by 'research conversation'. You might have come across it as an informal term for interviews as a data collection method, but that's not what we mean here. When someone decides to conduct research on a particular topic, what they will naturally do is read the literature that relates to that topic, and join the conversation about that area. When a researcher publishes their work, others can then read their contribution to the conversation, and reply by using that work to inform their own thinking, pieces of research and publications. Thomson (2022) describes the notion of joining a research conversation really well:

> connecting your research with other writings in the field means that you aren't engaged in a monologue over in your own little corner, but are talking with a community which is interested in the same question, topic, puzzle. And by plugging your work into what has gone before you are helping the scholarly community to build knowledge and develop greater understandings. When you refer to other writings, you are also orienting your readers – they can place your work within the discussions they know about.

Thomson talks about how knowledge is built upon; you can imagine wooden building blocks where what goes on top is only possible because of the foundations of what is underneath. This has certainly been the case in our research. Currently we are conducting research to develop understandings about what nature engaging and enhancing experiences can look like for children aged up to 2 in Early Childhood settings (Froebel Trust, 2025). It means we've joined two research conversations. The first is about what very young children do in their Early Childhood setting. Our contribution to this research conversation builds upon previous research that has been conducted about children aged up to 2 in Early Childhood settings, such as Goouch and Powell's (2013) The Baby Room project, which looked at what kind of experiences babies and toddlers had in baby rooms in Early Childhood settings. So, we have joined the research conversation about what babies are doing in Early Childhood settings. We have also joined a research conversation about what nature enhancing and nature engaging pedagogies might look like, by publishing online content for Early Childhood practitioners and parents to use to learn more about young children, the outdoors and nature (The Open University, 2023).

We know that others are now reading our literature and joining our research conversation; such as by citing us as background research in an evaluation of a project across North Wales called *Babi Actif*, which is a project aimed at supporting parents in being active outdoors during pregnancy and with their babies and toddlers aged up to 2

(Babi Actif, 2023). It shows that since joining the research conversation, others are beginning to chip in with their thoughts, ideas and findings to help us develop their understandings.

If you are an undergraduate student, you might not be thinking about publishing your work with a wider audience (although you should, and Part IV: *Telling the World about Your Early Childhood Research* will cover this!). But even if you think that others won't be responding to your research and ideas, it's still important that you see yourself as responding to theirs, through citing the literature they have published.

How Can We Make Sure We Are Using the Most Appropriate Type of Literature?

So now you know what we mean by literature, and why it's important to join a research conversation, we can now think about what literature we should be reading and referring to. We've already considered popular and scholarly sources and thinking about these can be an important place to start in selecting the types of literature that are typically appropriate for university students to cite. But as we said earlier, just because something is a scholarly source it doesn't mean you should definitely use it, and just because something is a popular source, it doesn't mean you should definitely not use it.

To help you decide what sources of literature to use, it can be useful to assess its quality. There are several strategies you can use to make sure that the literature you are using is fit for purpose. One of the strategies is considering the markers of quality of a piece of information (Bolshaw and Josephidou, 2018). Important markers of quality are a source's resonance, truthfulness and integrity, timeliness, style, relevance and provenance of the author. Using a 'markers of quality checklist' such as that in Table 4.1 may serve as a useful prompt to think critically about the information you are coming across.

If you think back to Chapter 2 (*Issues of power in Early Childhood Research*), we thought about how it's important that we invite more voices to the Early Childhood Research conversation, because traditionally some voices have been left out and others given excessive prominence. We considered how indigenous voices and children's voices have been marginalised while research published in the Global North and research published in English have dominated. We want to stress that it's very important you are listening to a wide, inclusive range of voices, of voices who traditionally may have been marginalised, silenced or overlooked. Because some of these voices continue to be marginalised, silenced or overlooked, you might be less likely to find them as scholarly sources of information, because these voices have been excluded from becoming scholars or seen as experts in their fields. It also might mean, in terms of the markers of quality checklist, that the authors may not have the provenance you might expect, that the style and expression requires some linguistic tolerance (Teszenyi, Varga Nagy and Pálfi, 2022), that it might not have been cited by as many sources as others or that it is published in less traditional ways (such as blogs). This means that you may feel justified in using sources that are further down the popular-scholarly hierarchy than you would typically, or don't respond to the markers of quality checklist as favourably, because you recognise you are listening to voices that are trying to join the research conversation but have traditionally been marginalised or overlooked.

Table 4.1 Markers of quality checklist (adapted from Bolshaw and Josephidou, 2018)

Marker of quality	Questions to ask yourself
Resonance	• Does it resonate with you, as the reader, and further your knowledge? • Have other academics and authors responded to it positively? • How often does it appear to be cited by authors?
Truthfulness and integrity	• Is information presented in an objective way? • Does the author have a vested interest in presenting a particular point of view? • Who are the intended audience of the piece of information?
Timeliness of the information	• How old is the piece of information? • Has relevant context (e.g. policy and legislation) changed since it was written?
Style	• Does the information look professionally presented? • Can you see any spelling or grammar mistakes? • Is it using appropriate language?
Provenance of the author	• Is the author well known in their field? • What is the author's discipline? How might that impact on the perspective they take? • Can you find other things they have published? • Who else has cited their sources of information?
Relevance of the information presented	• Is the information presented in a sufficient level of detail? • Does the source have an appropriate emphasis on the topic you are exploring? • Where was the information published, or the research conducted? Is it in the same geographic context that you are writing about?

Activity 4.1   Using Markers of Quality

To develop your ability to use the markers of quality to assess whether what you are reading is appropriate, have a go at applying them to a source of literature you have found. Choose a topic relating to Early Childhood that interests you. It could be something like child poverty, promoting reading, children's mental health or their digital wellbeing. Find a source of information about that topic from (a) a newspaper article, (b) a peer-reviewed journal article and (c) a charity or government report. How could you critique these three sources in line with the markers of quality? Remember that 'to critique' doesn't mean 'to

(Continued)

criticise', but rather to evaluate the pros and cons of something. Working through a list of the markers and considering a critique for each one might help you:

Marker of quality

- Resonance
- Truthfulness and integrity
- Timeliness of information
- Style
- Provenance of author
- Relevance of the information presented

Reflection

Hopefully this activity has helped you put into practice the different ways in which you can critique a source of information. Take some time to reflect on how your critiques for the three different sources (newspaper article, journal article and report) differed. Did you notice they had the same advantages and disadvantages, or different ones?

WHEN TO READ THE LITERATURE

As we said earlier, sometimes students feel like they don't have time to read; in the past we've had students tell us it can feel frustrating to have devoted a chunk of time to reading and not have anything physical to show for it, because their assignment word count hasn't changed. But also, as we said earlier, reading is a key part of any research project, whether the literature referred to is predominantly providing a rationale for the topic chosen and supporting a consideration of the methodology and data collection methods, or whether the literature you are reading is itself your data. In this section we will consider two main reasons to read the literature: to inform your knowledge of your research topic or even to use the literature as your data.

Reading Literature to Inform Your Knowledge of Your Research Topic

The first type of reading you'll need to do when conducting a research project is to read literature that links to your research topic. We spoke in Chapter 3 (*Designing your research project*) about how this is something that you do to help you identify what is already known in relation to your topic. Those working at PhD level and beyond will also be reading the literature to identify what *gap in the literature* exists so they can base their research project around generating new knowledge. At undergraduate and postgraduate level, reading the literature will allow you to identify what questions appeal to you and what questions you might want to attempt to answer in relation to your particular context.

Firstly, this means you'll have to decide where you are going to look for your literature. Often students go-to is Google, or Google Scholar. There are advantages to using
Google Scholar, including one important one which we'll talk about a little bit later, but
there are disadvantages too. A couple of the disadvantages are that you might find it
frustrating to come across literature that you don't actually have access to, and the second is that you might come across literature that isn't high quality. Using a university
library search engine is a way to avoid both of those disadvantages. A library search
engine will be able to retrieve only sources you have full access to, and that have been
selected by a subject librarian at your institution. This acts like an extra 'verification
check' in terms of the quality of the sources you are using.

Secondly, this means you'll have to identify what *key words* are relevant to type into
your library search engine. What's tricky about Early Childhood is that there are many
synonyms for some of the key words that are used. In research we conducted about the
impact of staff qualification levels in Early Childhood on the experiences of, and outcomes for, children and families, we found that there was a wide variety of terms used
(Josephidou et al., 2021). For instance, while in England we might refer to an Early
Childhood setting as a 'nursery', elsewhere the same provision may be called a 'kindergarten' or 'daycare'. Some research papers might use the term 'children' while others
refer to them as '0–5s' or '0 to 5s'. Using a variety of key words increases your chances
that you'll come across all the relevant literature that links to your topic and that you
won't overlook anything important. Table 4.2 lists some of the synonyms we had to use
to ensure we had a good overview of all the relevant literature for our topic.

Table 4.2   Synonyms for key terms in Early Childhood Research

Category	List of synonyms
staff	"early years practitioner"; practitioner; educator; teacher; "early years teacher"; EYPS; EYP; pedagogue; professional; workforce; Professionalisation; "graduate practitioner"; "childhood practitioner"; "Early Childhood educator"; "Early Childhood teachers"; "childcare supervision"; "nursery nurse"; nanny; childminder; "lead practitioner"; "(teaching) assistant"; HTLA; LTA; TA; "family support worker"
children	infants; babies; toddlers; pre-schoolers; child; "birth to 5"; 0 to 5; 0–5; 0–8; "birth to 8"
ECEC	"Early Childhood education"; nursery; preschool; pre-school; daycare; childcare; "Early Childhood education and care"; kindergarten; "early years"; policy; quality; playgroup; pre-primary; pre-elementary; pedagogy; "child care"; setting; provision
families	parent; sibling; mother; father; brother; sister; relative; family; "hard to reach"; carer

It's likely that, when you are looking for literature, you come across more than you
can manage. Think about how you can narrow down what your search retrieves by
thinking about the filters it's possible to apply through the university search engine you
are using. Students commonly might apply filters based on things such as the age of the

source, type of source, subject or name of publication. Table 4.3 gives more details about each of these things.

Table 4.3 Common filters that are applied when searching the literature

Filter	Reason for using it
Date of publication	You might want to filter by the date of publication, so that you only retrieve sources published in a certain time period, for instance the last 10 years, or since a particular policy or legislation has been in force.
Type of source	You might want to filter by the type of source, so you only retrieve sources that are the most scholarly, such as books and journal articles. You may be able to filter to retrieve only journal articles that have been peer-reviewed, too. When something has been peer-reviewed, that's like an additional 'verification check' by experts in the field that has been done to check something is worthy of publication.
Subject	It's often possible to filter by subject, where you could click "Early Childhood" or similar to retrieve results from your discipline.
Name of publication	Sometimes students find their search terms return information that isn't as relevant because it comes from other disciplines such as health. Filtering by the name of publication to retrieve only journals from within the discipline of Early Childhood can be one way of ensuring the articles you access are more likely to meet your needs.

Finally, we said earlier that although your university search engine should be your go-to, there can be advantages to using Google Scholar. One of these is the ability to see who has cited a particular piece of work (some library search engines provide this function too). A publication which has been cited in a large number of pieces of literature may have more resonance, which you'll remember is a marker of quality you can use to assess a source. It is contributing to more research conversations, too.

Reading Literature as a Form of Data Collection

As well as reading the literature to inform your knowledge of your research topic, some people also choose to use the literature as their data, by conducting a piece of research called *literature review*. Undertaking a literature review as your research project still means that you have to design your piece of research in a similar way to how we outlined in Chapter 3 (*Designing your research project*) by starting with identifying your research topic, position and research question before thinking about your methodology. There are two methodologies that are typically adopted for those seeking to use literature as their data: *narrative reviews* and *systematic reviews*. Greenhalgh, Thorne and Malterud (2018, p. 2) note that systematic reviews are 'generally placed above narrative reviews in an assumed hierarchy of secondary evidence', although argue that they should be seen as complementary because they have different purposes. The main difference, we would suggest, is that systematic reviews, as the name implies, take a purely systematic approach in how the data is gathered and findings drawn together; Page et al. (2021, p. 2) describe them as 'a review that uses explicit, systematic methods to collate and synthesize findings of studies that address a clearly formulated question', whereas narrative reviews have a less specific process (but not less rigorous) to follow, where 'the onus is on you to find relevant literature, assess it, and weave it into a meaningful account' (Thomas, 2025, p. 7).

Narrative reviews are the kind that undergraduate students are more likely to undertake although their name isn't particularly helpful; Thomas (2025, p. 119) notes how the term doesn't reflect what a literature review needs to do, as 'a review scans, searches, finds and integrates'. A narrative review should 'provide interpretation and critique; their contribution is deepening understanding' (Greenhalgh, Thorne and Malterud, 2018, p. 2). Thomas (2025) suggests that there are five different structures you might adopt:

- **A funnelled approach**, in which your review starts with more general information before funnelling down to literature that is more specific to your topic.
- **A thematic approach,** in which you group the literature by theme.
- **A chronological approach,** where you present the literature in broadly chronological order to demonstrate how thinking may have changed over time.
- **A comparison-based approach**, which focuses on making a comparison between literature that has difference in areas such as the methodology, or contrasting findings.
- **A mixed approach,** which uses more than one of the above approaches.

Systematic reviews have a procedure which is 'painstaking and time-intensive and which it is unlikely that student researchers will have the time or resources to undertake' (Thomas, 2025, p. 133). To illustrate this, in a recent one that we conducted, we screened almost 14,000 articles that were retrieved by our search strand, before eventually identifying 41 that met our inclusion criteria (Kemp, Josephidou and Bolshaw, 2025). Systematic reviews aim to address 'narrowly focused questions; their key contribution is summarising data' (Greenhalgh, Thorne and Malterud, 2018, p. 2). But if you are thinking about doing a systematic literature review, you might want to consider using the process outlined by the PRISMA (Preferred Reporting Items for Systematic Reviews and Meta-Analyses) approach (Page et al., 2021). Page et al. (2021) have created a useful checklist for when planning systematic reviews to ensure that you've included everything you need and followed a systematic process. Alternatively, you might also want to look at Gough, Oliver and Thomas' (2017) text, which explains procedures for conducting systematic reviews developed by the Evidence for Policy Practice Information (EPPI) Centre.

Activity 4.2   Comparing Narrative and Systematic Reviews

We have been involved in conducting both narrative and systematic literature reviews and have selected two for you to have a look at. Read through them both and draw up a list of how you think they compare in terms of their methodology:

Kemp, N. and Josephidou, J. (2023) 'Babies and toddlers outdoors: a narrative review of the literature on provision for under twos in ECEC settings', *Early Years: An International Research Journal*, *43*(1), pp. 137–50.

Kemp, N., Josephidou, J. and Bolshaw, P. (2025) '"Tiny humans" outdoors: understanding the factors that mediate opportunities for babies and toddlers', *Children's Geographies*, *23*(2), pp. 219–36.

Reflection

You have probably noticed that there are similarities and differences between them. For instance, both focus broadly on the same topic of babies' and toddlers' outdoor experiences. Both of them take a thematic approach to analysing the findings. You will also have noticed that there are overlaps in the literature cited, too. But there are differences. For instance in our systematic review we had clearly defined which four databases we would search for literature using clearly defined search strategies (Kemp, Josephidou and Bolshaw, 2025). In our narrative review we searched across six databases but also consulted personal contacts and authors to check for additional sources that might be relevant (Kemp and Josephidou, 2023).

Case Study 4.1   Doing a Literature Review for an Undergraduate Dissertation

Foluke wants to do a literature review for her undergraduate dissertation about the development of forest school provision in England. She is leaning towards a narrative approach but has concerns that they are not seen as rigorous enough. However, she knows that systematic reviews are incredibly time-intensive and are often completed by a team of people rather than one individual. For advice on which approach she should take, she has a look at Greenhalgh, Thorne and Malterud's (2018) journal article about the perceived superiority of systematic reviews over narrative ones. It reassures her that narrative reviews 'are not unsystematic (in the sense of being *ad hoc* or careless' (2018, p. 3) and that there are limitations to systematic reviews that shouldn't go unstated, such as their focus on summarising data rather than building understanding, which is what she wants to do in relation to forest school provision. After a chat with her dissertation supervisor she decides that a narrative approach is more appropriate for her.

KEY POINTS FROM THE CHAPTER

- It's important to think about how when people publish their study, they are joining a research conversation about their topic.
- Reading literature is key to help build your understanding of your research topic.
- Use criteria such as markers of quality (Bolshaw and Josephidou, 2018) to help you assess the literature you are reading.
- You might use literature as your data, by conducting a narrative or systematic literature review.

FURTHER READING

1   Gary Thomas' (2025) book about conducting literature reviews is an incredibly useful text for advice and guidance on how to search the literature. It provides useful guidance for those wishing to do a narrative or systematic literature review, too.

Thomas, G. (2025) *How to Do Your Literature Review*. London: Sage.

2   In Chapter 2 (*Issues of power in Early Childhood Research*) we referred to a piece of literature by McMellon and Tisdall (2020) in which they conducted a literature review of articles from one particular journal, *The International Journal of Children's Rights*, to identify what the literature said about children and young people's participation in the 30 years since the adoption of the UNCRC.

McMellon, C. and Tisdall, E.K.M. (2020) 'Children and young people's participation rights: looking backwards and moving forwards', *International Journal of Children's Rights*, 28, pp. 157–82.

REFERENCES

Babi Actif (2023) *Babi Actif: creating a culture of active families*. Available at: www.babiactif.co.uk/wp-content/uploads/2024/01/Babi-Actif-English-report.pdf (accessed: 31 July 2025).

Bolshaw, P. and Josephidou, J. (2018) *Introducing Research in Early Childhood*. London: Sage.

Froebel Trust (2025) *A Froebelian inspired nature pedagogy in urban babyrooms*. Available at: www.froebel.org.uk/research-library/a-froebelian-inspired-nature-pedagogy-in-urban-babyrooms (accessed: 31 July 2025).

Goouch, K. and Powell, S. (2013) *The Baby Room: Principles, Policy and Practice*. Milton Keynes: Open University Press.

Gough, D., Oliver, S. and Thomas, J. (2017) *An Introduction to Systematic Reviews*. London: Sage.

Greenhalgh, T., Thorne, S. and Malterud, K. (2018) 'Time to challenge the spurious hierarchy of systematic over narrative reviews?', *European Journal of Clinical Investigation*, 48(6). DOI: https://doi.org/10.1111/eci.12931.

Josephidou, J., Rodriguez-Leon, L., Bennett, S., Bolshaw, P., Musgrave, J. and Rix, J. (2021) *Where measurement stops: A review of systematic reviews exploring international research evidence on the impact of staff qualification levels in ECEC on the experiences of, and outcomes for, children and families.* A TACTYC funded report. Available at: https://tactyc.org.uk/wp-content/uploads/2022/01/Where-measurement-stops_FINAL_Dec2021.docx (accessed: 31 July 2025).

Kemp, N. and Josephidou, J. (2023) 'Babies and toddlers outdoors: a narrative review of the literature on provision for under twos in ECEC settings', *Early Years: An International Research Journal, 43*(1), pp. 137–50.

Kemp, N., Josephidou, J. and Bolshaw, P. (2025) '"Tiny humans" outdoors: understanding the factors that mediate opportunities for babies and toddlers', *Children's Geographies, 23*(2), pp. 219–36.

Page, M.J., Moher, D., Bossuyt, P.M., Boutron, I., Hoffmann, T.C., Mulrow, C.D. et al. (2021) 'PRISMA 2020 explanation and elaboration: updated guidance and exemplars for reporting systematic reviews', *British Medical Journal, 372.* DOI: https:// doi:10.1136/bmj.n160.

Teszenyi, E., Varga Nagy, A. and Pálfi, S. (2022) 'Re-imagining socialist childhoods: changing narratives of spatial and temporal (dis)orientations', *Journal of Childhood, Education and Society, 3*(3), pp. 212–17. DOI: https://doi.org/10.37291/27176 38X.202233252.

The Open University (2023) *Young children, the outdoors and nature.* Available at: www.open.edu/openlearn/mod/oucontent/view.php?id=141651&section=__ acknowledgements (accessed: 31 July 2025).

Thomas, G. (2025) *How to Do Your Literature Review.* London: Sage.

Thomson, P. (2022) *What does 'connect your work to an ongoing conversation' mean?* Available at: https://patthomson.net/2022/03/14/%EF%BF%BCwhat-does-connect-your-work-to-an-ongoing-conversation-mean/ (accessed: 31 July 2025).

5
ENSURING WE STAY ETHICAL

CHAPTER OBJECTIVES

By the end of this chapter, you will:

- Appreciate the key differences between ethical values and ethical compliance
- Identify how considering ethical values through all elements of the research process can address power imbalances in research
- Understand how ethics are a key consideration when thinking about reliability and validity.

INTRODUCTION

In the previous chapter, you thought about how understanding the key literature in your area of focus can be a vital provocation in terms of knowing what you want to find out, and how you are going to go about this. However, you could be ready to go, have the perfect research design, you even have a setting in which to conduct fieldwork, but this is where you must stop and think carefully about the ethics of your work. It is not permissible to carry out research without first having ethical approval; usually this will be granted by the higher education institute where you are carrying out your research as a student. To obtain this approval, you will need to complete an application and submit this to a panel of academics who will review, make suggestions and ultimately, when they are happy with the way you wish to proceed and are confident that you have met laid down ethical guidelines, will approve your proposal. We have noticed that would-be researchers can feel negative about this step and see it as a tick box exercise, however we argue that it is a useful task to complete because it will help you refine and develop your project.

Until you have ethical approval you must not proceed. As part of your application you may also have to submit any questionnaires, interview questions or other research tools you intend to use. This can be a particularly difficult thing to pin down at an early stage, ironically the very stage that you need to gain ethical approval; but grit your teeth and bear in mind that this process will support you in ensuring you are rigorous in your research design and also that you are not proposing something that will not work. Bear in mind that ethics panels are made up of very experienced academics so they will help you to recognise some of the flaws in your potential research decisions. In some institutions, at undergraduate level, it may be just your dissertation supervisor who reviews your application and grants you ethical approval, but they will draw on the expertise of their colleagues if there is anything that concerns them or that they are unsure about.

This chapter focuses on the ways in which undergraduate researchers must ensure 'ethical compliance' and hold 'ethical values' (Bolshaw and Josephidou, 2018) throughout all stages of the research process. It specifically considers the ways in which ensuring we stay ethical can help mitigate the power imbalances that exist in ECEC research, for instance in literature cited, participant selection, research methods, data analysis and dissemination of research. The chapter will also consider what is meant by validity and reliability in relation to staying ethical in Early Childhood Research.

ETHICAL VALUES AND ETHICAL COMPLIANCE

In this first section of the chapter we are going to consider the *must* and the *should* of ethical research. It is important to realise that there are minimum requirements you must fulfil to ensure that ethics committees are satisfied you are going to proceed in research ethically and so sign off your proposal. These will differ according to the experiences and perspectives of your panel. They will not always have the same subject knowledge as you so it is very important that you set out your proposal clearly and explicitly so that they can make an informed decision. You may have to describe to them ideas and issues that are outside their experience but that you perhaps take for granted. For example, you may decide that you would like to ask children to talk about photos you have taken of them playing in the early years setting in a project which focuses on children's understandings of play. If you work in a setting, this may be part of your everyday practice, where you take photographs to share with parents, discuss with children and to record learning. However, unless the panel have a good understanding of the role of documentation in early years pedagogy, they could raise ethical questions which you may believe to be 'overkill'; it is your responsibility to explain clearly the context of these methodological decisions you have made.

There are other considerations you may like to reflect on if you particularly want to address any power issues that potentially exist in your research and how your values may inform the ways you proceed. We would argue this is vital when your research involves young children. This consideration will be important long before you meet any participants; it will inform how you search the literature, how you recruit participants and how you develop your research approach.

Ethics and Power Imbalances: Using the Literature

In Chapter 4 (*Joining a research conversation*), you learnt how thinking about which literature conversations you want to join is an important part of the research focus, but how do you ensure you do this in an ethical way? This is a consideration that may not arise for your review panel, depending on their own experiences, but you must address it if you are committed to addressing issues of power in research. How will you ensure that you pay attention to different voices, are all voices represented in the research you review, and if not, will you draw attention to this? Finally, has ethics been addressed in terms of authorship of papers and who is given credit for this? You will not be able to answer all these questions, but they are important considerations for the ethical researcher.

When you conduct a literature search ethically, you will ensure that you are not just drawing from those areas of the world that dominate in Early Childhood Research such as USA, Australia, Europe etc. Researchers all over the world have had to accept the fact that to be published in revered journals, their work needs to be written up in English. This is problematic in terms of power issues and authentic understanding of context and specific terminology which is culturally bound and not easy to translate. In recent years there has been a push back and a realisation of the arrogance inherent in an English language-biased approach. However, English does still dominate. It is good, during your literature search, to not add the filter for English language only; this will help you gain an awareness of what other literature exists and shows you have been systematic in your approach even if you cannot read it. We did this for our *From Weeds to Tiny Flowers* report (Kemp, Josephidou and Bolshaw, 2023) and found several articles not in English. However, we were able to eliminate these papers as not appropriate for our report, by reviewing abstracts with colleagues who could read and understand the languages used – and a little bit of support from Google Translate!

One thing we realised very quickly in the above report was that in the papers reviewed, certain voices dominated while others were not represented. We ended up reviewing 41 papers which included research from 15 countries; if you look at the table below you can see which these countries were:

Table 5.1 The countries represented in the *From Weeds to Tiny Flowers* report (adapted from Kemp, Josephidou and Bolshaw, 2023)

Country	Number of papers included in the review (n = 41)
USA	9
Australia	8
England	4
Canada	4
Finland	3

(Continued)

Table 5.1 (Continued)

Country	Number of papers included in the review (n = 41)
Germany	3
Norway	2
New Zealand	1
Hungary	1
Chile	1
Spain	1
Netherlands	1
China	1
Sweden	1
Ghana	1

You will see from Table 5.1 that certain countries dominate the research discussion we were contributing to, i.e. babies and toddlers outdoors, and that most countries were from the Global North. The papers from Australia included only one which addressed indigenous voices, the paper from Ghana was carried out by a research team from the USA and Ghana and while it was good to see the voice of underrepresented countries included, the focus was on malaria prevention rather than any celebration of cultural practices compared to many of the other papers we reviewed.

Research is continually evolving and there has been a drive in recent years, particularly in the wake of #MeToo and the Black Lives Matter movement, to seek more ethical ways of including more diverse voices in research. One such way has been the Contributor Roles Taxonomy (NISO, n.d.). This initiative is a way of ensuring that all contributions to a piece of research are recognised and valued, not just those of the main academic author(s). This initiative recognises that there are 14 different contributions that can be made to a piece of research, which we have set out in the Table 5.2. We are not suggesting that you need to consider all these elements in your own work, but it is a useful overview to have when you are reading others' work. As we review the literature ethically, we should value studies that have taken this approach and there may also be elements you would like to consider when you write up your own work. We have added a third column to the table so that you could think about any considerations you could make.

This section has considered how the key literature can be reviewed in an ethical manner including reviewing who has written the research, geographical contexts and opportunities to foreground more marginalised voices. For the next section, we are going to think about how you might think about ethics in terms of your research design.

Table 5.2 Contributions to the research process (adapted from Contributor Roles Taxonomy (NISO, n.d.))

Possible contribution	Definition in practice	What could this mean in your EC research project?
Conceptualisation and methodology	Developing ideas about research aims and design.	How will you acknowledge those people who have helped you develop your ideas, your proposal and your completed work?
Data collection	Who collects the data.	You would probably do this yourself, but you may ask participants to do some for you or you may ask gatekeepers to collate some data for you, e.g. examples of children's drawings from teachers.
Data curation	Managing and organising the collected data.	In an undergraduate research project this should be work you undertake yourself.
Analysis	How you analyse your data.	This will be work that you should do yourself, however you should note if you use any software to support the analysis, e.g. Nvivo. Some researchers also ask participants to help with an analysis and so they should be acknowledged.
Funding	Both if an organisation has funded the project and if someone has supported in finding funding.	Generally would not be applicable to undergraduate research, however there are some opportunities; e.g. some students are awarded funding to attend an undergraduate research conference to present findings such as The British Conference of Undergraduate Research at Newcastle University.
Project administration	How the activities in your research are planned and carried out.	This is your responsibility, however don't underestimate how much you will need to draw on the expertise, understanding and collaboration of those in the field such as practitioners, headteachers etc.
Resources	Any materials that have been offered that support your project.	Will you need to acknowledge the provision of any resources, e.g. from an early years setting (i.e. policies/children's work etc.)
Supervision	How you are supported, mentored and supervised to carry out your research.	Will you remember to thank your supervisor in your acknowledgements as you write up your research, or indeed any other gatekeepers who support and supervise your research work?
Writing up	Writing up your research report.	This is your responsibility – with support from your supervisor. However, you may also get feedback from your participants.
Presentation	How you present your findings for dissemination purposes.	This is your responsibility in terms of putting together your research report, however you may decide to present your findings in a variety of ways for a variety of audiences – you may need to draw on the expertise of others to do this, so don't forget to acknowledge them.

Ethics and Power Imbalances: Selecting Your Methods

As you have engaged in your literature search you will no doubt have been able to read about different methodologies appropriate for your area of focus. This is a really good way to become informed about appropriate data collection methods which you can then adapt for your own design. However, there are some pitfalls you should be aware of, so it is important to read critically and think carefully about approaches that have interested you. For example, you may want to consider the date of research, the geographical context or the scale of the research.

Date

Carefully consider the date of the research paper you are reading and then think about the methodology chosen before you decide to replicate. For example, Warin (2000) asked children to be photographed in gender-specific clothes such as a pink frilly dress, to explore children's perceptions of gender (Bolshaw and Josephidou, 2018). Twenty plus years ago this may have appeared to be an appropriate methodology to explore young children's identity but given the polarising and contentious issue that the topic of gender has subsequently become, would Warin still choose this approach if she was carrying out this work today? Reflecting on this question, Warin states:

> ... this is a good example of a dated ethical approach. I would do this very differently if I were to do something similar now. Actually I would not be doing the study in the same way at all now as my thinking and theoretical stance have changed. At that time (nineteen nineties when I was doing the study – my PhD study) I was still using Kohlberg's ideas about the ages at which children recognise their gender group membership which assumes and works with a gender binary approach. My recent publications demonstrate a very different approach celebrating queer theory and non-binary approaches. (J. Warin, personal communication, 17 April 2024)

Presumably it would also now be difficult to gain ethical approval for such an approach.

Context

It is also important to consider the geographical and cultural context of the research. For example, you may read of an appealing methodology that appears to work well with preschool children and decide you would like to adapt it for your own work. Before you proceed look carefully at the geographical context and therefore the age of the children. School starting ages differ country to country so a methodology with 6-year-olds at preschool in Germany may not be appropriate with 3-year-olds in England.

Scale

In section three of this chapter, we will think about ethics during the dissemination process, but it is also important to think about this while designing your research.

You may read of a research design that appeals to you because of the interesting findings that it produced. However, look carefully at the scale of the research – is this really something that you could replicate in terms of number of participants, length of project, amount of data collected? If not, you need to look back again at your research question, the doable nature of your study and the claims and recommendations, you want to be able to make; these are all part of the ethical process when undertaking research.

As we have seen in this section, ethical considerations are a key part of research design, along with the areas touched on above you will want to think very carefully about how different approaches will be ethically appropriate for different kinds of participants, approaches that will allow participants to feel comfortable, share their perspectives and therefore contribute to knowledge. The next section will consider more fully how you can take an ethical approach when finding participants.

Ethics and Power Imbalances: Selecting Your Participants

In the previous section, you thought carefully about how your methods need to be thought through ethically; at the same time you will be thinking about who you would like your participants to be and how you will go about recruiting them. If they are children, or people working within an institutional setting, there will be others to act as gatekeepers so it is important to consider how you can work in an ethical way with these gatekeepers.

Before undertaking any piece of research with participants, you will need evidence that you have gained their consent. This part of the process means that you will need to show that you have informed them about the purposes of the research and their role in it, they know what will happen with the data they contribute to, and that they can withdraw at any time. This is a lot of information to share, and it is important that it is done in an accessible way and that participants can ask questions. There is also a delicate balance to be struck between providing enough information for participants to make an informed decision and not overwhelming them with information. It can be tricky to ensure that participants have understood what they are consenting to; they may be unfamiliar with terminology and concepts articulated by the researcher. As Warin states, 'Even when working with adults "informed consent" is a much more complex business than it a first appears, since researchers must make difficult decisions about the quantity, quality, and timing of information' (2011, p. 807). By sharing information about the research in a way that the participants can understand they are then able to give their consent. We have constantly come across difficulties in this area. Participants can be very eager to be included when they hear about our research but then when they need to read detailed information sheets (as required by ethical panels) and sign formal consent forms, they can often decide at this point that the project is no longer for them.

And what about those who cannot read detailed information sheets or sign their names on consent forms, for example what about young children? The methodology literature is full of ideas as to how assent can be obtained from young children (consent needs to be given by a parent or carer). But how would a researcher know if a child had truly given their consent? For example, when we have carried out research in schools and shared what we are going to do with the information the children have given us, we have noticed that, depending on the age group, there can often be misunderstandings. For example, we noted on one occasion that the children thought we were going to write a storybook with the data, although on reflection, perhaps that was a great idea, and we should have done! However, the reality is that the children clearly didn't completely understand what they were consenting to. Other issues for us have been when parents have chosen to opt their children out of a research project taking place in school so that the children had no say in the matter at all.

As far as those children who do give their consent are concerned, they may feel obliged to say yes to an adult figure in authority; in fact we could argue that they have been conditioned to do so in an educational setting. The ethical researcher must be aware that giving consent is a continual process of 'ethics in practice' (Warin, 2011) not a one-off tick list event. This involves watching the children's body language for any signs they may be giving that they are not comfortable participating.

When working with child participants aged 3, Flewitt (2006) described how she felt confident that they demonstrated an adequate understanding of how the research might impact on them, so that they were truly offering informed consent. In her view, they demonstrated this by asking questions about whether taking part would interfere with their play time; she also let them handle the video equipment she intended to use and thus felt they showed a good understanding of the data collection methods that would be employed. Another device she utilised effectively was to get the parents to explain the research to the children because she knew they were best placed to articulate it in a way their individual children would understand.

If you are conducting research in an educational setting, you will also need to have consent from the gatekeepers in that setting which could include headteachers and class teachers, setting managers and room leads. This situation can also bring with it its own problems; you may have a headteacher who finds your area of focus fascinating and therefore is very keen for you to carry out your research, whereas the busy class teacher, in whose class you wish to work with children, just hasn't got the buy in – it is just one more thing for them to fit into a crowded timetable. When this has happened to us before, we have noted that there is a gap between awareness of the project, including its importance, and the motivation to be involved. Those with whom we have been able to share why we think our research is important are more inclined to come onboard than those who have been told the research is going to 'happen to them'; this may seem a common-sense point to make but is a real issue in the considerable hierarchies of educational settings. Of course, the inverse is also possible, where a practitioner is very keen for you to carry out research in their setting, but you may have to convince the manager as gatekeeper about the importance and viability of what you want to do.

Activity 5.1   Using Ethical Guidelines

There are many ethical guidelines you can draw upon while thinking about the ethics application for your research. Indeed, you will have to cite the ones you have used. Do a simple internet search now and see how many you can come up with. You could use two of these and do a simple compare exercise. Look for common threads and major differences.

Reflection

How many did you manage to find? Two of the guidelines often used by researchers in Early Childhood are the BERA (British Educational Research Association) guidelines (2024) and the EECERA (Ethical Code for Early Childhood Researchers) guidelines (Bertram et al., 2024). Either of these would be appropriate for you to reference in your ethics submission. The BERA guidelines are appropriate for anyone doing educational research and the EECERA guidelines have been written by those with a specific expertise in Early Childhood. You may also find it interesting to look at the Save the Children Ethical Guidelines (Feinstein and O'Kane, 2008) as they have tried to incorporate children's suggestions and address some issues of power.

ETHICS IN ANALYSIS

Let's imagine that you are successfully moving on in your research project, including addressing any ethical issues that may arrive. You have gained ethical approval, successfully obtained consent from your participants and have gathered some lovely data that you are excited about beginning to analyse. You may be feeling at this point that you can be quite complacent about ethics, that it is all in hand. However, we would argue this is not the case; remember our previous point about thinking about ethics throughout all the research process. During the process of analysis you will be making important decisions about what to include and what to exclude, bringing your own values and perspectives to inform these decisions. Here it is pertinent to consider two key research terms: reliability and validity; you may come across them in your reading. These are important terms to consider although it must be stressed that they are 'borrowed' from scientific research and therefore are not always appropriate to use in social science research which is concerned with people's behaviours. Thomas (2017) infers that the disciplines of the social sciences may feel it is necessary to use the language of scientific research to justify their position in the academic world. This is particularly true of qualitative research which relies on words to paint a picture of a social situation or phenomenon and whose findings are often based on researcher interpretations. However, we do need to think about the rigour of our research and to do this we need to pay attention to both validity and reliability, albeit in a slightly more nuanced way. The important thing here is to consider our integrity as researchers and how that informs the decisions we make when analysing the data. We will now consider how we can use the terms validity and reliability to help us think about integrity in our own work thorough our analysis.

Thinking About Validity

Edwards (2010) believes that *'Validity* is often a vexed issue in *qualitative research* approaches' (p. 162). This is an important point to bear in mind as Early Childhood Studies small-scale research projects are often qualitative. However, regardless of its problematic use in Early Childhood Research, it is good for you to consider the idea of validity as you proceed. Edwards helpfully suggests a focus on the term 'authenticity' to understand validity in the context within which you are researching, e.g. how have you managed to authentically capture the perspectives of your participants? Cian (2021) offers the term 'trustworthiness' as a synonym for validity and we think this is a useful term to consider. How can the reader trust that your findings are informed by a rigorous analysis of your data? It may be useful here to frame this as a question-and-answer response between reader and researcher.

- The reader asks: How can I trust the recommendations you make at the end of your research report?
- The researcher responds: If you look at the Findings you will see that the recommendations are based clearly on them.
- The reader asks: Yes, I have read the Findings but how I can trust that what you say you have found out is true?
- The researcher responds: Well, this is a good point. I am not saying what I have found out is the only truth. I am saying this is my interpretation. You can trust that I have told you exactly how I analysed my data, what I have both kept in and omitted. I set out what I believe are the limitations of my research and I have shown you a sample of the raw data collected in the appendices.

You can see here that the key word is trust. You need to give the reader all the information they need to make an informed decision about the validity or trustworthiness of your work.

Thinking About Reliability

The notion of reliability is slightly more problematic in a small-scale qualitative study as this idea is usually based around replicability, i.e. that someone could follow your data collection methods and arrive at similar findings. Of course, given the small sample of participants you will work with and the context of your research, it is unlikely that someone will find out the same as you in a different context with different participants. In fact, we would suggest that even if the same research were conducted in the same space with the same participants, different conclusions would be made, such is the nature of qualitative research. However, there are aspects of reliability which will be useful to you as you read other's work and think about your methodology. For example, systematic reviews of children's voice research such as Sun et al.'s (2023) demonstrate how questions directed at children can be piloted and then adapted to lead to more informed responses and therefore more reliable data. What this means for you in your own small-scale work is to look at questions that have been used before in other studies to unearth specific perspectives.

Activity 5.2   Addressing Ethics

Find a peer-reviewed research article concerned with young children. If you are not sure where to start, try these journals:

- *EECERJ: European Early Childhood Education Research Journal*
- *Early Years: An International Research Journal*
- *JCES: Journal of Childhood, Education and Society*

For your chosen article, note if the authors have commented on the three areas of ethics, reliability and validity. Do they make any comments about power relationships at all? Are you satisfied with the information given or do you think you need to know more to make an informed decision?

Reflection

In response to this activity we consider three articles, one from each journal we have mentioned. Table 5.3 demonstrates what we found out:

Table 5.3   Articles addressing ethics, reliability, validity and power

Article	Ethics	Reliability	Validity	Power issues
Seo, J. (2025) 'South Korean Early Childhood educators' perceptions of North Korean defectors and unification education', *JCES*, 6(1), pp. 1–20.	Detailed paragraph (p. 6)	As regards the sample chosen (see p. 8)	Not mentioned	Acknowledges power between participants and gatekeepers (see p. 6)

(Continued)

Table 5.3 (Continued)

Article	Ethics	Reliability	Validity	Power issues
Groeneveld, M.G., Linting, M. and Vermeer, H.J. (2024) 'Children's involvement in home-based childcare: are boys more susceptible to caregiver sensitivity than girls?', *Early Years*, 45(2), pp. 367–81.	Two sentences include information on parental consent and ethical approval obtained (p. 372)	Training was given to those undertaking data collection and analysis (p. 372) 'interrater reliability' was considered (p. 373) reliability addressed in limitations (p. 378)	Not mentioned although they do explain they are using a research tool 'validated' by a professional body (p. 372)	Not addressed
Vuorisalo, M., Peltoperä, K. and Lucas Revilla, Y. (2025) 'Pedagogical practices for the infant-toddler's first day of transition from home care to Early Childhood education and care', *European Early Childhood Education Research Journal*, pp. 1–14.	Includes a section entitled Ethical Considerations (p. 4)	Not addressed.	No but there is a paragraph on limitations in the conclusion which offers some useful detail (p. 10)	Not addressed

You will see from the table that not all articles address all the issues we have set out in this chapter and as such this is a question of your ethical values, what you want the reader to know so that they can understand better your work and its potential impact.

Case Study 5.1 Ethics and Secondary Data

Kerem has gained ethical compliance to begin his research study into how celebrities present their young children; he is going to use secondary data by looking at posts on the top five (in terms of followers) celebrity baby Instagram accounts over the course of a month. His completed ethics form has now been approved by his tutor. However, as he gathers the data, he begins to question his own ethical values and how they are going impact on his analysis and write up. For example, he feels uncomfortable about some of the ways that the children are portrayed and realises he could come across as quite judgemental. At the same time, he realises that these celebrities and their children will never be able to respond to his analysis (they will probably never be aware of it!). He decides to take a step back from analysing the gathered data inductively, and to discuss with his tutor a possible conceptual framework he could use which would reduce any judgemental tone he is looking to avoid.

KEY POINTS FROM THE CHAPTER

- No research should be carried out until ethical approval has been obtained; for an undergraduate piece of research this may need to be gained through your supervisor.
- Completing and getting feedback on an ethics approval form can greatly help you in refining your research design.
- A consideration of your ethical values, which may not be necessary to gain ethical approval, can help you to address any power imbalances in your research work.
- Ethics should be considered throughout the research process.
- Thinking about validity and reliability in both your own work and research you read will support you in making claims from your findings.

FURTHER READING

1   Although Flewitt's paper is quite old now, it is nevertheless a useful read because of how she describes the children's understanding of ethics and consent:

Flewitt, R. (2006) 'Using video to investigate preschool classroom interaction: education research assumptions and methodological practices', *Visual Communication*, 5(1), pp. 25–50. DOI: https://doi.org/10.1177/1470357206060917

2   This is the latest version of the EECERA ethical code which will support you in your ethical decisions, both from a compliance and a values point of view:

Bertram, T., Pascal, C., Lyndon, H., Formosinho, J., Gaywood, D., Gray, C., … Whalley, M. (2024) 'EECERA ethical code for Early Childhood Researchers', *European Early Childhood Education Research Journal*, 33(1), pp. 4–18. DOI: https://doi.org/10.1080/1350293X.2024.2445361.

3   To support your thinking about validity in your small-scale qualitative project, this is a very useful article:

Cian, H. (2021) 'Sashaying across party lines: evidence of and arguments for the use of validity evidence in qualitative education research', *Review of Research in Education*, 45(1), 253–90. DOI: https://doi.org/10.3102/0091732X20985079 (original work published 2021).

REFERENCES

Bertram, T., Pascal, C., Lyndon, H., Formosinho, J., Gaywood, D., Gray, C., … Whalley, M. (2024) 'EECERA ethical code for Early Childhood Researchers', *European Early Childhood Education Research Journal*, 33(1), pp. 4–18. DOI: https://doi.org/10.1080/13 50293X.2024.2445361.

Bolshaw, P. and Josephidou, J. (2018) *Introducing Research in Early Childhood*. London: Sage.

British Educational Research Association [BERA] (2024) *Ethical Guidelines for Educational Research*. 5th Edition. Available at: www.bera.ac.uk/publication/ethicalguidelines-for-educational-research-2024 (accessed: 30 May 2025).

Cian, H. (2021) 'Sashaying across party lines: evidence of and arguments for the use of validity evidence in qualitative education research', *Review of Research in Education*, 45(1), pp. 253–90. DOI: https://doi.org/10.3102/0091732X20985079.

Edwards, A. (2010) 'Qualitative designs and analysis', in G. MacNaughton, S. Rolfe and I. Siraj-Blatchford (eds), *Doing Early Childhood Research*. Abingdon: Routledge, pp. 155–75.

Feinstein, C. and O'Kane, C. (2008) *Ethical guidelines for ethical, meaningful and inclusive children's participation practice*. Available at: https://childethics.com/wp-content/uploads/2013/09/Feinstein-OKane-2008.pdf (accessed: 17 June 2025).

Flewitt, R. (2006) 'Using video to investigate preschool classroom interaction: education research assumptions and methodological practices', *Visual Communication*, 5(1), pp. 25–50. DOI: https://doi.org/10.1177/1470357206060917.

Groeneveld, M.G., Linting, M. and Vermeer, H.J. (2024) 'Children's involvement in home-based childcare: are boys more susceptible to caregiver sensitivity than girls?', *Early Years*, 45(2), pp. 367–81.

Kemp, N., Josephidou, J. and Bolshaw, P. (2023) *From weeds to tiny flowers: Rethinking the place of the youngest children outdoors*. The Froebel Trust. Available at: FT-From-Weeds-to-Tiny-Flowers-Miday-way-report-Nov-23-Kemp-Josephidou.pdf (accessed: 30 May 2025).

NISO (n.d.) *Contributor role taxonomy* (CRediT). Available at: https://credit.niso.org/ (accessed: 30 May 2025).

Seo, J. (2025) 'South Korean Early Childhood educators' perceptions of North Korean defectors and unification education', *JCES*, 6(1), pp. 1–2.

Sun, Y., Blewitt, C., Edwards, S., Fraser, A., Newman, S., Cornelius, J. & Skouteris, H. (2023) 'Methods and ethics in qualitative research exploring young children's voice: a systematic review', *International Journal of Qualitative Methods*, 22. DOI: https://doi.org/10.1177/16094069231152449.

Thomas, G. (2017) *How to Do Your Research Project: A Guide for Students*. London: Sage.

Vuorisalo, M., Peltoperä, K. and Lucas Revilla, Y. (2025) 'Pedagogical practices for the infant-toddler's first day of transition from home care to Early Childhood education and care', *European Early Childhood Education Research Journal*, pp. 1–14.

Warin, J. (2000) 'Gender consistency at the start of school', *Sex Roles*, 42(3–4): pp. 209–31.

Warin, J. (2011) 'Ethical mindfulness and reflexivity: Managing a research relationship with children and young people in a 14-year qualitative longitudinal research (QLR) study', *Qualitative Inquiry*, 17(9), pp. 805–14. DOI: https://doi.org/10.1177/1077800411423196.

PART III
METHODS AND ANALYSIS

6

TAKING AN AUTOETHNOGRAPHIC APPROACH

CHAPTER OBJECTIVES

By the end of this chapter, you will:

- Understand what autoethnographic approaches in research look like
- Recognise why autoethnographic approaches may be effective in Early Childhood Research
- Recognise some challenges in autoethnographic research and how you can mitigate against these
- Identify how marginalised voices can benefit from an autoethnographic approach.

INTRODUCTION

In this chapter we will introduce you to a methodology that you may not have come across before but will certainly be of interest if you have a research concern with the learning and development of young children. This approach is called autoethnography and it is becoming more and more prevalent because of its capacity to address gaps that other methodologies are unable to. We are going to consider how this popularity has come about including how power issues mean it is not always seen as valuable. We believe it is an important way of adding to the breadth of voices that make up Early Childhood Research and hope that by the end of the chapter you will have enough understanding to be able to attempt a small-scale study in this way for yourself. We will also reference ethnography and show how this links to autoethnography while considering the important issue of rigour. The theme of power is one that will continue to run through this chapter as we consider how autoethnography can mitigate against power imbalances by promoting voices seldom heard in research (Maude and Davies, 2025).

AUTOETHNOGRAPHY: WHAT'S IT ALL ABOUT?

In this section we will define the term autoethnography and unpack some of the terminology and concepts which underpin it. Before we can dive into a consideration of this methodology however, we do need to understand how it has developed as a research idea and how it has arisen from an approach called ethnography. It is important to appreciate as a novice researcher why you might want to try it out so a consideration of rationales will also be included here.

Defining Autoethnography

At a very simple level, autoethnography is about conducting research on yourself. You might not have realised that people conduct pieces of research solely with themselves as the participant; one such useful example is Henderson's study (2017) in which she explores her role as an early years practitioner. It's fair to say that if you look at a handful of books about research methods, they will not necessarily have any information about this approach. Mukherji and Albon (2018) do address it, explaining that it is an approach that disrupts the notion that research should always be carried out 'with *other* people' (p. 302) but rather that 'the *self* can be a legitimate subject for research' (p. 302). They note, as we have done, that in qualitative research, the researcher must always be transparent about their own positionality, i.e. their impact on the research, however autoethnography takes a step further than this. Mukherji and Albon (2018) also note how it is a useful approach for professionals who wish to gain an insight into their practices, as Henderson (2017) did, and as such link it to action research approaches. They suggest that 'journaling' is a strategy for the researcher to gather data on their self and we will see what this method might look like further on in this chapter.

So, what is the relationship of autoethnography to an approach called 'ethnography'? This latter methodology has as its intention an objective to 'understand people, and why people do the things they do' (Aubrey et al., 2005, p. 111). Data is generally gathered through spending prolonged periods of time in the contexts being researched to undertake observation of practices and behaviours. One such famous example in Early Childhood, that you have no doubt come across, is the work of Tobin (see for example Tobin, 2021), which looked at different ECEC practices in diverse cultural and geographical contexts. Autoethnography, on the other hand, looks at our own practices (i.e. those of the researcher) within a specific context, whether that be the workplace, the home, or some other space. So, it could tell us something about ourselves and our own particular characteristics or about particular contexts; these kind of findings are revealed for example in Paula Stone's work where she looked at the interaction between her own background as a white working-class woman and the context of higher education that she found herself in (Stone, 2020).

The History of Autoethnography

As we have suggested, autoethnography has its roots in ethnography which is an oft used approach in Early Childhood to understand the lives of children in context. In some ways ethnography has had a problematic history as a research approach because it may sometimes take a deficit view of the behaviours and practices it is investigating. It is interesting therefore that it has given birth to an approach that could address power imbalances. Edwards (2021) suggests that some ethnographic researchers, rather than focusing on other people in the contexts they were researching, instead considered their own reactions and that it was this practice that introduced the notion of autoethnography as a valid approach. She also describes how various types of autoethnography have evolved so that there are several ways that this kind of research can be carried out. For example, she highlights how you could collect data by looking back at events that happened in the past or you could collect data on something you are currently experiencing. You may also collect data along with others who are experiencing a context along with you; so, for example, a group of practitioners might decide to collect autoethnographic data on their experiences of working in the baby room.

Reasons to Use Autoethnography

We would suggest there are two main reasons why you may feel autoethnography is a good approach for you to adopt as you think about your research project. The first reason is a purely practical one; it may be very difficult for you to obtain any empirical data. This happened for example in the Covid lockdown when many students had to change their dissertation research plans. Even post lockdown, students may find it difficult to get Early Childhood settings to welcome their research project, given the financial and social problems that have subsequently been of impact. The second reason that you may choose to adopt this approach could be that you see its potential in addressing some of the power issues we have noted in this book so far. Autoethnography could be particularly relevant if you believe you are one of the more marginalised voices in society because of, for example, your gender, ethnicity, socioeconomic status etc.

Let's address this latter point first, i.e. how autoethnography can address power issues in research. Primarily autoethnography can be an approach that aligns with concerns about social justice. Adams et al. (2014) record their belief that 'the stories we tell', this being the data in autoethnography, 'enable us to live and to live better … to lead more reflective, more meaningful, and more just lives' (p. 1). They set out some useful characteristics of autoethnography that you may like to bear in mind as you design your project:

- You use your own experiences.
- You reflect on your interactions with other people.
- You reflect on your interactions with, and in, different contexts.
- Your findings don't offer definite answers and solutions rather they reflect a sense of finding your way.
- You reference the work of others so that your work is intellectual and rigorous while including a creative and affective aspect.
- Your work is underpinned by an aspiration for social justice.

(Adapted from Adams et al., 2014, p. 1)

As far as the point about practicality is concerned, there may be a variety of reasons that good plans to collect empirical data go awry. We have already used the example of students completing dissertations prior to the Covid lockdown who had to immediately change their plans. There are many other events, of course, that could happen to prevent the collection of empirical data. In such circumstances, one option would be to do a desk-based literature review as a piece of research; however, another option could be to collect some autoethnographical data, all the while bearing in mind that you should not define your methodology until you have defined your question. However, perhaps you believe you are a member of a marginalised group in society because of your gender, class, ethnicity or even profession; if so, consider if you have something important to say as part of this marginalised group.

In the previous paragraph we mentioned that you may feel marginalised because of your profession, and this could be certainly true if you are an Early Childhood practitioner. In her foreword to the book *Autoethnography in Early Childhood Education and Care* (Henderson, 2017), Cathy Nutbrown makes the point that so many texts focus on telling practitioners what they should be doing. She talks about how this book 'scrapes away at layers of policy' by allowing practitioners to talk about how they 'feel', particularly when they are having to enact policy that they believe is at odds with what the children in their care really need. It is a book which truly foregrounds the voice of the practitioner. This is noteworthy because as Henderson suggests, echoing many others who have come to the same conclusion, Early Childhood practitioners have been continually marginalised, perhaps because they are predominantly women.

In this section you have been asked to consider various rationales for using the autoethnographic approach. We have discussed how the power issues that run throughout this book may in some cases be addressed by using autoethnography. We have also considered how it may be a practical choice. Have a go now at an activity which asks you to reflect on various plans for research and consider which could be autoethnographical.

Activity 6.1   Taking an Autoethnographic Approach

Have a look at these examples. Can you identify which are taking an autoethnographic approach?

Table 6.1   Research scenarios and autoethnography

Research scenario	Is this autoethnography?
Student A decides to find out whether children in her setting are making gendered play choices.	Y/N
Student B decides to investigate what practitioners' views are about gendered play choices.	Y/N
Student C decides to analyse her own reflections on children's play choices in the setting.	Y/N

Reflection

Did you find this activity difficult? If your response was, they could all be autoethnography, then you do have a point; the important question to bear in mind is what the data will be that each student analyses. If Student A makes observations of the children and asks them questions to answer her research question, then this is not autoethnography – although it could be ethnography. However, if she decides to reflect on her own practices in the setting and how she perhaps unwittingly provides gendered opportunities and writes these reflections down as data to analyse then yes this could be an autoethnographical approach. The same point could be made for Student B's research; they may decide to interview practitioners (not autoethnography) or they may decide to write up their own reflections on what is happening in the setting in terms of practices and their response to this (autoethnography). Student C clearly wishes to undertake a piece of autoethnographical research.

In this section we have been introduced to the approach called autoethnography including learning how it can be defined, how it developed and when you may think about using it. In the next section of the chapter, you will be able to learn not just the what but the how – i.e. if you have determined it is the approach for you then how should you begin and what do you need to bear in mind?

USING AN AUTOETHNOGRAPHIC APPROACH

In this section we are going to respond to the important question that you may be asking by now, i.e. 'This sounds interesting – but how do I use the autoethnographic approach?' The very first consideration you will need to think about is whether this is the best methodology to answer your research question and what your rationale would be. Then, having decided to go forward, think about the type of data you could gather. We will have a look at some of the ways you could do this, including looking at some real examples. Then in the final part of this section, we will explore the different ways you could analyse the data once you have collected it. Of course, there will be overlaps with data analysis in other kinds of methodologies and data collection methods so you will be able to make links and decide which is the best way to proceed for your own project.

Getting Started

So where to start? In this section we will discuss the concept of 'noticing' and how this can lead to exploratory research. We will encourage you to think about ideas and issues you have noticed in a professional context such as an Early Childhood setting you work in or a school you volunteer in. Then we will explore how this noticing could lead to a research question.

'Noticing' may seem a simple and perhaps unacademic term but it is an important one to consider. You may remember that we mentioned this in Chapter 3 (*Designing your research project*). This is because it is noticing that leads to questions that then lead to action, i.e. carrying out a piece of research. The term was one coined by the academic John Mason (you may be able to get hold of his book *Researching Your Own Practice; The Discipline of Noticing* (2001)). In a paper published in 2021, Mason develops further the idea and sets out how 'the Discipline of Noticing' is important for 'sensitising oneself to notice possibilities for action' (p. 231). He further states that it is foremost a 'systematic method for conducting research into one's own practice' (p. 231). So, if you relate this to yourself it could be what you have noticed if you work in a setting, or if you attend a baby group as a parent, for example; it is about your own 'lived experience' (Frechette et al., 2020). These don't need to be big things that you notice but rather the everyday actions, reactions, practices and behaviours.

The next step would be to think about how what you have noticed impacts on you, or how you react and whether you notice you have any impact on the situation. To help you do this, we have set out in Table 6.2 what this looked like for three students who had a go at this exercise; we have added a final row so you could add your own example.

Table 6.2 Noticing and impact

Noticing	Context	Impact on me	How I impact on the situation
Freddie: I notice the practitioners, including myself, don't like taking the babies outside.	Baby room	I feel guilty because I know it is good for the babies, and I know I should be modelling good practice.	I keep talking about how important it is but – it's just that – all talk.
Gita: I notice that when the children play football outside it can seem quite aggressive.	Reception class	I feel uncomfortable as the boys seem to display quite macho behaviours that are not inclusive (which also makes me feel cross).	I often stop the play or try to include a wider range of children to take part.

Noticing	Context	Impact on me	How I impact on the situation
Ivan: I notice lots of the girls wear pink, including my own, even though as parents we seem to be trying to not conform to gender stereotypical practices.	Parent and toddler group	I feel embarrassed that other parents might be judging me.	I try to persuade my daughter to wear more gender-neutral clothes or I end up making a joke of it to the other parents – I definitely let them know the pink clothes are not my choice!
Over to you: I notice....	[Consider a context]	[Reflect on how what you have noticed impacts on you]	[Do you notice any impact you have on the situation?]

Can you see that by completing Table 6.2, you are moving gently towards a piece of research? The next step then would be to come up with a doable research question. This is what the undergraduate researchers in Table 6.2 came up with:

- **Freddie:** How do my practices and my talk about practice align as an Early Childhood practitioner working with babies?
- **Gita:** What strategies do I use to encourage the children to be more inclusive as a teaching assistant in a Reception class?
- **Ivan**: How do I talk about my parenting practices with other parents in a social setting when children are present?

You will see that all questions include 'I' and this is perfectly acceptable in autoethnographic research even though in other academic writing you may be encouraged not to. Have a go and see if you can come up with a research question based on your own noticing.

In this section of the chapter, you have been introduced to the notion of 'noticing' and seen how powerful this can be when planning a research study. We have also set out the relationship between noticing, reflecting on this noticing and using this reflection to come up with a useful research question. A key question at this point might be 'Why bother?' 'Why would such a small-scale piece of research based on one person's reflection be of use?' This is an important question to ask and demonstrates that you are focusing on the purpose of research which should always be an important consideration. Thinking of the examples we have given above, the purposes could be:

- To develop own practice when working with young children
- To impact positively on practice within a setting
- To be able to understand own parenting behaviours.

If the students then successfully complete a research project and then share (perhaps even publish) their findings they could also:

- Impact on others' practice

  - *Contribute to the knowledge we have about practitioner/parenting practices*
  - *Contribute a voice that may not often be heard in research (i.e. the voice of the practitioner, working class parents or parents from specific ethnic groups, disabled parents) and therefore be contributing to a dismantling of power issues in research.*

Different Approaches to Gathering Data in Autoethnography

So far, we have seen the important relationship between noticing – reflection – question – purpose. The next thing we need to consider is what kind of data we could gather. The important aspect of autoethnography is to ensure that the data gathered, and the analysis of the data are considered separately, otherwise the writing up of the project may merely be an opinion piece with no apparent rigour. We will discuss rigour in autoethnography in more depth later in the chapter but for now bear in mind that as we discuss data gathering in this section that it is just that, i.e. data not findings. It is what you do with the data that will turn them into findings. There are different ways that you could gather data – one of the simplest ones would be to choose the narrative form which you could later analyse in much the same way as you would analyse narrative observations. We will return here to our student researchers and show how they did this in different ways.

Freddie: How do my practices and my talk about practice align as an early years practitioner working with babies?

I decided that I would make a note of the different conversations I had about practice during the day either with parents or other practitioners. I knew I had to be very careful not to note down what they said as this was not part of my research approach or would not answer my research question. What I did was at the end of every day while waiting for the bus, I would send myself a voice note which I could then transcribe when I had more time at the weekend. In my voice note I made sure I answered three simple questions (which really helped me if I was feeling a bit tired). The three questions were:

- *What three aspects of practice did you discuss with anyone today (e.g. the outdoor area/changing nappies/sleep time)?*
- *What are your main thoughts about these three areas (i.e. Babies should... Practitioners should... Parents should...)?*
- *How did you feel after these discussions and why?*

I did this every working day for a month (i.e. 5 × 4 = 20 lots of data) and ended up with enough data to be able to analyse to come up with some findings. I missed one or two days when I was poorly, but it didn't impact too much. I did notice I changed my behaviours a little because I knew I was gathering data on myself but then I was able to include this in my reflection on question 3.

Gita: What strategies do I use to encourage the children to be more inclusive as a teaching assistant in a Reception class?

I have a notebook and pencil that I keep with me all the time in the classroom, so I just quickly made a note of any interventions I had made trying to support the children to be more inclusive. I did this four times a day, i.e. break in the morning and afternoon, lunch time and home time. Then before I left school each day, I would sit in my car with a cup of coffee and look at my notes and write them up more fully in longhand. I tried to do this over a half term so had about six weeks' worth of notes. Some days I was just too busy, but I would say I managed to keep to this routine at least four times a week so had 24 lots of data. Of course, my interactions with the children would have been impacted by knowing I was going to write them up as data, but I was able to reflect on this in my write-up. Of course, I had to be very careful that I was not writing up observations of the children – apart from anything, I didn't have ethical approval for this. I concentrated more on responding to questions which required me to consider my own response and feelings such as:

- *Why did you feel the need to intervene? (i.e. I believed/felt that toys were not being shared)*
- *What did you do?*
- *How did you feel?*

Ivan: How do I talk about my parenting practices with other parents in a social setting when children are present?

I have been in the practice for a while now to keep a journal. It is an important part of my day since I have been on paternity leave as I feel it engages my brain in a different way. Once the children are in bed I sit down with a cup of tea and reflect on my day. I was able to include this practice as part of my data collection and decided to reflect on the conversations I had about parenting during the day. I don't make a note of who I have talked to, but I do make a note of the context, i.e. where I was and how big the group was, the topic of conversation, how I had contributed and how I had felt. I did this for about six weeks, and this included toddler group once a week, coffee at someone's home twice a week, getting together with another family at the weekend. I did find this difficult to fit in some times and had to ask my partner to support me by giving me a bit of space in the evening to write up if the children needed a bit more input. It was worth it though – and I found it quite empowering to be able to reflect on my own practices as a parent.

Now you have read about how these three students collected data, we hope you may feel encouraged to have a go yourself.

In this section we have considered the three different ways that three undergraduate researchers chose to collect autoethnographic data for their three distinct research projects. You probably noted they were all aware of how they affected the data, and this self-awareness will be an important part of their write-up. You may probably be also thinking that the data collection is very similar to reflections that you engage in as part of your professional practices. In fact, reflections would be a great source of data, provided all necessary ethical requirements were met, however what turns these reflections into rigorous research is all part of the next important step, i.e. how these narratives are analysed.

How to Conduct Analysis When Using This Approach

In this section we are going to look at how our novice researchers could analyse the data they have collected. There are many ways that this data could be analysed but we are going to look at a method called Thematic Analysis made famous by Braun and Clarke (2021). Braun and Clarke introduced this approach to analysis to counteract some of the accusations about lack of rigour that can be directed at qualitative approaches. They wanted to set down a rigorous approach to analysis so that it offered the potential for more consistency between qualitative researchers rather than a free for all approach. We have added an example below of how you might choose to analyse your data if you are an undergraduate student working on a small-scale project, here using an autobiographical approach. We haven't used the full approach that Braun and Clarke set out, but we have suggested a way that we believe is suitable for an undergraduate piece of research.

As a first step, you should read through the data you have collected several times, so you feel that you know it well. This is the exciting bit, and you will no doubt begin to find patterns and themes that jump out at you. Once you feel quite familiar with your data, begin to underline in different colours some of the key ideas that you find interesting or that you can immediately see will help you answer your research question. Sometimes, but not always, you might see ideas referenced that you have read about for your literature review.

Neil was collecting autoethnographical data on his role as a male Early Childhood practitioner. Most days after work he tried to write a reflective comment in his journal of how his gender may have had an impact. Below you can see one such journal entry that he has subsequently read through to look for themes as described above:

> When I was having lunch today, my colleague asked me if I thought I behaved differently towards the children compared to the other practitioners (I am the only male). It's an interesting question! I definitely think that *the way I interact with young children is because I used to work in a primary school. I like them to be independent because that's what I learnt as a teaching assistant with children aged 5 to 11. I am good at tailoring activities in a way that best communicates with the*

*children and helps them to learn. <u>Some of the female practitioners are different</u> with the children to me but I think **that is more about my past experiences than the fact of my gender**. Although some of <u>the children</u> <u>don't feel comfortable</u> working with me especially a few of the girls. For example, <u>when they are</u> <u>crying, they</u> <u>won't come to</u> me, they'll want to go to a female member of staff. <u>I think I do have a</u> <u>male style because of my sports coaching background</u> **but I don't think it differs too much.**

Of course this is just a snapshot of Neil's data, but he found some ideas that seemed to be threaded through his reflections. He decided to use the themes of:

There's no difference

Practitioner as professional

<u>Male and female practitioners are different</u>

and was able to write about these themes in his findings, using quotations from his data to support his use of these themes. He was very careful not to suggest that he had found an absolute truth (which you wouldn't in qualitative research anyway) but rather that these were his perceptions as a male practitioner in a female-dominated profession.

ENSURING RIGOUR WHEN USING AN AUTOETHNOGRAPHIC APPROACH

As we discussed in the previous chapter, rigour is so important in research, regardless of the methodology used. There are certain accusations made of autoethnographic approaches and it is important to address these in your work. Firstly, some accuse it of reinforcing privilege: if I do not belong to a marginalised group and use autoethnography then my voice will continue to dominate. We would encourage both to reflect carefully on how you might be marginalised before you adopt this methodology but then also foreground your own privilege. For example, Neil believed that as he had protected characteristics, it was an appropriate choice for him; at the same time, he did acknowledge in his work that he may be able to climb the career ladder faster than his colleagues because he was a man.

Another accusation is that such research is too subjective and perhaps self-indulgent. This is where rigour in analysis is important. If you can show explicitly how you have gathered your data, including your positionality, analysed it and used some key litera-ture to consider your findings then you are demonstrating the same research practices as a researcher who has worked with other participants to gather data. Some may argue that autoethnography is too small in scale, it has only one participant and even that is the researcher, so how could it possibly contribute? We would argue you are contribut-ing a lived experience as the expert in your own life, so this supports the building up a picture about an issue or context.

Case Study 6.1 Exploring a Sense of Place

Fatima had been reading about children developing a sense of place and so was interested to explore it in her own life for a small-scale study. She had grown up in a seaside town and wanted to understand more about the spatial connections that children might make. She decided to list ten landmarks in her hometown that were particularly meaningful to her. She came up with:

- Primary school
- Toyshop
- Promenade
- Clock tower
- Pier
- Beach
- High school
- Crescent Bay
- The park
- The townhall

Each week for five weeks, she would write a reflection of about one side of A4 on two of these places. To help her do this in a systematic way she had a few prompt questions such as:

- Why is this an important landmark to me?
- How can I best describe it?
- What is a key memory I have attached to this place?

By the end of the five weeks, Fatima then had over ten sides of A4 that she could begin to analyse in much the same way as Neil above. It is important to add here that initially Fatima had 'bus shelter' on her list; however, as she began to respond to the questions about the bus shelter, she realised there were some memories attached to this place that made her feel particularly sad. Having discussed with her tutor, she decided to avoid exploring any places that might be triggering for her.

KEY POINTS FROM THE CHAPTER

- Autoethnography is an appropriate research design to consider if you are undertaking a small-scale Early Childhood Research project.
- It is an important approach in adding to the breadth of voices that make up Early Childhood Research.
- It is an approach which does have various challenges but there are strategies to mitigate against these.

- Autoethnography can address power imbalances in research by foregrounding more marginalised voices if undertaken appropriately.
- Demonstrating rigour in autoethnography is particularly important; this can be done by showing how you have gathered your data, including your positionality, analysed it and used some key literature to consider your findings.

FURTHER READING

1   Henderson's book is a great read if you are interested in how autoethnography can support reflection on Early Childhood practice.

Henderson, E. (2017) *Autoethnography in Early Childhood Education and Care: Narrating the Heart of Practice.* Abingdon: Routledge.

2   In Mukherji and Albon's useful book, they have a great chapter on 'Journaling as a research tool' (Chapter 16) which will be helpful if you would like to carry out autoethnography.

Mukherji, P. and Albon, D. (2018) *Research Methods in Early Childhood.* 3rd Edition. London: Sage.

3   Reading a full thesis is a big commitment but, by dipping into Paula Stone's work, 'Confronting myself: Using auto/biography to explore the impact of class and education on the formation of self and identity', you will get a wonderful flavour of the potential of autoethnography, including how key literature can support the researcher in understanding their data.

Stone, P. (2019) *Confronting myself: Using auto/biography to explore the impact of class and education on the formation of self and identity.* Available at: www.researchgate. net/profile/Paula-Stone (accessed: 24 June 2025).

REFERENCES

Adams, T.E., Holman Jones, S. and Ellis, C. (2014) *Autoethnography (Understanding Qualitative Research).* Oxford: Oxford University Press.

Aubrey, C., David, T., Godfrey, R. and Thompson, L. (2005) *Early Childhood Educational Research: Issues in Methodology and Ethics.* London: Routledge Falmer Press.

Braun, V. and Clarke, V. (2021) *Thematic Analysis: A Practical Guide.* London: Sage.

Edwards, J. (2021) 'Ethical autoethnography: is it possible?', *International Journal of Qualitative Methods, 20.* DOI: https://doi.org/10.1177/1609406921995306.

Frechette, J., Bitzas, V., Aubry, M., Kilpatrick, K. and Lavoie-Tremblay, M. (2020) 'Capturing lived experience: methodological considerations for interpretive phenomenological inquiry', *International Journal of Qualitative Methods, 19.* DOI: https://doi.org/10.1177/1609406920907254.

Henderson, E. (2017) *Autoethnography in Early Childhood Education and Care: Narrating the Heart of Practice*. Abingdon: Routledge.

Mason, J. (2001) *Researching Your Own Practice: The Discipline of Noticing*. Abingdon: Routledge.

Mason, J. (2021) 'Learning about noticing, by, and through, noticing', *ZDM Mathematics Education, 53*, pp. 231–43. DOI: https://doi.org/10.1007/s11858-020-01192-4.

Maude, K. and Davies, L. (2025) *Diversity, Equity, Inclusion and Teaching*. London: Sage.

Mukherji, P. and Albon, D. (2018) *Research Methods in Early Childhood*. 3rd Edition. London: Sage.

Stone, P. (2020) 'Confronting myself: using auto/biography to explore the impact of class and education on the formation of self and identity', *European Journal for Research on the Education and Learning of Adults, 12*(3), pp. 1–14.

Tobin, J. (2021) 'Learning from comparative ethnographic studies of Early Childhood education and care', *Comparative Education, 58*(3), pp. 297–314. DOI: https://doi.org/10.1080/03050068.2021.2004357.

7

CREATIVE APPROACHES TO RESEARCH

CHAPTER OBJECTIVES

By the end of this chapter, you will:

- Understand why creative approaches can be useful in foregrounding more marginalised voices
- Recognise how secondary data can be used creatively
- Consider how you may be able to adopt a creative approach in your ECEC research.

INTRODUCTION

If you imagine someone thinking creatively, what are they doing? This is what we are going to focus on in this chapter – how research can be approached in creative ways that encourage the researcher to move away from more traditional forms of data collection towards methods that may be more effective at involving participants in an inclusive way, answering the research question and overcoming barriers to access that the researcher may have.

This chapter begins by introducing what creative approaches are and how they may be a way of capturing perspectives that might not be captured in more traditional ways, of supporting participants to think differently about their perspectives and of considering secondary data, too. We will then explore in more depth how to use creative approaches by bearing in mind how the approach must not overpower the research question, how some participants in particular may benefit from such an approach and how the breadth of what counts as secondary data should not be overlooked. Finally, we will explore some of the challenges when using creative approaches and how to overcome these, for instance in maintaining rigour, in ensuring that the approach doesn't dominate over the aim and research question, and in considering that not only should data be collected in creative ways, but that it can be analysed and presented using a creative approach as well.

We hope that by the end of this chapter you will be inspired to try a creative approach to research, particularly as one of the strengths is that it can enable people to develop their research skills when they don't have a space, such as an Early Childhood setting or school, to do this in.

WHAT ARE CREATIVE APPROACHES?

Let's begin by thinking about what we mean by creative approaches. It might conjure up images of people, perhaps child participants, doing things that are often seen as creative endeavours, such as painting, drawing or making collages. While we might include these as examples of creative approaches, what we actually mean are approaches to data collection that go beyond what we consider to be more traditional methods of data collection, such as interviews, observations, questionnaires, surveys and experiments. We know that these methods don't work as well for marginalised voices, whether that's the researcher or the participant, in allowing them to share their views and voice. We also know that these traditional approaches don't always address the power imbalances that may exist between the researcher and the participant. This section of the chapter will think more about what creative approaches are and why you might use them.

A Way of Listening to Voices That Wouldn't Be Captured in More Traditional Ways

One of the advantages of taking a creative approach is that it can be a way of capturing perspectives and voices that wouldn't be captured in more traditional ways. We said earlier that more traditional methods include observations (see Chapter 10), questionnaires and surveys (see Chapter 11) and interviews (see Chapter 12). Take a moment to think about which participants these types of methods work for. What types of characteristics do you think participants need to be able to share their voice using one of these approaches? You may think that these methods might be effective with adults who speak the same language as you and are comfortable with reading and writing in that language, too. But then you might be able to identify that there are other groups, such as young children, people with SEN or with whom you do not share a common language, for whom these methods would not be an effective way to gather their perspectives.

Table 7.1 identifies the limitations that some of these traditional methods may have in capturing perspectives and voices and the ways in which they might not address power imbalances between the researcher and participant.

Table 7.1 Disadvantages of traditional methods of data collection

Method	Critique
Interview	• Relies on the participant being verbal • Relies on the participant speaking the same language as the interviewer, or the interpretation of a translator
Surveys and questionnaires	• Relies on the participant being able to read and write in the language the questionnaire has been produced
Observation	• May rely on the participant being unaware they are being observed • Can be subjective

For the researcher, these methods also rely on:

- Access to participants, which is often face-to-face
- Access to gatekeepers such as managers of Early Childhood settings or headteachers of schools
- Additional financial costs, such as for transportation.

Using a creative method can remove some of the limitations of capturing perspectives of participants and reduce some of the practical difficulties that researchers may face in accessing participants.

A Way of Supporting Participants and Researchers to Think Differently About Their Experiences

Even with participants who you might not (or they might not) consider to be marginalised, another strength of taking a creative approach can be that it supports participants to think in different ways about their experiences. For example, at the time of writing we are attempting to collect data about parents' perspectives of their babies' outdoor experiences by using a photovoice methodology, which was originally developed by researchers called Wang and Burris (1997). It was developed as a participatory action research approach for marginalised groups with public health but has been adapted and used in other disciplines such as education. It takes an approach whereby participants are encouraged to take photographs which they then reflect upon, which act as a stimulus for conversation and leads towards community action. One example of how it has been used in practice is by Booth and Booth (2003) who used the approach to 'see the world through the eyes of mothers with learning difficulties' (2003, p. 431).

Booth and Booth (2003) talk about how one of the features of the photovoice approach is that the participants themselves are responsible for how they are portrayed and depicted; it demonstrates the participants' viewpoint and way of seeing the world. They write:

Photovoice involves giving people cameras and using the pictures they take to amplify their place in and experience of the world. It puts people in charge of how they represent themselves and how they depict their situation. The process challenges the established politics of representation by shifting control over the means for documenting lives from the powerful to the powerless, the expert to the lay-person, the professional to the client, the bureaucrat to the citizen, the observer to the observed. Photovoice is all about point-of-viewness: it sets out to capture and convey the point of view of the person holding the camera. Photovoice invites us to look at the world through the same lens as the photographer and to share the story the picture evokes for the person who clicked the shutter. (Booth and Booth, 2003, p. 432)

Their participants were 16 mothers who attended a weekly support group specifically for mothers with learning difficulties, who were given a disposable camera and asked to take photos of people, places and things that were important to them. After they were processed, each participant had the option to share the photos with the researcher and took part in an individual discussion about the photographs and what they represented. If you were asked to take photos of things that were important to you, what would you capture? Family members? Pets? Your workplace? Your bedroom? What do you think these photos would tell somebody else about your life and about what was important to you? Analysis of the photos from the mothers with learning difficulties revealed the importance that the participants placed on their children, specific places such as their home and gardens and also on their friends. The researchers also noted particular things that they were surprised were absent from the photographs, such as partners, extended family and support services. What do you think this may tell us?

Booth and Booth's (2003) research was conducted near the turn of the 21st century using disposable cameras, and indeed some participants had never used a camera before. Over 20 years later, we may see social media profiles as examples of curated content in which people choose how they represent themselves and view their world. For instance, Gray, Norton and Breault-Hood (2018) explored Facebook and Instagram posts that used two hashtags (#NatureGirls and #outdoorwomen) to explore how the posts (or 'cultural texts', p. 158 that were published in the public domain portrayed women in the outdoors and how authentic they were of representing identities of women outdoors. If you use social media, you might be able to think about how you could use this approach to explore what is being posted about a topic that is interesting to you. We had a go by looking at posts that used the hashtags #babiesoutdoors and #toddlersoutdoors and found it interesting to consider what images were shared and who (and, importantly, who didn't) feature in the photographs. What hashtags might you explore?

While Booth and Booth (2003) used an approach in which the participants themselves took ownership of their portrayal, others have considered how participants may have been represented in popular media and used that as a stimulus for discussion. For instance, Edmondson and King (2016) use extracts from four film and television dramas that feature social workers as a stimulus for a focus group interview with social workers themselves. The participants were given a brief overview of the dramas and the historical context at the time of its release and then invited to watch extracts as a basis for a discussion about how social work has been and is portrayed within UK media. A common theme was that of the social worker as 'childcatcher', with one participant describing how social workers were represented in the films as those who 'nab people's children' (2016, p. 647). Similar techniques have been used with child participants, too; later we'll consider Zsubori's (2024) research which used video clips of Disney and Disney-Pixar princesses such as Pocahontas, Mulan and Jasmine as a basis for discussions with 38 children aged between 7 and 10 about their understanding of gender.

A Way of Exploring Secondary Data Such as Children's Picture Books

Creative approaches can also be used to explore secondary data. Secondary data is data that already exists, rather than the researcher going out and collecting it themselves in the field. Think about the types of popular sources you encounter that feature children or those that care for them in some way. For example, you might watch television programmes or films that feature child actors or read fiction books that have characters who are children, or you might read newspaper or magazine articles about them. They might not be about children themselves, but those who play a role in their lives.

You can also consider media sources such as books, films and magazines that are aimed at children themselves and use those to examine how children and childhoods are portrayed and what they might say to children. One of the most common types of media source that are presented to children in their homes, Early Childhood settings and schools is picture books. Body and Lacny (2022) considered how children's picture books represent philanthropic acts. To explore this, they used a snowball sampling method to examine over 500 children's picture books published either in the UK or the US, and from this sample identified 104 which considered philanthropic acts in some way. This might have been volunteering through giving time, resources or money, or campaigning for a particular cause like improving a local park.

Do you think that you could replicate something like Body and Lacny (2022), perhaps by going to a local library and examining the books on offer in relation to your research topic? For instance, Koss (2015) analysed who was represented in children's picture-books, in terms of ethnicity, gender and disability. To examine this, she identified 455 books published in 2012 in the US and coded them to identify how ethnicity, gender and disability were represented in the book both as a whole and in relation to the main characters (when the book had main characters) by assessing them in a quantitative way. She found that the characters were predominantly white. There was a fairly even distribution between male and female characters, although the female characters were much more likely to take on stereotypical gender roles like teacher or stay-at-home parent. While 44% of texts were identified as having a character with a physical disability, predominantly this was due to characters who were wearing glasses – when these characters were removed this figure reduced to just 9%.

Activity 7.1   Exploring Play and Gender in Children's Magazines

Jimmy is an undergraduate student considering his final year dissertation. He is interested in how children's magazines portray play in relation to gender and emails to ask your advice:

> *Hi, how are you doing? I'm just thinking about my dissertation. I grew up reading weekly comics for children and, looking back, I think there may have been differences in how boys and girls were portrayed when they were playing. Do you think this is something I could investigate? Any help appreciated – thanks!*

Take some time to compose a reply to Jimmy about how he could approach this.

Reflection

There are many things you might have recommended to Jimmy for his study. Here's one possible response:

> *That sounds like a great idea! One thing I'd consider is choosing a few children's magazines and getting hold of a few copies of them over a period of months. Have a reason why you've chosen those particular ones – perhaps because of the readership reach? Or because of a recommendation – the Scottish Book Trust (2024) have a list of recommended comics and magazines. Then have a think about what you are actually going to look for; it could be just images that portray aspects of play, or the text as well. Make sure you record these in a systematic way like in a table because that'll make it easier when it comes to analysis.*

HOW TO USE CREATIVE APPROACHES

Let us now explore how to use some creative approaches to the research process.

Start With a Research Question, Not an Approach

In the past we've both encountered students who, when we ask them how they are thinking of approaching their research project, start by telling us what method they would like to use. Although the prospect of using a creative approach might appeal to you, it's important to remember that you need to start with a research question, not an approach, as we considered back in Chapter 3 (*Designing your research project*). You might find that some research questions lend themselves more to creative approaches, whereas others will be better answered by traditional data collection methods such as observations, interviews or questionnaires.

That doesn't mean, of course, that these traditional methods of data collection can't be supplemented with a creative angle, which is an approach Zsubori (2024) adopted when exploring children's understanding of gender. While she used traditional methods such as conversational interviews and observations with the participants, she recognised that starting the interviews by showing the children short video clips of Disney princesses helped facilitate a 'comfortable 'child-friendly' atmosphere' (p. 202) as well as providing a starting point for a conversation about gender using the concept of princesses and what an 'ideal' princess should be.

Think Carefully About Which Participants You May Give a Voice To

As we've said earlier in this chapter, there are particular groups of participants that creative approaches may be more suitable for, such as those who are vulnerable or marginalised. Zsubori (2024) describes how children have previously been seen as vulnerable and 'one homogeneous demographic comprised of incompetent objects' (p. 200), although she herself did not position her child participants as such. And think back to how Wang and Burris (1997) developed the photovoice approach for marginalised groups, and how this was used to explore the experiences of mothers with learning difficulties (Booth and Booth, 2003), a group who may be considered to be both marginalised and vulnerable.

Using photographic research with people with learning disabilities has also been used by Aldridge (2007a) as a way of including vulnerable people in research. She argues that taking such an approach focuses on what they are capable of (when often the incapabilities of vulnerable respondents are focused on), it demonstrates their point of view in a way that the researcher themselves taking photographs would not and also allows participants to showcase their skills. She powerfully argues that 'If the participants in research cannot tell us, but are able to show us, their experiences through photographic participation methods (as in this case) then this only emphasizes the positive, inclusive advantages of using such a technique, particularly for the participants themselves' (Aldridge, 2007a, p. 12). She has also used the technique with children with care responsibilities (Aldridge, 2007b). She argues that in her research with vulnerable children they often do not wish, or are unable, to make verbal contributions and thus are at risk of being excluded from research studies. A creative approach that uses photographic participation methods can give these children a voice as well as 'help challenge fixed perceptions and assumptions about children's lack of competency as decision makers or active citizens, and can help to highlight children's agency and resilience rather than their susceptibility' (Aldridge, 2014, p. 117).

Don't Forget the Breadth of Secondary Data You Could Explore

One example of how advertisements have been used as a form of secondary data to consider the portrayal of babies and toddlers has been conducted from an Australian context (Lupton, 2014). Lupton (2014) collected content about children aged up to approximately 2 years old from the print and online versions of two Australian newspapers over a period of eight months and also accessed advertisements featured on an Australian version of the parenting website *BabyCenter* for one month. She then analysed the images and articles using qualitative analysis to find out how infants were embodied by the text and images, for instance considering how the babies' bodies were portrayed and what spaces they are seen to inhabit. Her analysis led her to four themes in how infants are embodied: as precious, pure, uncivilised and vulnerable. Table 7.2 shares examples of these portrayals from the data.

Table 7.2   Examples of how babies' bodies were portrayed in Lupton's (2014) research

Discourse	Example from the media
Precious	• A television advertisement for nappies where infants are snuggling with their parents and experiencing intimate moments of care. • A television advertisement for an IVF clinic showing real footage of a baby's birth in which they are placed on the mother's chest.
Pure	• A magazine advertisement for eco-friendly carpet showing a sleeping baby lying on the carpet with a leaf in their hand. • A television advertisement for all-natural yoghurt showing babies eating non-foods like crayons and sand, before showing a baby eating the yoghurt.
Uncivilised	• Online comments about an online newspaper article about parents travelling with babies in aeroplanes, which complain about babies' behaviour and criticise parents for taking them on flights. • The letters section of a print newspaper saying that while it's acceptable for owners to take dogs to cafes, babies and small children should be banned due to their behaviour.
Vulnerable	• A television advertisement for spray cleaner showing a mother using a spray cleaner with baby eating in a high-chair and then crawling in the house, including in the bathroom. • An article in a weekend newspaper magazine about a baby who suffered severe side effects following a flu vaccination.

It is important to remember that Lupton is writing from an Australian perspective and collected her sources in 2011, so there might be differences now in terms of geographic region and the time period. You might be interested in spending a month making a note of all the television advertisements you come across that feature children to see how they are portrayed, recording key information such as the date, time, length of advert, channel and product being advertised. Alternatively, you could explore some newspapers online to find articles about children, or perhaps browse some magazines to find print advertisements that have children in.

Activity 7.2   Developing a Creative Approach for Care-Experienced People

Imagine you have a research question which seeks to explore the narratives of children who are care-experienced (i.e. who have been in or are in care). What creative approaches can you think of that may explore these perspectives? Take some time making some notes.

Reflection

There are several ways you could choose to explore the narratives of young people who are care-experienced. If you wanted to take a desk-based approach, you could look at children's fiction such as Wilson's (1991) *The Story of Tracy Beaker*, and the subsequent television series, which has been explored in research for instance by Damayanti and Asmarani (2022) who look at how the protagonist experiences 'the absence of mother's love' (p. 57).

Depending on your level of study, it might be tricky to gain ethical approval to recruit care-experienced participants for your study. But if you are able to, you could use a creative approach such as the photovoice methodology, as used with care-experienced youth by Conley Wright and Collings (2025), or an arts-based approach as adopted by McCusker et al. (2025) in which, in part, participants were supported to create a podcast about their experiences. If you are thinking that these approaches would not be suitable for young children, you could consider the way that Winter (2012) asked children in care who were aged between 4 and 7 to create 'reality boxes' out of craft materials and a shoe box in which 'the outside of the box was to be used to help children construct an image of themselves that best reflected how they thought they came across to the outside world (their public person). The inside was used to construct images of their feelings and perspectives (their private person) regarding their lives at home and in care' (2012, p. 371).

WHAT ARE THE CHALLENGES WHEN USING CREATIVE APPROACHES?

Although creative approaches can be fun to employ, there are challenges to them, too. Two of the main challenges are of ensuring rigour and the approach dominating the research process.

The Challenge of Ensuring Rigour

One challenge that can occur when a researcher uses a creative approach is ensuring that it still maintains rigour. What it means to ensure rigour can mean different things to different people, but generally it is understood to mean making sure you are being thorough and careful in the approach that you take. MacNaughton and Hughes (2009) define it nicely when they describe the rigour of a research study as 'the hallmark of its quality' (p. 122). They add 'the more thorough and careful you are in planning your project, collecting data, analysing it and drawing conclusions from it, the more rigorous your research project' (p. 122).

Ensuring rigour is something we have seen students struggle with in the past when taking a creative approach. As with traditional methods, researchers must make sure that they take a systematic approach to their data collection and analysis and must be able to justify the research decisions that they have made. For instance, earlier we spoke about Body and Lacny's (2022) exploration of how children's picture books represent philanthropic acts. They outline clearly how they identified the original 500+ books that they investigated through using a snowball sampling technique of asking teaching professionals via social media, investigating lists of recommended picture books published by organisations like BookTrust, exploring those for sale in bookshops and available in local libraries. Rigour was then ensured in how the data was analysed by using a systematic content analysis procedure in order to identify key codes and themes.

The Challenge of the Approach Dominating the Research Process

A second challenge that can occur when a researcher takes a creative approach is that the approach comes to dominate the research process and the researcher loses sight of the purpose of their study. It's important that although it can be exciting to 'think outside the box' when it comes to your data collection, you don't let that interfere with your quest to answer your research question. To overcome this challenge, researchers must ensure that there is alignment between the research question, the aim of their study and the approach they are taking to their research. We've had experiences in the past where our creative research approach has been in danger of dominating the research process, at the expense of answering the research question. In Chapter 12 (*Interviewing adults and children*) we'll tell you about some research we conducted in which we wanted to understand the gendered nature of the early years workforce (Bolshaw, Josephidou and O'Connor, 2016). As part of this, we used a creative approach called 'the teddy interviewer', in which our teddy bear wanted to know from the children what to expect when he started nursery, which would lead on to a conversation about who he might find working at the nursery.

Yet have a look at this excerpt from one of the interviews. Can you see what problem we encountered?

Jo:	... this is our friend Teddy and we've brought him into your school today because he has got lots and lots of questions....
Nancy:	My Teddy is even bigger....
Jo:	Even bigger, well he is just a little Teddy and we have tried to answer....

Jamie:	I've got two big teddies.
Jo:	We've tried to answer his questions….
Beth:	My mummy has … my nan has got a ginormous one it goes all the way up to the ceiling….
Jo:	Shall I tell you something….
Beth:	My and also she … she….
Jo:	Beth, Beth, can I just tell you some of the other things he has been asking us and then in a minute can you keep that thought in your brain and then will you tell us all about your teddy in a minute is that okay….

While attempting to use the creative approach of a teddy interviewer, what we found was that the children were much more interested in telling us about their teddies than finding out what teddy might want to say to them! We did, eventually, manage to use the stimulus of teddy to encourage the children to talk about their own experiences of Early Childhood education, but you can see from our example how one challenge is that the approach may dominate and create barriers to effective data collection.

Case Study 7.1   Exploring Picture Books

During a university module about multicultural perspectives of childhood, students considered the way in which different ethnicities were portrayed in a variety of domains. One student, Helen, chose the domain of children's picture books to explore what messages young children may receive about their racial identity based upon the stories they may read or be read in their homes and Early Childhood setting.

Helen uses a list produced by World Book Day 2025 of their Top 25 Picture Books and gets hold of a copy of each of the 25 from her local library. She then creates a data collection table where, for each book, she can note details of the main character, any supporting character, traits and features of the characters, how often their image appears in the texts and who is featured on the front cover. She uses the data collection table to build up a picture about what messages young readers of these texts might receive about race.

KEY POINTS FROM THE CHAPTER

- Creative approaches are approaches to data collection that go beyond what we consider to be more traditional methods of data collection, such as interviews, observations, questionnaires, surveys and experiments.
- Creative approaches can be effective in listening to marginalised voices and addressing power imbalances that can exist between the researcher and the research participants.

- Creative approaches with participants include photo voice methodology, 'teddy interviewer' and photo elicitation.
- Creative approaches can also be used when looking at secondary data, such as picture books, social media posts, advertisements or films.
- Researchers should consider whether a creative approach is important not only for data collection, but also for data analysis or dissemination.

FURTHER READING

1 Body and Lacny (2022) draw upon the work of Grant (2019) when they consider how to analyse their data. Grant's book *Doing Excellent Social Research with Documents* explores how to explore sources such as news articles, historical documents, social media posts and advertising in research and how to use 'documents as data'.

Grant, A. (2019) *Doing Excellent Social Research with Documents: Practical Examples and Guidance for Qualitative Researchers*. Abingdon: Routledge.

2 Booth and Booth's (2003) research using the photovoice methodoloy with mothers with learning difficulties is a really powerful read because of the insight that it gives into their participants' lives.

Booth, T. and Booth, W. (2003) 'In the frame: photovoice and mothers with learning difficulties', *Disability & Society*, *18*(4), pp. 431–42.

REFERENCES

Aldridge, J. (2007a) 'Picture this: the use of participatory photographic research methods with people with learning disabilities', *Disability & Society*, *22*(1), pp. 1–17.

Alridge, J. (2007b) Pictures of Young Caring: Full Research Report. *ESRC End of Award Report, RES-000-22-1321*. Swindon: ESRC. Available at: https://reshare.ukdataservice.ac.uk/850092/1/Report_RES-000-22-1321.pdf (accessed: 5 March 2025).

Aldridge, J. (2014) 'Working with vulnerable groups in social research: dilemmas by default and design', *Qualitative Research*, *14*(1), pp. 112–30.

Body, A. and Lacny, J. (2022) 'Philanthropic tales: a critical analysis of how philanthropic citizenship is represented in children's picture-books – problems and possibilities', *Education, Citizenship and Social Justice*, *18*(2), pp. 182–96.

Bolshaw, P., Josephidou, J. and O'Connor, S. (2016) 'Exploring children's perceptions of the gendered nature of the early years workforce', 69th Annual OMEP World Conference. Conference Centre Tamaris, Opatija, 20–24 June.

Booth, T. and Booth, W. (2003) 'In the frame: photovoice and mothers with learning difficulties', *Disability & Society*, *18*(4), pp. 431–42.

Conley Right, A. and Collings, S. (2025) 'Conceptual meanings of permanency: photovoice with care-experienced youth', *Journal of Youth Studies*, *28*(1), pp. 236–53.

Damayanti, B.P. and Asmarani, R. (2022) 'The absence of mother's love experienced by the main female character in Jacqueline Wilson's The Story of Tracy Beaker', *Culturalistics: Journal of Cultural, Literary, and Linguistic Studies*, 6(3), pp. 57–65. DOI: https://doi.org/10.14710/culturalistics.v6i3.1599.

Edmondson, D. and King, M. (2016) 'The childcatchers: an exploration of the representations and discourses of social work in UK film and television drama from the 1960s to the present day', *Journal of Social Work*, 16(6), pp. 639–56.

Gray, T., Norton, C. and Breault-Hood, J. (2018) 'Curating a public self: exploring social media images of women in the outdoors', *Journal of Outdoor Recreation, Education & Leadership*, 10(2), pp. 153–70.

Koss, M.D. (2015) 'Diversity in contemporary picturebooks: a content analysis', *Journal of Children's Literature*, 41(1), pp. 32–42.

Lupton, D. (2014) 'Precious, pure, uncivilised, vulnerable: infant embodiment in Australian Popular media', *Children & Society*, 28(5), pp. 341–51.

MacNaughton, G. and Hughes, P. (2009) *Doing Action Research in Early Childhood Studies: A Step by Step Guide*. Berkshire: Open University Press.

McCusker, P., McMellon, C., Roesch-March, A. and Bartlett, T. (2025) 'Feeling well, feeling cared for? Using participatory and arts-engaged research to improve understanding and professional responses to the mental health needs of care-experienced young people', *Educational Action Research*, 33(1), pp. 153–71.

The Scottish Book Trust (2024) 'All reading is good reading: comics and magazines'. Available at: www.scottishbooktrust.com/articles/all-reading-is-good-reading-comics-and-magazines (accessed: 5 March 2025).

Wang, C. and Burris, M.A. (1997) 'Photovoice: concept, methodology, and use for participatory needs assessment', *Heath Education Behaviour*, 24(3), pp. 369–87. DOI: 10.1177/109019819702400309.

Wilson, J. (1991) *The Story of Tracy Beaker*. UK: Doubleday.

Winter, K. (2012) 'Ascertaining the perspectives of young children in care: case studies in the use of reality boxes', *Children and Society*, 26, pp. 368–80.

Zsubori, A. (2024) 'The Good, the Bad and the Disney: employing princesses to examine Hungarian tweens' understanding of gender', *European Journal of Cultural Studies*, 27(2), pp. 195–214.

8

CENTRING THE VOICE OF THE CHILD

CHAPTER OBJECTIVES

By the end of this chapter, you will:

- Understand that there are some research designs which are most appropriate for centring the voice of the child
- Consider how some research designs may diminish the voice of the child while claiming to hear them
- Consider what is meant by the 'voice of the child', and how it links to the ways in which adults position and value children
- Identify why centring the voice of the child is so important and how it is a social justice issue.

INTRODUCTION

You may remember that in Chapter 2 (*Issues of power in Early Childhood Research*) we examined issues of power in research and thought about how power imbalances could be addressed. We would like now to build on this important discussion. One of the things that makes us proud about Early Childhood Research, and which makes research in this discipline so special, is the fact that it often attempts to address power imbalances by centring the voice of the child. Chapter 2 addressed the fact that research is always context bound; we described it as being undertaken by certain people, engaging with certain other people in certain locations. When these certain people include children then decisions must be made by adults about how loud they are going to allow the voice of the child to be. But what does 'The voice of the child' mean? Obviously, we are not talking about volume here but rather issues of opportunity, consideration and respect. One of the first things we will do in this chapter is to consider how this well-used phrase can be defined; at the same time we will examine how it links to issues of social justice. We will look at the meaning behind this term in different contexts and explore some different research designs and accompanying methods that have centred the voice of the child particularly well. At the same time, we will consider why it is so important to adopt this perspective in research. We believe you will discover that 'the voice of the child' continues to be a problematic phrase, not just because it is linked to issues of power and control.

WHAT DOES THE VOICE OF THE CHILD MEAN?

In this section of the chapter we are going to consider what the phrase 'the voice of the child' means. You will come across several definitions and they do not necessarily all agree. One of the reasons for this is because the concept of a child has changed over time, including how we consider what a child is capable of and what expertise they may have. An interesting point to consider is how different ways of 'hearing' children have emerged over time. At the same time, some argue the child's voice is becoming more and more diminished. It is important to remember that promoting the voices of children is to do with improving their lives (Mahony et al., 2024, p. 3) and if this is not happening through the research then we need to question what our motives are for adopting such an approach.

A Social Justice Issue

Mahony et al. (2024) claim that little has been written about the younger age group (i.e. birth to 8 years) when ideas around listening to children are considered. They remind us that this is a social justice issue if we consider that 2.4 billion of the world's population (8 billion) are under 18 with 656 million of these being under 5. They refute the well-used notion of children being the future of the world, claiming rather that children 'are integral to the world today' (p. 5).

The two main articles of the UNCRC (12 and 13) (United Nations, 1989) set out the child's rights to have their views heard although there is some deficit language here, particularly if we think of the very youngest children such as babies and toddlers. For example, the phrase 'the child who is *capable* (our italics) of forming his or her own views' is used; immediately this word 'capable' introduces issues of power because who gets to decide who is or isn't capable? Of course it is an adult! Furthermore, it states a requirement to consider 'the views of the child ... in accordance with ... age and maturity' (p. 5); once again it is the adult who is deciding if the child is both old enough and mature enough for their views to be considered. Article 13, encouragingly, recognises that children may share their views in many ways and therefore stresses that the 'right shall include freedom to seek, receive and impart information and ideas of all kinds ... either orally ... in the form of art, or through any other media of the child's choice' (p. 5). This doesn't appear to include body language, however, which we may feel is important for very young children such as babies.

Listening as a Challenge

Listening to children authentically is a challenging endeavour which must involve a respectable disposition towards their ways of communicating and a determination to value what they share. It is very easy to enter the researcher/child encounter with an adult agenda and a mindset of parachuting in to mine the child for data to ultimately complete a successful small-scale study. The challenge, as a researcher, is to put your agenda on the back burner and then really look for ways that the children are communicating their ideas, not just responding to your questions, but sharing what is important to them. For example, you may want to find out from children what they like in their local area, expecting them to talk about the park, the seaside and the playground. However, they, in contrast, may want to talk about the minibeasts in their garden, what they had for tea (chips, and yes that has happened to us) or about their daddy's job. This is probably difficult as a novice researcher as you may feel under pressure to collect your data in a limited timeframe. But really try to listen to what the children want to tell you, in their own diverse ways, about what is important in their lives; you may learn a lot from them, and you are in a very privileged position doing a small-scale piece of research in that you have this unique opportunity to listen and hear a few children in this kind of research encounter.

How Do I Know You Are Listening?

The use of the word 'voice' implies that there is a speaker and a listener. Mahony et al. (2024) unpack the term 'listening' to consider what we really mean by it. They reference the fact that it is more often a term used in education, it is the adult who speaks and the child who listens; the listening child pays attention to the adult so that the adult can have an impact by sharing knowledge and so that the children can learn. We see this often in the primary school where young children are frequently told 'Show me you are listening (eyes front, legs crossed, finger on lips).' I wonder how young children would describe what an adult looks like when they are truly listening; how do they know that the adult is listening?

Activity 8.1   Defining Listen, Voice, Expertise

In this activity you are going to reflect on what you have read in the section above and consider what your own definition of the three important terms, 'listen', 'voice', 'expertise' might be. After you have done this, we would like you to consider how your chosen definition will impact on your research practice and what this would look like with young children. We have chosen three specific ages to focus on to help you consider how you may need to be flexible and responsive depending on children's ways

(Continued)

of engaging with and responding to you (although of course we are not saying that these are necessarily defined by age, and it is important not to make assumptions of what a child is capable of).

Complete Table 8.1 to show how you might define these terms for three different ages and stages of young children.

Table 8.1 Defining listen, voice and expertise

	Definition		
Term	Baby (birth to 12 months)	Toddler (2-year-old)	5-year-old
Listen			
Voice			
Expertise			

Now you have thought about your definitions think about what this would look like in practice, if you were working with these children in research, and then complete Table 8.2.

Table 8.2 Practical application of listen, voice and expertise

	Practical application		
Term	Baby (birth to 12 months)	Toddler (2-year-old)	5-year-old
Listen			
Voice			
Expertise			

Reflection

How did you find this activity? When we carried out this activity, as you can see in Table 8.3 and Table 8.4, we initially intended to have different definitions for the different stages, but we were surprised to find that we wanted to keep the same definition regardless of age and stage. This may surprise you too if you think about how chatty a child in their first primary school class might be. The message this definition reinforced for us was how much a baby might be able to tell us if we learnt to listen.

Table 8.3 Attempting to define listen, voice and expertise

	Definition		
Term	Baby (Birth to 12 months)	Toddler (2-year-old)	5-year-old
To listen	To watch, notice, observe closely, be attuned to, to question (oneself).	To watch, notice, observe closely, be attuned to, to question (oneself).	To watch, notice, observe closely, be attuned to, to question (oneself).

	Definition		
Term	Baby (Birth to 12 months)	Toddler (2-year-old)	5-year-old
Child's voice	What the child can tell us through actions, emotions, utterances, facial expressions how they might be feeling or what they might be thinking.	What the child can tell us through actions, emotions, utterances, facial expressions how they might be feeling or what they might be thinking.	What the child can tell us through actions, emotions, utterances, facial expressions how they might be feeling or what they might be thinking.
Expertise	What the child knows and shares about their own life, context, feelings, emotions, experiences.	What the child knows and shares about their own life, context, feelings emotions, experiences.	What the child knows and shares about their own life, context, feelings, emotions, experiences.

Table 8.4 Attempting to define the practical application of listen, voice and expertise

	Practical application		
Term	Baby (birth to 12 months)	Toddler (2-year-old)	5-year-old
Listen	I will think about the different ways I can listen and the different communication methods that children use.	I will think about the different ways I can listen and the different communication methods that children use.	I will think about the different ways I can listen and the different communication methods that children use.
Voice	I will look for ways to note how children's behaviours and practices may be trying to communicate something.	I will look for ways to note how children's behaviours and practices may be trying to communicate something.	I will look for ways to note how children's behaviours and practices may be trying to communicate something.
Expertise	I will ensure I see the child as competent and able to have and share their expertise.	I will ensure I see the child as competent and able to have and share their expertise.	I will ensure I see the child as competent and able to have and share their expertise.

In this section of the chapter we have focused, once again, on the idea of voice, building on some of the ideas we introduced in Chapter 2. We have seen that it is a concept that can be defined in different ways, particularly when we are thinking about very young children. One of the reasons for this is because the idea of what a child is has changed over time, although if we look at recent world events, we might think that the UNCRC has had very little impact at all. There may be a bleak picture in terms of how children are listened to, as inequalities increase across the globe.

CENTRING THE VOICE OF THE CHILD

Up to now we have talked about the importance of centring the voice of the child in research; it would be good to look at how research designs can encourage this. Phillips and Ritchie (2025) draw our attention to the fact that even though 35 years have passed since the establishment of the UNCRC, some children's lives have become considerably worse. Drawing on UNICEF documentation they use the terminology of 'the global anthropogenic-catalysed polycrisis' (p. 1) to describe how 'COVID-19, climate disasters, wars, and dislocation' (p. 1) are having a holistically negative impact on children. They cite statistics from the war in Gaza to illustrate how most victims are children with, at their time of writing, over 17,000 deaths being those of children. Of the children killed, 30% of them were under 5.

Establishing Trusting Relationships

The report 'Voice of the Child: learning from case reviews' was published by the NSPCC in 2024. The report focuses on what has been learnt and how practice can be improved in terms of safeguarding children; this is a particular context but one which can also support us in considering how we can listen to children's voices in research.

The authors stress that the voice of the child is not only 'what children say' and that it applies just as much to children who are 'non-verbal and pre-verbal'. Instead, they argue that it is about children's holistic behaviour. The only true way to hear children, they suggest, is through taking time to establish trusting relationships and providing environments that are conducive to listening and 'children sharing their thoughts and experiences' (p. 2). In the context of the case reviews, these thoughts are about crucial decisions to be made about children's lives, which they can offer some expertise on. Two of the barriers described that prevent the voice of the child being heard is a lack of trust between adult and child along with an over focus on the needs of the adult. They suggest that when things have gone wrong for children, as illustrated in these case reviews, then it is because their views have not been sought enough. Sometimes this was because the children themselves had 'complex communication needs' (p. 3) and strategies were not put in place to support these children in sharing their views. The sad and frustrating thing is that these are not new ideas but are comments that seem to have been discussed for years; for example, an Ofsted report 15 years earlier in 2010, 'The voice of the child: learning lessons from serious case reviews', was saying similar things.

Listening and Hearing

The title of Helen Roberts' chapter 'Listening to children and hearing them' in *Research with Children; Perspectives and Practices* (Christensen and James, 2017) illustrates well some of the tensions which arise when adults claim they are trying to listen to children's views, not just in research but across the social world. Roberts recognises that in many ways we have become much more skilled in listening to children but wonders if we have also progressed in our skills of hearing them. She defines hearing in this context as 'taking account in a meaningful way of what they have to tell us' (p. 142). She notes that researchers are still learning that sometimes their ways of engaging children, albeit with the best of intentions, can be 'exploitative, simply another box to be ticked, or a voice of endorsement on an adult project' (p. 142). She also raises the issue, we have already noted, that if only selected children are heard then this is not just exclusionary, but it is also a threat to validity. In the same way, have those voices of children who are included been 'edited and sanitised' (p. 2) by the very adults who claim they are foregrounding them?

Roberts was writing this chapter from her position as head of Research and Development at Barnardo's so we can see an alignment with her perspective and the thoughts in the NSPCC report that we have mentioned above. She discusses how without the input of children's ideas and perspectives it is impossible for them as an organisation to evaluate their practice, or indeed influence policy, so that children are seen as 'a reservoir of expertise on their own lives' (p. 144). She takes the issue of policy to illustrate this expertise; for example she states that the notion of poverty may be 'contested in academic articles and political debates' (p. 3), yet a child's vivid description of their experiences of living in poverty is harder to dismiss. She also notes the issues around water metering, school exclusions and parents with HIV highlighted by children as areas of concern in the charity's research and development work, long before they were picked up by policy. In the same vein, Cooper et al.'s work (2023) which focused on the impact on families of having a parent in prison, highlighted important information on the impact on children and how they can best be supported. See for example Charles explaining to the researcher the impact of his parent's imprisonment on his body:

> Charles: *So, I drew around myself on a big piece of paper and I put orange where I would get angry and use when I get angry. I drawed orange all over my fist, on my knees, on my legs, on my head and I think that's it.*
>
> Researcher: *So, you drew all around your body and showed all the bits where you perhaps felt angry in your body?*
>
> Charles: *Oh yeah, I think my face because I would shout a lot and in the middle on my chest I drawed what was inside of me, my own version of a monkey* (pp. 74–5)

In the foreword to Cooper et al.'s report, Catherine Kevis draws our attention to the hidden victims of crime, i.e. the children of parents who are sent to prison for crime-related activity, an issue the report describes as 'secondary prisonisation'. She remarks that very little is known about these children because up till now they have held very little interest for those involved in policymaking even though there may be issues of inter-generational, anti-social behaviour that could be addressed if they were.

Child Centredness in Research

Notions of child centredness in research and particularly the growing tensions between this and other calls for a de-centring of childhood are explored by Orrmalm et al. (2024). They draw on the notion of childism (Wall, 2023), a term which recognises a certain prejudice against children in our society, and 'post-child' (Aitken, 2018), a posthuman term which conceptualises how children are more-than-adult and how they negotiate, and impact on, the spaces they encounter. In Orrmalm's section, she uses the term 'ghostly participation' (p. 15) to describe how children do not necessarily need to be physically present to impact on spaces. She describes the powerful image of a swing 'creaking' in the abandoned playground to illustrate how we might think differently about child-centredness, including thinking about it in terms of absence. She suggests that absence can be about 'forgetfulness, lack of attention' (p. 14), what can't be said or what hasn't been considered.

The term 'childism' is used by Alminde (2024) to discuss children's participation in family law courts in Denmark. Although she describes how legislation has been put in place to allow this and that practice has greatly developed, nevertheless their voice can still often be 'undermined or excluded' (Abstract) depending on how the term 'listening to children' is enacted. Alminde uses what she terms a 'childist' lens (p. 1) in her article to examine how children are supported in these courts to express their opinions about important decisions being taken in parental divorce cases which will impact directly on their future experiences and opportunities and, as such, their wellbeing. She refers to Davies' idea of 'listening as usual' (2014, 2015) and emergent listening to disrupt the notion that an adult's views are more important than a child's. It is a way of seeing children as 'competent agents' (p. 1) who can both impact on others but also be impacted on in their turn. She claims this view of childism is an important lens to challenge notions of 'adultism' which places adult knowledge and ways of being as being the most desirable.

Children's participation can be limited by adults, perhaps because they are seen as 'people of tomorrow' as Korczak (1929, cited in Mahony et al., 2024, p. 5) suggests and because of their 'not-yet-adult status' (Alminde, 2024, p. 2) which is seen as the most desired status.

Activity 8.2   Who Makes the Decisions?

In the article by Alminde (2024) discussed above, she talks about the importance of re-figuring and re-orientating 'the underlying norms and structures that condition the position of children' (p. 2). With this in mind it would be relevant to think about how children are positioned within your setting or within your home and perhaps reflect on ideas of adultism. This activity is not without its tensions: as we have discussed in Chapter 2 an individual child is an expert in their own life – not all children's. Just as it can be problematic to give undue emphasis to the adult perspective so too can it be problematic to give undue emphasis to the child's. However, the aim of this activity is to get you to look at practices in a different way, for example through the lens of 'childism' to see if it could help you in your research approach or indeed in your area of focus.

Using Table 8.5 we would like you to think of a particular child, or group of children, in a particular setting, whether that be your home or your place of work. We have thought of some of the routines the child/ren might be involved in and would like you to think about who makes these decisions predominantly. Of course, it may be a negotiated or guided decision so you may want to tick both child and adult. We would like you to reflect in the final column though on why it matters who makes the decision in this scenario. Remember we are certainly not looking for any 'right' answers here – it is a reflective activity to help you develop your thinking about how children can be 'competent agents' and what that might look like.

Table 8.5 Making decisions

Question	Child	Adult	Does it matter?
Who decides when they eat?			
Who decides what they eat?			
Who decides when they sleep?			
Who decides when they tidy up?			
Who decides what they learn?			
Who decides what they wear?			
Who decides if they are indoors or outdoors?			
Who decides when their nappy needs changing?			

Depending on your context, that may have been a challenging activity. It would be good to reflect on what you may have learnt from undertaking it. In the reflection section below, we will see how Early Childhood student Alicia completed the table and how it helped them develop their thinking about her research.

Reflection

Alicia works as a teaching assistant in a primary school class where the children are 4 and 5 years old. She collaborates with the teacher to establish some of the routines and decisions that are made during the school day – including when the children can contribute to those decisions. You can see her reflections in Table 8.3.

This activity was useful for Alicia, and she shared her thoughts with the teacher. They decided they would really like to listen to the children's views on 'tidy up time' in case there was something they were missing so Alicia designed a project to allow her to capture their perspectives. She got the relevant permissions to film different tidy up

(Continued)

times over a week and then she used these films to discuss with the children in informal interviews.

Table 8.6 Decision rationales

Question	Child	Adult	Does it matter?
Who decides when they eat?	Y	Y	There is a set lunch time, but the snack table is set out so that children can have a drink and healthy snack when they need one. Some children are very hungry when they arrive at school whereas others just want to get going with activities. I think it is important that the children understand their own feelings of hunger and thirst and how to respond rather than always being told when it's time to eat.
Who decides what they eat?	Y	Y	Some children bring lunch from home, so I imagine they negotiate that with their parents. Others can choose from the cooked lunch options. Sometimes, the cook will include things we have grown in our vegetable garden which is very exciting. It would be good though it they could contribute to the menu more – I wonder what they would choose?
Who decides when they tidy up?	N	Y	This is interesting for me – because it seems to be the only routine that the children do not impact on – we tell them it is 'tidy up time'. They don't always appreciate having to finish their play, but we have to fit in with the routines of the day. This might be an interesting area to explore in research with the children – I could possibly learn something from their expertise that I could then share with the class teacher.
Who decides what they learn?	Y	Y	We have a good balance of adult directed activities and child led activities. I notice that in the child led they are often using what they have already learnt in adult led work and of course we design our adult led activities based on what we have seen the child doing in play. It's good that both child and adult recognise each other as 'expert'.

Question	Child	Adult	Does it matter?
Who decides what they wear?	Y	Y	The school has a uniform, and I think parents have been consulted on this but pretty sure the children haven't! I wonder what they would say if we asked them. I have indicated both adult and child choose because the children do make some decisions about whether they wear coats outside, if they take their shoes off inside and of course they may spend most of the day wearing something from our wide selection of dressing up clothes.
Who decides if they are indoors or outdoors?	Y	Y	Most of the day, children can choose whether they are inside or outside. The teacher and I are committed to this – we have noticed that some children just learn better outside.
Who decides when they go to the toilet?	Y	Y	This is an interesting question. We have easily accessible toilets in the classroom so the children can use them whenever they want without asking – although we do ask them all to go when they go to wash their hands before lunch.

THE STUDENT RESEARCHER AND THE VOICE OF THE CHILD

You may be thinking at this point, that although you can see both the benefits and the ethical rationale for focusing on research which centres the voice of the child, it is probably something that a highly skilled and experienced researcher would undertake. However, we would argue that it is a methodology that suits a student researcher well. You may even be working with young children and so will have no problem finding a group of children to research with. If this is the case, we would really encourage you to consider children's voice research.

The Least Adult

Why is this kind of research particularly suitable for student researchers? It is useful to think about the term 'least adult' when seeking to answer this question. This is a term coined by Mandell (1988). Mandell describes how when researching with children there are three roles that the researcher can adopt; these are 'detached observer', 'semi participatory' and 'complete involvement'. The latter role is also described as that of the 'least adult' as a way that the researcher can position themselves in order to address power imbalances. If you work in a setting, you may be able to identify with this position well; have you had a string of beads plonked over your head? Have you been told 'you're the baby' in the home corner by a 4-year-old? Have you been presented with a 'cup of tea' from the water tray by a 3-year-old? We certainly have! By engaging with us in this way, children were perhaps demonstrating that they didn't see us as 'proper' adults, that they felt an equality with us, that they saw us as the 'least' adult within that space. They were relaxed and confident and happy to interact – this is exactly the kind of environment you would like to be researching with children in. We are not suggesting that it is a strategy without issues, however. Yet Garratt (2021), drawing on research work in Dublin primary schools focusing on racism, suggests that the least adult role is:

> a technique that encourages researchers to shed adult power and signifiers,
> to become as immersed in children's worlds as possible. The logic behind
> this method is that the researcher must be orientated towards children differently
> than other adults, in order to access what is often kept concealed from them. (p. 1)

So you are in a perfect position to explore capturing the child's voice in research as a student researcher. Your study is small scale, so you don't have any concerns about collecting data from great numbers of children. You may already be working with children, so have easy access to those with whom you are already attuned so that you don't have to spend a long period of time in building up a trusting relationship; if they are children you know well, you may also be familiar with the different ways that they choose to share their understandings and views.

Case Study 8.1   Wearing School Uniforms

Hasim wanted to find out about school uniforms and why they were important; he noticed that many countries didn't have them. He designed his research to find out from adults and parents, at his local primary school, why they were used. One of his parent participants jokingly said, 'Oh you should ask my child about that – he has lots to say – he would like to come to school dressed as Spiderman every day!' Hasim realised he was missing a trick not asking the children, so he submitted an updated ethics form and talked informally to the children as they were playing on the playground, noting down any interesting remarks. Children approached him when they knew that he wanted their opinions. Some talked about how the uniforms were uncomfortable and 'scratchy', some talked about never being able to find their own jumper because they all looked the same. One child said how much they loved non-uniform days for special occasions. These were all messages that he hadn't picked up from the parents and teachers who were very interested to have this detail. As a result, the school decided to have every Friday as a non-uniform day and it made a lovely end to the week for everyone.

KEY POINTS FROM THE CHAPTER

- The choice of research design can both promote or diminish the voice of the child.
- The concept of 'the voice of the child' is not without issues and it is important to acknowledge this if attempting to use child participation methods.
- Sometimes these issues arise because of contradictory definitions of the concept.
- Regardless of the difficulties around the concept, this should not be used as an excuse to exclude children from research or aspire to hear their voice.
- As a student researcher, particularly if you are working with young children, children's voice research is a good option to consider.

FURTHER READING

1   This report sets out the findings of a project which was looking at the idea of 'secondary prisonisation' for children when their parent is sent to prison. It very clearly includes the voice of the child.

Cooper, V., Payler, J., Bennett, S. and Taylor, L. (2023) *From arrest to release, helping families feel less alone: An evaluation of a Worcestershire pilot support project for families affected by parental imprisonment*. The Open University, Milton Keynes. Available at: https://oro.open.ac.uk/88511/ (accessed: 1 July 2025).

2   If you are interested in finding out more about the least adult role, this paper is a very interesting read.

Garratt, L. (2021) 'Embodying the least-adult role', *British Educational Research Journal*, *47* (5), pp. 1194–1208.

3   This article, written by several authors, is a great one to dip into as they all explore what being child centred in research means to them individually.

Orrmalm, A., Sjöberg, J., Sparrman, A., Tiefenbacher, R., Löw, J., Annerbäck, J., Sköld, J., Holmbom Strid, E., Hedrén, S., Lago, L., Anatoli, O., Hrechaniuk, Y., Prout, A. and Tesar, M. (2024) 'Centring children in research: a collaborative exploration into child-centredness as method and theory', *Child Studies*, (6), pp. 11–32. DOI: https://doi.org/10.21814/childstudies.5745.

REFERENCES

Aitken, S. (2018) *Young People, Rights and Place*. London: Routledge.

Alminde, S. (2024) 'Listening to children: a childist analysis of children's participation in family law cases', *Social Sciences*, *13*, 133. DOI: https://doi.org/10.3390/ socsci13030133.

Christensen, P. and James, A. (2017) *Research with Children: Perspectives and Practices*. Abingdon: Routledge.

Cooper, V., Payler, J., Bennett, S. and Taylor, L. (2023) *From arrest to release, helping families feel less alone: An evaluation of a Worcestershire pilot support project for families affected by parental imprisonment*. The Open University, Milton Keynes. DOI: https://doi.org/10.21954/ou.ro.000159bf.

Davies, B. (2014) *Listening to Children: Being and Becoming*. New York: Routledge.

Davies, B. (2015) *Emergent Listening*. Open Lecture at DPU. October 27. Available at: https://dpu.au.dk/viden/video/listening-to-children (accessed: 17 October 2025).

Garratt, L. (2021) 'Embodying the least-adult role', *British Educational Research Journal*, 47(5), pp. 1194–1208.

Mahony, L. McLeod, S., Salamon, A. and Dwyer, J. (2024) *Early Childhood Voices: Children, Families, Professionals*. New York: Springer.

Mandell, N. (1988) 'The least-adult role in studying children', *Journal of Contemporary Ethnography*, 16(4).

NSPCC (2024) *Voice of the child: Learning from case reviews*. Available at: https://learning.nspcc.org.uk/media/ccqcd2e2/voice-of-the-child-learning-from-case-reviews-briefing.pdf (accessed: 2 July 2025).

Ofsted (2010) *The voice of the child: Learning lessons from serious case reviews*. Available at: https://assets.publishing.service.gov.uk/media/5a74a872ed915d0e8bf1a15f/The_voice_of_the_child.pdf (accessed: 2 April 2025).

Orrmalm, A., Sjöberg, J., Sparrman, A., Tiefenbacher, R., Löw, J., Annerbäck, J., Sköld, J., Holmbom Strid, E., Hedrén, S., Lago, L., Anatoli, O., Hrechaniuk, Y., Prout, A. and Tesar, M. (2024) 'Centring children in research: a collaborative exploration into child-centredness as method and theory', *Child Studies*, (6), pp. 11–32. DOI: https://doi.org/10.21814/childstudies.5745.

Phillips, L. and Ritchie, J. (2025) 'Contemporary challenges for children's rights, well-being, justice and equity: policy, community activism and pedagogy', *Global Studies of Childhood*, pp. 1–6.

Roberts, H. (2017) 'Listening to children: and hearing them', in P. Christensen and A. James (eds), *Research with Children: Perspectives and Practices*. Abingdon: Routledge, pp. 142–59.

United Nations (1989) *United Nations Convention on the Rights of the Child*. Treaty no. 27541. Available at: www.unicef.org.uk/wp-content/uploads/2016/08/unicef-convention-rights-child-uncrc.pdf (accessed: 16 December 2025).

Wall, J. (2023) 'From childhood studies to childism: Reconstructing the scholarly and social imaginations', *Children's Geographies*, 20(3), pp. 257–70.

9

CENTRING THE VOICE OF THE VERY YOUNG CHILD

CHAPTER OBJECTIVES

By the end of this chapter, you will:

- Understand why it is important to listen to the voice of the very young child
- Recognise some strategies in being able to listen to the voice of the very young child
- Appreciate some of the challenges that exist in doing this.

INTRODUCTION

In Chapter 8 (*Centring the voice of the child*) we began to think about how, although the concept of 'the voice of the child' is not unproblematic, it is important to consider how to centre the child's voice and acknowledge that there are particular research designs that are appropriate for this and other research designs that may diminish the voice of the child. In this chapter we continue this discussion but focus particularly on very young children, who we are defining as babies and toddlers aged birth to 2 years. Children of this age may be especially seen as using other ways to communicate than use a verbal 'voice'. This certainly doesn't mean that they don't have valuable things to tell us about their lives, if as researchers we consider carefully what strategies and research designs are most appropriate to use. And the same principles about listening to their voice hold true as for older children: it's important to listen to babies and toddlers because it's a social justice issue embedded within the UNCRC (United Nations, 1989) and also because listening to them can, and should, improve their lives.

In this chapter we will consider some starting points for listening to very young children, think about some approaches to data collection that have been used by researchers aiming to gather the perspectives of very young child participants, acknowledge that there are some challenges in centring the voice of the very young child and explore how these challenges might be able to be overcome.

STARTING POINTS FOR LISTENING TO VERY YOUNG CHILDREN

If you are thinking about conducting research which aims to listen to the voice of very young children, there are several starting points you can begin with. These include supporting a pedagogy of inclusive participation for young children, thinking about the significant adults close to them and focusing on what very young children *can* do, rather than what they *can't*.

Support a Pedagogy of Inclusive Participation for Very Young Children

The more that we value very young children's expertise and capabilities generally, the more that these will, by extension, be valued when researchers seek to conduct research with them. If you are already working with young children, think about how developing the opportunities that they naturally have to participate will build their participatory abilities and reinforce a narrative that very young children do have expertise and competence. Developing a pedagogy of inclusive participation may involve facilitating opportunities that allow young children to make decisions in their play, use open-ended materials, have autonomy, respond to their own interests and build their own knowledge. In their ethnographic study of a classroom for 2-year-olds over a three-year period, Ceballos, Saiz-Linares and Susinos (2024) found that building opportunities for inclusive participation gave way 'to understanding children as subjects of rights, in possession of their own culture and agents with the ability and knowledge to understand, make decisions and give meaning to their experiences' (p. 378).

Those working or volunteering with very young children may also like to reflect on how the Reggio Emilia approach facilitates a democratic culture that values inclusive participation. Ghirotto and Mazzoni (2013) share how within an infant-toddler centre in Reggio Emilia, Italy, Early Childhood educators noticed that the 2-year-olds were interested in using open-ended materials to construct representations of their city. They took the children to the local library to find books about city landscapes and took other opportunities to follow their interest in their city. After several weeks, the educators asked the children to create a new place for their city and the 2-year-olds decided they wanted to develop 'a round garden with white stripes in it' (p. 305) to grow vegetables. You might be thinking 'how brilliant that the 2-year-olds were able to have a say about the setting's outdoor space in such a way!' But what happened next might surprise you. The educators invited grandfathers (who had gardening expertise) into the setting to help build the garden. But the grandfathers disagreed that the garden should be a circle shape, as a square shape would give the plants better space to flourish. They worked with the children to redesign a square-shaped garden, which was eventually built. You might be thinking 'is that inclusive participation that the adults overrode the children's wishes?' But the authors note that 'participation means to support children's agency in a way that allows children to realise their ideas'. Supporting inclusive participation doesn't mean necessarily letting the children do what they want, it means adults listening carefully and actively to what the children are saying with their voice (verbal or otherwise) and offering scaffolding to build their knowledge, develop their thinking and then realise their ideas.

Think About the Adults Close to Them

Very young children cannot survive in isolation, so it can be useful to think about which adults are close to them and how they might play a role in the research process. Young children often exist as part of a dyad (a group of two people) or a triad (a group of three people). Can you think of examples of who might be part of their dyads and triads? You might have come across literature that talks about the mother–infant dyad; that is, seeing the child and their mother as a group together rather than two individuals. You might also be familiar with the concept of a child's microsystem from Bronfenbrenner's (2005) bioecological theory of human development; if you think about the relationships that a child is likely to be part of within their microsystem, such as with their parents, siblings, early years practitioners or neighbours, then those are the people that are close to them and might be in a dyad or triad with them.

There are many pieces of research that have sought to listen to the voice of the very young child by utilising dyads or triads, often using similar creative approaches to the ones we outlined in Chapter 7 (*Creative approaches to research*). For instance, Venturelli and Cigala's (2016) research uses the caregiver–child–parent triad to explore the drop-off experience for toddlers at nursery. They note that previous studies about the daily micro-transition that a child experiences into their Early Childhood setting have rarely considered the perspectives of all three stakeholders, yet 'adopting a triadic perspective means that we can see welcoming as a relational space in which a unique triadic child–parent–caregiver interaction takes place with all participants having an active role' (p. 3).

Others, such as Ataol et al. (2022) have used the term 'team members' to describe the relationship between mothers and their toddlers in research that explores what inclusive urban environments look like for babies and toddlers. They state that 'the participation of mothers as "team members" in representing their very young children derives learnings about very young children's daily lives since very young children's daily lives are structured not by individual aims and performance but by joint action with their caregivers, especially mothers as the dominant caregivers' (2022, p. 1179). We love the idea that mothers and their babies are on the same team who have joint agency, joint geographies and undertake joint action. Who else do you think very young children are on the same team as? Can you think of ways you could involve them in the research process?

Start With What Very Young Children *Can* Do, Rather Than What They *Can't*

When you think of children aged between birth to 2, what do you imagine? There's a big difference between a newborn and a 2-year-old, but there are still some similarities between them. Some might be toddling, some wiggling, some chatting, some gurgling. We like to focus on what young children *can* do, rather than what they *can't*. So, think about how they *can* move, *can* communicate and *can* express themselves, rather than reinforce a deficit perspective that often surrounds very young children. We find this is a good starting point for listening to very young children.

We remember vividly a conversation we had with someone in which, when we were talking about doing research with very young children, they expressed the view 'but what do babies know!?' This has stuck with us as babies have been described as 'the most powerful learning machine in the universe' (Gopnik et al., 1999, p. 1) who 'far from being mere unfinished adults … are exquisitely designed by evolution to change and create, to learn and explore' (Gopnik, 2010, p. 81). This description of babies as not 'mere unfinished adults' resonates with how Alminde (2024, p. 2) describes how children in general are seen through the deficit lens of having a 'not-yet-adult status'. It reinforces why it's important that researchers challenge this common deficit perspective of very young children by taking opportunities to raise the profile of their capabilities and expertise. In Chapter 8 (*Centring the voice of the child*) you read how we defined a child's expertise as what they know and share about their own life, context, feelings, emotions and experiences, and we reiterated a commitment to seeing babies and toddlers as competent and being able to have and share their expertise. Take a moment to consider – what do you know that babies and toddlers have expertise in? What do you know about what they *can* do which may facilitate us to be able to learn from their expertise?

Activity 9.1   What Can Very Young Children Do?

It can be hard to reflect on what very young children *can* do, rather than what they *can't*. Often their abilities are compared to that of older children and of adults and the differences between them position babies and toddlers as deficient or defective, rather than just *different*. Take some time to complete Table 9.1, which focuses on what very young children often can do. There are many different types of behaviour, but for this activity we have focused on just three. At the same time, reflect upon whether this is an easy task for you, or whether it is easier to outline what babies and toddlers can't do.

Table 9.1   Acknowledging what babies and toddlers can do

Type of behaviour	Example
Moving	*E.g. kicking their legs*
Communicating	*E.g. gurgling*
Using their senses	*E.g. turning their head in response to a noise*

Reflection

How did you find completing that task? Here are some of the ways in which very young children show what they can do.

Table 9.2 Examples of what babies can do

Type of behaviour	Example
Moving	Kicking their legs, grasping their fingers, holding, patting, throwing, rolling, crawling, shuffling, toddling, walking, pulling themselves up, climbing
Communicating	Gurgling, crying, screaming, smiling, babbling, pointing, singing, pointing, chattering
Using their senses	Turning their head in response to a noise, looking towards the light, mouthing objects, feeling textures, tasting food, splashing in water

WHAT STRATEGIES CAN BE USED TO CENTRE THE VOICE OF THE VERY YOUNG CHILD?

When thinking about how to centre the voice of the very young child in research, there are certain approaches to data collection and research designs that you might want to consider. Many of these approaches rely on taking videos or photographs. These include methodological approaches that utilise wearable 'baby-cams', approaches which use video footage or photographs to support reflections that may give insights on very young children's perspectives and also sensory video ethnography.

Methodological Approaches With Wearable 'Baby-Cams'

When we think about gathering people's perspectives, we typically don't mean their literal perspective (i.e. point of view) but collecting data that captures a very young child's literal viewpoint using a wearable camera like a GoPro is a method sometimes used to centre the voice of the very young child. Capturing footage from this perspective, rather than via a traditional hand-held or fixed-mounted camera, can help researchers, practitioners and family members to think differently about babies' perspectives and how they view the world.

For instance, in the Australian context Elwick (2015) filmed an Early Childhood practitioner interacting with a baby on two video cameras simultaneously. She then showed the footage to both groups of Early Childhood educators and to the practitioner who had been filmed herself, to compare the differences in how the instance was perceived dependent on whether it was filmed via a fixed tripod-mounted camera and a body-worn 'baby-cam'. Elwick (2015) found that reflecting on baby-cam footage can create a more decentred viewing experience for the audience, support the viewer to notice things that otherwise may have been overlooked and challenge practitioners' perceptions of babies' capabilities. The practitioner who featured in the footage noted how big she appeared to be in the baby's gaze and how that reinforced the importance of getting down to babies' levels when interacting with them. Elwick (2015) argues that reflecting on footage recorded via baby-cams may support babies to share their 'own perspectives' (p. 323) and to participate in research by taking an active role in the generation of data.

Similar wearable camera technology has been used with slightly older children, too. For instance, Burbank, McGregor and Wild (2018) explored young children's experiences of museums by collecting data which, in part, took the form of recordings from GoPro cameras that were worn by children aged between 3 and 6 during a museum visit. They cite Green (2016), who argues that wearable video cameras capture 'children's unique perspectives of being-in-the-world, depicting what they see, hear, say, touch, and their interactions with others' (p. 277). Green offers a range of advantages of wearable cameras which are applicable to very young children too, including:

- They allow the researcher to see what the child sees.
- They put size into perspective, by highlighting the relative height of the child in comparison to adults or environmental features.
- They reduce the power imbalance between the child and the researcher, as the need for the adult to be nearby is removed.
- They 'tell the whole story' (p. 286) as, unlike fixed-mounted cameras that a researcher might place in one particular location and may not capture everything fully, wearable cameras are able to record a whole instance or interaction without interruption and thus can capture a child's experience more fully.
- They are non-intrusive and children often forget that they are wearing them.
- They can be enjoyable for children who understand their function; Green (2016) notes how one child displayed pride that he was able to take an investigative role.
- They could support children to take part in data analysis through reviewing and discussing the video footage together.

Burbank, McGregor and Wild (2018) share other advantages of wearable cameras, including that:

- Participants may behave more authentically as the researcher is not present.
- They provide insights into how young children move, and what they touch and feel.
- Their footage 'allows intimate access, without overt researcher interference, to other modes or "hundred languages" … with which young children express themselves during their visits' (p. 321).

You might be able to think of other advantages too, such as how it may be easier for a child to withdraw their consent by deciding to remove their camera or to switch it off, without having to explicitly inform the researcher that they no longer want to take part. Yet this method is not without its limitations. What do you think some of the difficulties might be in placing body-worn cameras on babies or young children? Both Green (2016) and Burbank, McGregor and Wild (2018) talk about the risks that a child might switch a camera off accidentally. Green (2016) also highlights the challenge that the storage space needed to save GoPro footage can be large, and that it is possible that the camera angle can shift as the child moves so should be regularly checked to see if it requires readjustment.

Using Videos or Photos to Support Reflections of Very Young Children's Experiences

Using video footage or photographs of very young children to support those close to them, or even the very young children themselves, to engage in reflections about their experiences can be an effective way to attempt to centre the voice of the very young child. We have already considered how Elwick (2015) shared footage of a practitioner's interaction with a baby with the practitioner herself. Others, too, have used photographs and video footage in conjunction with reflective conversations to build up a fuller picture of the child's experiences.

For instance, in the UK context this method has been used to develop a reflective model, Video Interaction Dialogue (VID), in which Early Childhood practitioners watch back footage captured via hand-held cameras of their interactions with babies and then reflect upon the footage with the researcher in 'reflective dialogues' (Guard, 2023). The VID model is comprised of three themes – interact, reflect and empower – and nine principles within those. It is designed to 'make visible the voice initiations of babies to Early Childhood educators and offers scope to reconceptualise the way in which babies' voices can be seen, heard, and acknowledged in Early Childhood settings' (2023, p. 608). In Guard's (2023) study, she found that practitioners identified VID as a way for Early Childhood practitioners to reflect on which babies' voices were uncovered. She also identified how these opportunities for those working with babies to reflect are important because babies are marginalised politically and thus by extension those who work with them become disempowered (both 'institutionally and societally' (p. 620)); the process of reflecting on interactions that Early Childhood practitioners have with babies empowers them by growing their confidence, facilitating their agency and strengthening their relationships with very young children.

While Guard (2023) used video footage to support adults to reflect on babies' experiences, Salamon (2015) used photographs to support babies to engage in reflection on their own experiences. Do you remember Green's (2016) suggestion that it is possible to involve children in analysis of video footage? The same is true with photographs too. Salamon (2015) encouraged babies to reflect on their experiences, by observing them, reflecting upon the observations and then introducing the babies to photographs taken during the observations to assess their reactions to them. The photographs acted as pedagogical documentation (Rinaldi, 1998), 'to help them [the babies] "revisit" and "rethink" their experiences in the research' (p. 1016). Salamon (2015) notes how initially she lined the photographs up in an ordered way on a table but the babies were reluctant to engage and when they did, they 'did not appear to care as much about who was in the photo as they did about what it felt and tasted like, how it looked and bent and bounced and slid under their hands and bodies' (p. 1025). So, she reflected on this and changed her approach and instead offered a smaller number of photographs to babies in a pile to see how they would engage with them. Doing this meant that the babies engaged with the photos for longer periods of time and in ways which were individual to them, for instance passing them back and forth to other children. This demonstrates how, when attempting to centre the voice of the very young child, it is important to be reflective throughout the research process to assess whether the approach may need to be changed to support the participants' participation and engagement.

Sensory Video Ethnography

Finally, cameras have also been used as a data collection method to listen to the voice of very young children when taking an ethnographic approach. Ethnography is a research approach where the researcher aims to closely study a particular social or cultural group of people by participating in the group to gain an 'insider's perspective' (Kramer and Adams, 2017, p. 458). Orrmalm (2023) focused on babies' perspectives in their home environments in Sweden by undertaking a *sensory video ethnography* (Pink, 2015, cited in Orrmalm, 2023), in which she recorded video footage via a handheld camera of her interactions with babies (hence the 'video' aspect) but also focused on 'embodied and sensory encounters between [herself] and the babies as a valuable part of what it means to do ethnographic method' (p. 3). Overall, she spent about 100 hours with seven families who had at least one child between birth and 18 months and collected about '70 hours of video material, 100 images and 60 pages of field notes'. In order to uphold the need to act ethically, particularly as babies themselves cannot give consent, Orrmalm (2023) did not initiate physical contact with the babies and let the babies take the lead when they chose to interact with her or the camera. As a result, Orrmalm (2023) encountered 'unplanned, troubling and messy moments' (p. 4) during fieldwork because data collection did not go as expected due to both her interactions with the babies and the babies' interactions with the camera, which led to feelings of 'losing control' (p. 9). She describes some of her video footage as 'a blurry mess' (p. 8) because of how one baby participant took hold of the camera, began to zoom in and out and changed what was being filmed so the researcher herself was captured in the footage. As a result, Orrmalm (2023) argues that researchers must 'stay curious' and 'stay cautious' (p. 10) when considering what babies' participation in research might consist of.

Activity 9.2   How Can We Define Very Young Children's 'Voice'?

Earlier we referred to how Burbank, McGregor and Wild (2018) identify that an advantage of wearable cameras allows researchers access to young children's 'hundred languages'. 'The Hundred Languages of Children' is a poem by Loris Malaguzzi (1996), pedagogical leader of Reggio Emilia, which talks about all the different ways that young children express themselves, such as through playing, loving and singing.

If you are unfamiliar with it, find a copy of 'The Hundred Languages of Children' online. Read through it. Use it as a basis for making a list of all very young children's 'languages'. Then think about how the researcher may need to behave in order to listen to those languages.

Reflection

You might have noticed that some of the 'languages' on your list overlapped with your responses to Activity 9.1 and your consideration of what babies and toddlers *can* do, rather than what they *can't*. Our attempt at writing a list of babies' languages included:

- Smiling
- Pointing
- Babbling
- Moving in response to music
- Listening
- Crawling to or away from something
- Crying
- Mark-making

When thinking about data collection methods that allow the researcher to listen to these languages, you may think it's clear that it involves getting to know the child closely to get to know their behaviour, ways of being and ways of communicating. It may also involve the researcher spending time with the child and adults who are significant to them in environments that are comfortable and familiar to them, so that they feel confident and secure to express their languages.

WHAT ARE THE CHALLENGES OF CENTRING THE VOICE OF THE VERY YOUNG CHILD?

Although it is important to conduct research that aims to centre the voice of the very young child, this doesn't mean that it is easy. Challenges to doing so exist. These include practical challenges, ethical challenges and societal challenges that must be overcome.

Practical Challenges

It can be difficult to get access to baby participants in an inclusive and ethical way. Whereas often research that attempts to centre the voice of the older child is conducted in their Early Childhood setting or school, very young children are less likely to be attending Early Childhood provision, and more likely to be spending time at home while their family members are taking maternity, paternity or parental leave. This means that those wishing to recruit baby participants may need to think about other settings in their microsystem that they may be visiting, such as postnatal courses or baby stay and play groups.

A second practical challenge is that the amount of time that very young children are awake can be significantly less than that of an older child. A responsive researcher must, therefore, take into account that they may need to factor in flexibility to their data collection to account for naps as well as other moments of personal care such as feeds or nappy changes.

Ethical Challenges

A second challenge of centring the voice of the very young child is ensuring both 'ethical compliance' and 'ethical values' (Bolshaw and Josephidou, 2018, p. 111). In terms of ethical compliance, it is, of course, impossible to gain informed consent from a baby to recruit them as a participant. In terms of ethical values, Elwick, Bradley and Sumsion (2014, p. 209) note that researchers hold an ethical responsibility 'to foreground the uncertainty of their endeavour – to acknowledge from the outset that to treat infants as genuinely human requires researchers to accept that they cannot know infants, their lives and experiences with any certainty'. Researchers who accept this premise must accept the limitations of what it is possible to know and comprehend about babies' perspectives. Despite this, there are strategies that researchers may take to gather babies' perspectives in ethically sensitive ways. By reflecting on baby-cam footage, as opposed to footage from a tripod-mounted camera, Elwick (2015) argues practitioners engage in 'ethical reflection' (p. 336) because they are challenged to view babies and their capabilities in new – potentially unsettling – ways, which may support babies in 'fully claiming their "participant stance"' (p. 336).

Alternatively, adopting an attitude of 'ethical symmetry' may support babies when undertaking participatory research that seeks to gather babies' perspectives (Salamon, 2015). Ethical symmetry is the notion that children should not be seen as the 'Other', but that they have both similarities and differences to adult research participants. Taking this approach means that child participants, albeit seen as capable, are not treated the same way as adults. This may impact on a researcher's theoretical framework, enactment of ethical principles or research methods in ways that avoid othering the child. Salamon (2015) argues that ethical symmetry can be realised with babies, in her case through building respectful relationships with her baby participants before commencing data collection and adapting the research process in reflexive ways in line with how babies may be guiding it.

Societal Challenges

A final challenge that can exist for those wishing to centre the voice of the very young child is that there is the danger that others in wider society may respond 'but who cares?' In Chapter 7 (*Creative approaches to research*) we shared a study by Lupton (2014) who explored how babies were commonly portrayed in advertisements as precious, pure, uncivilised and vulnerable. They weren't, however, portrayed as humans who have something important to say or who have the right to express their views freely (despite what Article 12 of the UNCRC may say). Wider society doesn't see the need to centre the voice of the very young child.

Wider society, perhaps, thinks negatively about very young children. If you heard someone be described as 'babyish', what would you think? That they were constantly processing new information and making synaptic connections at an astonishing rate? Or would you consider them to have some kind of character flaw that means they are somehow 'lesser' than the adults around them? Earlier on in this chapter we shared Guard's (2023) perspective that babies are marginalised. This is the reason that research that seeks to capture the voice of the very young child is so important, so that their status will be elevated and their worth recognised.

Activity 9.3   Overcoming Challenges

Researchers will always have challenges to overcome, whether they have very young child participants, older children or adults as participants or even no participants at all. Have a look at the list below where we've outlined some common challenges that researchers may encounter when conducting research that attempts to centre the voice of very young children. What strategies could you suggest to overcome these challenges? Then have a go at thinking of your own challenges and possible solutions.

- 'I can't find any literature about babies that relates to my research topic.'
- 'I am struggling to recruit baby participants.'
- 'My toddler participants are not able to give consent.'

Reflection

The challenges that you envisaged may have been pre-, post- or during data collection. The possible solutions that you might have suggested are outlined in Table 9.3.

(Continued)

Table 9.3 Solutions to challenges during the research process

Possible challenge	Possible solution
'I can't find any literature about babies that relates to my research topic.'	Book a tutorial with a university librarian for support and techniques on searching for appropriate literature.
'I am struggling to recruit baby participants.'	Consider spending time or volunteering at the type of places that young babies may visit with their caregivers, such as baby stay and play sessions, postnatal groups or library toddler song and story times.
'My toddler participants are not able to give consent.'	Be mindful of how very young children may demonstrate the withdrawal of consent, such as through moving away from the researcher, showing discomfort at being photographed or displaying emotions such as boredom or tiredness.

Case Study 9.1   Using Child-Centred Methods to Find Out What Babies Think of Spending Time Outdoors

Kubra, an Early Childhood Studies Year 3 student, wants to explore what babies think of being outdoors. She decides to approach a family friend she knows who has just had a baby to ask if she could spend some time with them in their home and garden to observe how the baby behaves to both the indoors and outdoors. She makes several visits to the family over the course of several months in order to get to know the baby well and build up a relationship with them. She is able to observe how the baby reacts to spending time outdoors and how the baby's behaviour sometimes appears to change when they are taken outside and records these moments using a video camera. She later shares the video footage with both the baby's mother and father for their reflections on their child's behaviour and what their baby's 'languages' may be telling them about their perspective of spending time outside.

KEY POINTS FROM THE CHAPTER

- In order to listen to the voice of the very young child, you may wish to utilise strategies like supporting a pedagogy of inclusive participation for very young children, thinking about the adults close to them and also starting with what they *can* do, rather than what they can't.
- There are several methodological approaches that have been used to centre the voice of the very young child. These include methodologies using cameras and those that seek to also capture the perspectives of babies' significant adults.

- There are many challenges that exist in centring the voice of the very young child. These include practical challenges, ethical challenges and societal challenges.

FURTHER READING

1 Orrmalm's (2023) video sensory ethnographic study with babies highlights some of the challenges in doing research that attempts to gather babies' perspectives and gives some lovely excerpts from her field notes about what seeking to involve baby participants in research can look like (such as a 9-month-old putting the camera power cord in their mouth before the Orrmalm could put it into the plug socket!):

Orrmalm, A. (2023) 'Doing ethnographic method with babies: participation and perspective approached from the floor', *Children & Society*, *34*(6), pp. 461–74. DOI: 10.1111/chso.12380.

2 Elwick, Bradley and Sumsion's (2014) article is a fascinating read that considers whether it's possible to conduct research that seeks to capture very young children's perspectives (they argue that it is potentially impossible to do):

Elwick, S., Bradley, B. and Sumsion, J. (2014) 'Infants as Others: uncertainties, difficulties and (im)possibilities in researching infants' lives', *International Journal of Qualitative Studies in Education*, *27*(2), pp. 196–213. DOI: 10.1080/09518398.2012.737043.

REFERENCES

Alminde, S. (2024) 'Listening to children: a childist analysis of children's participation in family law cases', *Social Sciences*, *13*(3), 133. DOI: https://doi.org/10.3390/socsci13030133.

Ataol, O., Krishnamurthy, S., Druta, O. and van Wesemael, P. (2022) 'Towards inclusive urban environments for infants and toddlers: assessing four urban neighbourhoods in Istanbul with mothers', *Children & Society*, *36*(6), pp. 1177–93. DOI: https://doi.org/10.1111/chso.12566.

Bolshaw, P. and Josephidou, J. (2018) *Introducing Research in Early Childhood*. London: Sage.

Bronfenbrenner, U. (2005) 'The bioecological theory of human development', in U. Bronfenbrenner (ed.), *Making Human Beings Human: Bioecological Perspectives on Human Development*. Thousand Oaks, CA: Sage, pp. 3–15.

Burbank, B., McGregor, D. and Wild, M. (2018) '"My special, my special thing, and my camera!" Using GoProTM as a complementary research tool to investigate young children's museum experiences', *Museum and Society*, *16*(3), pp. 311–33.

Ceballos, N., Saiz-Linares, A. and Susinos, T. (2024) 'A participatory and inclusive 2-year-old infant classroom', *Journal of Early Childhood Research*, *22*(3), pp. 359–80. DOI: 10.1177/1476718X231221364.

Elwick, S. (2015) '"Baby-cam" and researching with infants: viewer, image and (not) knowing', *Contemporary Issues in Early Childhood, 16*(4), pp. 322–38. DOI: https://doi.org/10.1177/1463949115616321.

Elwick, S., Bradley, B. and Sumsion, J. (2014) 'Infants as Others: uncertainties, difficulties and (im)possibilities in researching infants' lives', *International Journal of Qualitative Studies in Education, 27*(2), pp. 196–213. DOI: 10.1080/09518398.2012.737043.

Ghirotto, L. and Mazzoni, V. (2013) 'Being part, being involved: the adult's role and child participation in an Early Childhood learning context', *International Journal of Early Years Education, 21*(4), pp. 300–8. DOI: https://doi.org/10.1080/09669760.2013.867166.

Gopnik, A., Meltzoff, A.N. and Kuhl, P.K. (1999) *The Scientist in the Crib: Minds, Brains, and How Children Learn.* New York: William Morrow & Co.

Gopnik, A. (2010) 'How babies think', *Scientific American, 303*(1), pp. 76–81. DOI: 10.1038/scientificamerican0710-76.

Green, C. (2016) 'Sensory tours as a method for engaging children as active researchers: exploring the use of wearable cameras in Early Childhood Research', *International Journal of Early Childhood, 48*(3), pp. 277–94.

Guard, C. (2023) '"It's the little bits that you have enabled me to see". Reconceptualising the voices of babies using the video interaction dialogue model with early years educators', *Early Years, 43*(3), pp. 606–25. DOI: https://doi.org/10.1080/09575146.2023.2190498.

Kramer, M. and Adams, T. (2017) 'Ethnography', in M. Allen (ed.), *The Sage Encyclopedia of Communication Research Methods.* Thousand Oaks, CA: Sage, pp. 458–61.

Lupton, D. (2014) 'Precious, Pure, uncivilised, vulnerable: infant embodiment in Australian popular media', *Children & Society, 28*(5), pp. 341–351.

Malaguzzi, L. (1996) *The Hundred Languages of Children: The Reggio Emilia Approach to Early Childhood Education.* Greenwich, NJ Ablex Publishing Corporation.

Orrmalm, A. (2023) 'Doing ethnographic method with babies: participation and perspective approached from the floor', *Children & Society, 34*(6), pp. 461–74. DOI: 10.1111/chso.12380.

Rinaldi, C. (1998) 'Projected curriculum constructed through documentation – Progettazione: an interview with Lella Gandini', in C.P. Edwards, L. Gandini and G.E. Forman (eds), *The Hundred Languages of Children: The Reggio Emilia Approach – Advanced Reflections.* Greenwich, NJ: Ablex Publishing Corporation, pp. 113–26.

Salamon, A. (2015) 'Ethical symmetry in participatory research with infants', *Early Child Development and Care, 185*(6), pp. 1016–30. DOI: https://doi.org/10.1080/03004430.2014.975224.

United Nations (1989) *United Nations Convention on the Rights of the Child.* Treaty no. 27541. Available at: www.unicef.org.uk/wp-content/uploads/2016/08/unicef-convention-rights-child-uncrc.pdf (accessed: 16 December 2025).

Venturelli, E. and Cigala, A. (2016) 'Daily welcoming in childcare centre as a microtransition: an exploratory study', *Early Child Development and Care, 186*(4), pp. 562–77. DOI: https://doi.org/10.1080/03004430.2015.1044987.

10

CONDUCTING OBSERVATIONS

CHAPTER OBJECTIVES

By the end of this chapter, you will:

- Recognise some of the ways that observations can be used as a data collection method to challenge power imbalances and foreground children's perspectives
- Understand some different types of observation that are used in Early Childhood Research
- Identify some of the limitations to observations and how these can be minimised in your own study.

INTRODUCTION

You've probably carried out many observations already today. Perhaps you opened the curtains this morning and looked at the sky to decide whether to take an umbrella out with you. Or noticed how many people were at the same bus stop as you on your way home from work. If you work in an Early Childhood setting, perhaps you carried out an observation on a child today to assess them so that you can plan for their next steps. In a non-academic sense, we might define 'observe' as 'to look at' or 'to notice' and we carry out observations all the time. In relation to research, observations still rely on looking, or more specifically 'looking critically, looking openly, looking sometimes knowing what we are looking for, looking for evidence, looking to be persuaded, looking for information' (Clough and Nutbrown, 2012, p. 54) and there are a multitude of different ways to approach them as a form of data collection, which this chapter will consider.

We will begin by thinking about why observations can be an effective way to conduct Early Childhood Research because they can address power imbalances and foreground children's perspectives. We will then explore some of the different ways that observations can be conducted. We will then consider what some of the limitations might be to observations, but how these limitations can be minimised.

WHY USE OBSERVATIONS AS A DATA COLLECTION METHOD?

There are several reasons why you might want to consider observations as a data collection method. For instance, they can be an effective way to address power imbalances, they can build upon the professional strengths that the Early Childhood Researcher already has, and they can also help give a voice to those who may be marginalised, for instance those with a learning disability.

Conducting Observations Can Address Power Imbalances

Think about who typically has control in the data collection process – is it the researcher or the participant? Take questionnaires, for example. Who decides what questions to ask? Or consider interviews – who decides when to move onto the next question? Most of the time, it is the researcher making those decisions. But using observations as a data collection method can go some way to address this power imbalance by giving the participant the lead in what they do and how they behave. That is not to say that the participant's behaviour will not be affected by virtue of being observed; this is known as the Hawthorne Effect. The name comes from an industrial plant in Chicago, USA, where in the 1920s a researcher sought to investigate whether improving the lighting conditions would boost worker productivity. What, instead, was discovered was that worker productivity was increased as a result of the workers knowing they were being observed, and this phenomenon has become known as the Hawthorne Effect (Roethlisberger and Dickson, 1939, cited in Papatheodorou and Luff, with Gill, 2012). You might have experienced this yourself – perhaps if at work you've been subject to an observation by somebody senior, you might have noticed yourself behaving in a different way because you are conscious that someone is watching you.

In the studies on which the Hawthorne Effect was developed, the observers conducted non-participant observations, in that they did not interact with the participants but instead stood back. In terms of challenging the power imbalance that can exist between the researcher and participant, undertaking participant observations may be a better approach. For instance, Corsaro and Molinari (2017, p. 12) argue that 'several ethnographers have pointed to the importance of developing a participant status as an atypical, less powerful adult in research with young children'. In their case, Corsaro spent a year acting as a participant observer in a preschool class in Italy in which his 'very "foreignness" was central to his participant status' (2017, p. 12) because of his limitations in being able to communicate in Italian and his lack of knowledge of how the school operated. This meant that he was seen as an 'incompetent adult' (p. 12) by the children, and thus the power imbalance between the child participants and adult researcher was somewhat minimised. It is odd to consider, but have you ever thought about how you might have 'incompetent adult' characteristics that would support you in being a less powerful adult researcher?

Conducting Observations Can Build Upon Professional Strengths the Researcher Already Has

Often those who are doing research in Early Childhood may have worked or volunteered in an Early Childhood setting, in which observations of children can be a big role. Within the English context, the Early Years Foundation Stage (EYFS) Statutory Framework (Department for Education, 2025) talks about how practitioners will take part in ongoing assessment of children to ensure they understand children's interests and what they do, which will shape the provision they provide for them. To do this, practitioners should 'make and act on their own day-to-day observations about children's progress and observations that parents and carers share' (DfE, 2025, p. 19). Of course, the way in which a researcher may conduct an observation of a child may be very different to how an Early Childhood practitioner may observe their key child, yet many of the principles are the same. For instance, Louis (2022) argues that good observations:

- focus on what children say and do, 'not what we think they are saying or doing' (p. 5)
- give all the details necessary for informed decisions to be made
- are collected over several instances, so that those conducting them do not 'come to conclusions based on a single observation' (p. 5).

While Louis (2022) is talking about observations in relation to building up a deep picture of the child to extend their learning, the same principles for good observations hold true for those wishing to use observations as a data collection method. Thus, those researchers that already have experiences of observing children as part of their professional lives may find that using them as a data collection method builds upon skills that they already have and strengthens their abilities to observe as part of their working practices.

Conducting Observations Can Give a Voice to Those Who May Be Marginalised

We have already considered in this book how when we use the word 'voice', we aren't just referring to somebody's verbal communication but instead their perspectives and views in a broader sense. Observing children gives them the opportunity to show you their 'voice' in the form of their actions, gestures and behaviours when the alternative might be to ask their Early Childhood practitioner or family member about how they typically behave. One group who can often be marginalised in research are those with learning disabilities, particularly children. Yet observations can foreground the child's perspective, particularly if an approach such as In-the-Picture is adopted.

In-the-Picture has been described as a 'reflective, observational approach' (Rix, Parry and Malibha-Pinchbeck, 2019, p. 3) that was originally developed as a way of listening to the voices of children with learning disabilities (Paige-Smith and Rix, 2011).

The approach draws upon the Mosaic Approach (Clark and Moss, 2011) and comprises of four stages, which are known as 'perspectives':

1   Observing the child and recording the observation from the perspective of the child in the form of a first-person narrative observation (i.e. 'I am sitting on the grass ... I begin to crawl towards a daisy...')
2   Taking photos of what the child is showing an interest in (i.e. the daisy, not the child themselves)
3   Sharing the photos with the child to notice their responses
4   Reflecting with significant adults (i.e. family members or practitioners) after the observation and after the photos have been shared.

One strength of In-the-Picture is that through using the approach, the child is seen as having agency and their capabilities are highlighted. Writing narrative observations in the first person facilitates 'the child's lived experiences' (Paige-Smith and Rix, 2011, p. 31) to be captured and centres their perspective. Sharing photographs with them can help facilitate the child's active participation in the research process, while the reflective discussions with significant adults can help build an understanding of the child's perspective.

Activity 10.1   Asad on the Picnic Blanket

Here is an observation of a 10-month-old baby called Asad which is written in the third person. Have a go at re-writing it so it is written in the first person. Then reflect, does reading back the first-person narrative in comparison to the third-person observation change how you see the child? Then, think about what Asad's focus of attention is on and what you might take a photo of. And then finally, who might you have a reflection conversation with about your observation, and what sort of questions might you ask?

> *Asad is sitting on the picnic blanket under the tree with his father. He crawls towards the grass and touches it with his hand. He tries to pull the grass up several times until he manages it. He holds it to his face and attempts to put it in his mouth; his father says, 'no thank you', removes the grass from his hand and puts him on his lap.*

Reflection

When re-writing the third-person observation into a first-person account, you might have written something like this:

> *Daddy and I are sitting on a picnic blanket. I can see some tree branches swaying above me. I notice the grass beyond the picnic blanket and move*

onto all-fours so that I can crawl towards it. I stop when I get to the edge of the picnic blanket. I can reach the grass there. I touch the grass to see what it feels like. I wonder what it tastes like. I grasp the grass in my palm and try to pull it up but I don't manage it. I try again but it slips through my fingers. I try again and finally manage to pull some grass up. This makes me smile. I put it to my mouth but suddenly I hear my Daddy behind me say 'no, thank you'. He immediately puts his hands under my armpits and picks me. He puts me on his lap and uncurls my fingers. My grass falls away.

You might have decided to take some photographs looking up at the tree and of the grass at the edge of the picnic blanket to see how Asad responds to them. You might have chosen to talk to Asad's father to reflect upon your first-person observation and of how Asad reacted to the photographs of the tree and the grass. Perhaps you would ask him what you think Asad's intention was and why he might have been curious to put the grass in his mouth.

Does it make you feel differently about Asad reading the first-person observation rather the third person? You might think that he has more agency and control over his actions in the first-person narrative and it might have helped you to see things from his perspective.

HOW ARE OBSERVATIONS COMMONLY CONDUCTED IN EARLY CHILDHOOD RESEARCH?

When thinking about how to conduct observation research in Early Childhood, there are three key elements you need to consider. You need to think about the role that the researcher will take in the observation, the way in which the researcher will collect their data and the advantages and disadvantages of different types of observation methods.

The Role of the Researcher in Observations

Earlier we spoke about two different approaches that a researcher might take when conducting observations – do you remember them? The first was non-participant observations, which we introduced when we considered the Hawthorne Effect and the studies which informed it. While these studies did not have child participants, non-participation observations have shaped a lot of what is known and believed about young children. For instance, it was favoured by Maria Montessori, who had learned about the importance of observations in a clinical sense when she trained as a medical doctor. She used this knowledge when thinking about observations within Early Childhood education (Montessori and Gutek, 2004). The second approach you have been introduced to in this chapter is participant observation, which William Corsaro undertook in his ethnographic study in an Italian preschool (Corsaro and Molinari, 2017).

Different researchers will choose different approaches to observations because of their differing beliefs about how to generate knowledge about children (i.e. their epistemology as we discussed in Chapter 3 (*Designing your research project*)). Some people believe that to get an accurate picture of a child, it is crucial not to impact on how they behave. Those who take that perspective may favour non-participant observation, in which the researcher remains detached from the participants in order not to influence their behaviour. Others would argue that it is important to get to know a child well to build up an accurate understanding of their world, and that this is easier to do through participant observation, in which the researcher does interact and engage with the participants. And some researchers might favour a particular approach because of the observation method they have chosen; Podmore and Luff (2012) suggests that 'qualitative methods may demand a participatory role ... while quantitative observation techniques usually require a non-participant stance' (p. 90). Papatheodorou and Luff, with Gill (2012) state that in non-participant observation, researchers focus on 'scientific/objective recordings and understandings' (p. 79) rather than 'subjective understandings and meanings' (p. 79) that participant observations consider.

Similarly, some people believe that it is important that observations of different children are conducted in the same place so that external variables which might impact on the research are minimised, and thus they choose to carry out research in laboratory settings. Non-participant observations are sometimes carried out in laboratory environments, although they do take place in naturalistic settings (i.e. the actual places where young children spend time, such as their homes or Early Childhood settings) too, whereas participant observations are typically conducted in naturalistic environments. This aligns with the fact that often those who adopt a participant observation approach might already have a role in the place the observations are conducted, for instance an Early Childhood practitioner conducting research in their setting. If they aren't already familiar with the site of data collection, they might spend time joining in with the participants who are being studied to become familiar with them and their daily routines.

Methods of Observation

There are many different methods of observation that Early Childhood Researchers adopt. Table 10.1 outlines some of the most common ones:

Table 10.1 Observation methods

Method	Description of method	Example
Video, photo or audio recording	Observing using a camera or audio recording device to record what is happening.	Tina uses a hand-held camera to observe how a baby engages with a treasure basket.
Checklists	Observing while using a checklist to be able to tick off or tally when you observe a certain event, action or behaviour.	Ibrahima makes a checklist of different ways that toddlers move and tallies how often she sees a 3-year-old move in those ways during a forest school session.

Method	Description of method	Example
Event sampling	Observing in order to note down when particular events take place.	Paris observes practitioners in the baby room and notes every time they spontaneously sing a song or nursery rhyme.
Narrative observations	Observing while keeping a running written record of what you are seeing, often written up alongside the researchers' reflections on what they observed.	Leomie spends 30 minutes observing a small group of reception class children during their school assembly and writes notes on their actions and behaviours as well as what happens in the school assembly.
Sociograms	Observing which participants interact with each another.	Maya observes how babies interact with each other and their practitioners during 'garden time' in their Early Childhood setting.
Time sampling	Observing what is happening at a particular time at set time periods (for instance observing for 2 minutes every 10 minutes)	Sam observes the mark making area of a reception classroom and records what is happening there every 10 minutes for 2 minutes.
Tracking maps	Observing how someone moves around a space, using a diagram of that space to record the direction and time spent in each location.	Tadhg notes on a printed diagram of the toddler room how a 20-month-old girl moves around the space during the first 20 minutes she is in the setting each morning for a week.

Activity 10.2   Advantages and Disadvantages of Different Observation Methods

In this section we have considered how there are different types of observation that a researcher might employ. Different methods of observation have different advantages and disadvantages.

Take some time to complete Table 10.2 which asks you to consider what the strengths and limitations of each type of observation method might be. As you do this, think about whether there are some that better align to what you believe about how to go about generating knowledge about young children.

Table 10.2   Exploring the advantages and disadvantages of different observation methods

Type of observation	Advantages	Disadvantages
Audio/visual recordings	E.g. The researcher can look back on the observation if there is something they cannot remember.	E.g. The presence of a video or audio recording device may distract the participants.
Checklists		
Event sampling		

(Continued)

Table 10.2 (Continued)

Type of observation	Advantages	Disadvantages
Narrative observations		
Sociograms		
Time sampling		
Tracking maps		

Reflection

You might have found this a hard activity to complete, and do remember that in reality your chosen research question should inform your data collection method, rather than you choosing a data collection method and then finding a research question that fits, as we spoke about in Chapter 3 (*Designing your research project*). With that in mind, Table 10.3 gives suggestions of research methods you might use to address research questions you may have considered answering:

Table 10.3 Exploring the advantages and disadvantages of different observation methods

Type of observation	Advantages	Disadvantages
Audio/visual recordings	The researcher can look back on the observation if there is something they cannot remember.	The presence of a video or audio recording device may distract the participants.
Checklists	The researcher can measure instances and occurrences in an objective way.	The researcher might observe interesting things which are not identified on the checklist.
Event sampling	The researcher can note how often a particular event takes place and the specifics around it.	Researchers may not record what triggers an event as they may only start making notes once the event has commenced.
Narrative observations	The researcher is not constrained by only looking at or recording particular things or at a particular time.	It can be hard to observe while making notes that are detailed enough to be able to write up to give a narrative account of the observation afterwards.
Sociograms	The researcher may be able to identify who children interact with.	The researcher cannot explain what types of interactions children have, or other factors that may influence a lack of interaction between certain children.

Type of observation	Advantages	Disadvantages
Time sampling	The researcher is able to build an objective picture of what is happening at particular time intervals.	If the researcher sees something interesting outside of the period that they are observing, this will not be recorded.
Tracking maps	The researcher can record where, and where not, a child chooses to spend time.	The researcher does not have an insight into why, or why not, a child spends time in a particular place.

HOW CAN THE LIMITATIONS OF OBSERVATIONS BE MINIMISED?

In the past when we have spoken to students, they've been reluctant to carry out observations. This can be for a variety of reasons. Some students feel that their subjective nature is problematic, others state that the information they provide isn't useful because it focuses on the 'what' rather than the 'why', while others believe that observations bring about too many ethical challenges. This section will consider some of these limitations.

'Observations Are Too Subjective'

Yes, some observations may be subjective, but we don't think that that's a bad thing. As we've spoken about in Chapter 3 (*Designing your research project*), everybody approaches the world from their own worldview, based upon their own experiences and place in the world. A good researcher acknowledges how this will have shaped their interest in their research topic, how they approach their research question, how they collect their data and how they make sense of it.

Some researchers attempt to make their observations objective by using approaches such as tracking or mapping to record what a child does, or where they spend their time. Others employ checklists, as we spoke about earlier, that note quantitative data about how many instances children may do a particular behaviour or engage in a particular type of play. For instance, Morrissey, Scott and Wishart (2015) conducted observations in which they used checklists to count how many times babies and toddlers engaged in different types of play in the outdoor environment. Yet these approaches to observation are still subjective in the sense that the researcher themselves has decided who to track, where to map and what to count.

Other researchers, instead, lean into the notion that observations are subjective. Take, for instance, the Tavistock method of infant observation. Developed by Esther Bick, it is an approach to observation in which 'the role of the observer is to immerse themselves in the interactions that take place between the infant and others present' (Brooker, 2017).

Unlike other forms of observation, the researcher takes no notes and the observation (which should last at least 30 minutes) is not recorded through photographs or videos, but instead after it has finished the researcher writes up a transcript of what was observed. Brooker (2017) writes that this transcript 'aims to encapsulate not only what was seen, but significantly what was felt by the observer; the emotions, thoughts and feelings that were evoked'. In this case, the observation is subjective in the sense that what emotions and thoughts are evoked by one person may be very different to that of another. And that isn't a bad thing; it is up to the researcher to reflect on their positionality and how that shapes their research process, including during data collection.

If researchers are concerned about the subjective way in which they may analyse observations that they've conducted, a useful way to combat this is to work in partnership with another person, so that more than one pair of eyes are doing the observing. We spoke earlier about how in In-the-Picture observations the significant adults of those observed are invited to take part in reflective discussions about the observations, which allow their perspectives to shape findings. Alternatively, those seeking to use observations may analyse their data alongside another researcher, who will come with their own worldview through which they filter what they see. Discussing your data with another person, whether a participant or fellow researcher, will not make your observations more objective, but may support you to see your data through another lens.

'Observations Don't Explain the "Why", Only the "What"'

One other common complaint we hear about observations is that they tend to capture *what* happens, rather than *why* that instance occurs. For instance, imagine you are a researcher who is interested in how 2-year-olds engage with sand play in a preschool setting. You sit in the outdoor area observing what is happening around the sandpit. Several children are around the edge of the sandpit and another child approaches. This child is reluctant to engage and instead hovers nearby intently watching the other children. She appears to be interested in sand play but does not actively take part, despite encouragement from a practitioner.

Your observation may tell you what has happened – that a child appears to be reluctant to engage in sand play despite obvious interest – but doesn't tell you why that happened. Why do you think this might be? Perhaps the child isn't familiar with sand. Perhaps they don't like the texture. Perhaps they've had a prior experience of getting it in their eye or mouth. Perhaps they are wary of one of the other children who is already playing in the sandpit.

This is why observations can be useful to conduct as part of a multi-methods approach alongside another data collection method like interviews, such as in The Mosaic Approach (Clark and Moss, 2011). While a strength of interviews is that it allows the researchers to ask a participant about their experiences, views or practices, a limitation is that there is no certainty that what they say correlates with what they actually do. There might be discrepancies because of a wish to present themselves in a particular way to the researcher or simply because they've forgotten or misremembered details. Triangulating your data by conducting an interview after an observation can allow you to ask those who have been observed, or those who are familiar with them, about what you have seen and their reflections on it. This can offer a new perspective and help explain the 'why' whatever you have observed is happening. This was a practice used by the famous Swiss psychologist Piaget, whose ideas were informed by many observations on his own children, after which 'he interviewed each child to ensure that he was accurately interpreting their experiences' (Gray and Winter, 2011). If you don't think it is appropriate to ask the participant themselves, you can interview somebody else. Perhaps, when you ask a practitioner about why one child appears reluctant to engage in sand play, he tells you that the child in question had only just had their suncream applied and knew the sand would stick to their skin and cause discomfort. Triangulating your methods can help you draw conclusions about the answers to your research question and help you approach your data from another perspective.

'Observations Aren't Ethical'

Earlier we spoke about how one limitation of observations is the Hawthorne Effect, which is the idea that somebody's behaviour changes by virtue of them being observed. One obvious solution to this is to conduct covert observations in which the participants do not know they are being observed. But this brings about a dilemma – is it ethical to observe people without their consent? Your opinion on this may differ dependent on how you view children and your paradigm. Papatheodorou and Luff, with Gill (2012) consider how when conducting covert observations, there is a tension between the advantage they bring in that participants are more likely to display their typical behaviour and the limitation that those employing the method are prioritising their own data collection over the participant's right to informed consent.

Yet on the flipside, there are ways that an ethically sensitive approach can be taken in observations. In Chapter 8 (*Centring the voice of the very young child*) we introduced the notion of ethical symmetry, which was developed by Christensen and Prout (2002) as a way of addressing the power imbalance between child participant and adult researcher. You may remember we spoke about Salamon (2015) who used an approach of ethical symmetry when observing baby participants, which in her case involved getting to know the babies before commencing data collection and facilitating the babies to guide and shape the research process. Salamon's research took an ethnographic approach, like Corsaro, who we have also spoken about in this chapter. Ethnographic approaches often employ observations as a data collection method. The way in which researchers spend time getting to know their participants during ethnographic studies demonstrates an ethical value in wanting to build up a relationship with their participants to support them to build up accurate pictures of their lives.

Case Study 10.1   Conducting Research About How Toddlers Engage With Books

Wen is the toddler room lead at her setting and is curious to know how the children engage with books in the setting. She thinks about the way in which she could find out more about this and decides that conducting observations would be a good way to find out information that helps her answer her research question. Firstly, she considers what role that she might hold in an observation; as she already works with the toddlers and has a relationship with them, she thinks that a participant observation would be most appropriate. She then explores different observation methods and which one would be most appropriate to explore how toddlers engage with books. She narrows it down to two approaches – event sampling and checklists. She decides that she will first try event sampling and record events where children spend time with books. She thinks that then she will use this information to make a checklist of how the toddlers typically behave and interact with books, so that she can try using a checklist approach as well.

KEY POINTS FROM THE CHAPTER

- There are some important reasons why you might want to consider using observations as your data collection method.
- Observations can help address power imbalances, give a voice to people who are marginalised and can build upon strengths the researcher already has.
- There are several ways in which observations can be conducted. These include audio/visual recordings, checklists, event sampling, narrative observations, sociograms, time sampling and tracking maps.
- Some people think that there are limitations to observations, such as the fact they are subjective, they explain the 'what' rather than the 'why' and they can bring ethical challenges. However, these limitations can be embraced or minimised by those wishing to employ observations as a data collection method.

FURTHER READING

1   If you are interested in exploring how to use the In-the-Picture approach to observations, The Open University has produced some very useful online resources:

OpenLearn Create (2023) *Course: In-the-Picture*. Available at: www.open.edu/openlearncreate/course/view.php?id=3590 (accessed: 12 June 2025).

2   The book that Papatheodorou and Luff have written with Gill about doing child observations gives a comprehensive account of how to use observations as a data collection method:

Papatheodorou, T., Luff, P. and Gill, J. (2012) *Child Observation for Learning and Research*. Harlow: Longman.

REFERENCES

Brooker, K. (2017) *Observing to understand: Using the Tavistock method of observation to support reflective practice*. British Educational Research Association. Available at: www.bera.ac.uk/blog/observing-to-understand-using-the-tavistock-method-of-observation-to-support-reflective-practice (accessed: 12 May 2025).

Christensen, P. and Prout, A. (2002) 'Working with ethical symmetry in social research with children', *Childhood*, 9(4), pp. 477–97. DOI: 10.1177/0907568202009004007.

Clark, A. and Moss, P. (2011) *Listening to Young Children: A Guide to Understanding and Using the Mosaic Approach*. London: NCB.

Clough, P. and Nutbrown, C. (2012) *A Student's Guide to Methodology*. London: Sage.

Corsaro, W. and Molinari, L. (2017) 'Entering and observing in children's worlds: A reflection on a longitudinal ethnography of early education in Italy', in P. Christensen and A. James (eds), *Research with Children: Perspectives and Practices*. Abingdon: Routledge, pp. 23–42.

Department for Education (DfE) (2025) *Early years foundation stage (EYFS) statutory framework*. Available at: www.gov.uk/government/publications/early-years-foundation-stage-framework--2 (accessed: 12 May 2025).

Gray, C. and Winter, E. (2011) 'The ethics of participatory research involving young children with special needs', in D. Harcourt, B. Perry and T. Waller (eds), *Researching Young Children's Perspectives: Debating the Ethics and Dilemmas of Educational Research with Children*. London: Routledge, pp. 38–51.

Louis, S. (2022) *Observing young children: A Froebelian approach*. Available at: www.froebel.org.uk/uploads/documents/FT_Observing-young-children_Pamphlet_INTERACTIVE_REV-2.pdf (accessed: 12 May 2025).

Montessori, M. and Gutek, G.L. (2004) *The Montessori Method: The Origins of an Educational Innovation, Including an Abridged and Annotated Edition of Maria Montessori's The Montessori Method*. Lanham, MD: Rowman & Littlefield Publishers.

Morrissey, A., Scott, C. and Wishart, L. (2015) 'Infant and toddler responses to a redesign of their childcare outdoor play space', *Children, Youth and Environments*, 25(1), pp. 29–56.

Paige-Smith, A. and Rix, J. (2011) 'Researching early intervention and young children's perspectives – developing and using a "listening to children approach"', *British Journal of Special Education*, 38(1): 28–36. DOI: https://doi.org/10.1111/j.1467-8578.2011.00494.x.

Papatheodorou, T., Luff, P. and Gill, J. (2012) *Child Observation for Learning and Research*. Harlow: Longman.

Podmore, V. and Luff, P. (2012) *Observation: Origins and Approaches in Early Childhood*. Berkshire: Open University Press.

Rix, J., Parry, J. and Malibha-Pinchbeck, M. (2019). '"Building a better picture": practitioners' views of using a listening approach with young disabled children', *Journal of Early Childhood Research*, 18(1), pp. 3–17. DOI: https://doi.org/10.1177/1476718X19885990.

Salamon, A. (2015) 'Ethical symmetry in participatory research with infants', *Early Child Development and Care*, 185(6), pp. 1016–30. DOI: https://doi.org/10.1080/03004430.2014.975224.

11

SURVEYS AND QUESTIONNAIRES

CHAPTER OBJECTIVES

By the end of this chapter, you will:

* Understand the key differences between surveys and questionnaires
* Understand how surveys and questionnaires can be useful in Early Childhood Research
* Be able to adapt surveys and questionnaires for use with both adults and children of various ages
* Understand the strengths and limitations of surveys and questionnaires.

INTRODUCTION

There can be some confusion around the definition of surveys and questionnaires in research. Students are sometimes taught the simplified idea that a survey belongs with approaches which gather numbers as data (therefore more quantitative approaches) whereas questionnaires speak more to approaches which use words (therefore qualitative approaches); however, their definitions are more complex. We will try to unpack this complexity in this chapter so that you will understand how you could use both surveys and questionnaires in your small-scale project. To begin with, this chapter will explore what surveys are and how they can be used in Early Childhood Research. It will then consider questionnaires whether as a standalone method or alongside others. Before we begin, let us consider the two verbs 'to survey' and 'to question' and consider how doing so can help define how they are used in research us. Table 11.1 shares some ideas that several students came up with.

Table 11.1 Defining the verbs survey and question

To survey	To question
Find out what a large group of people think about an issue.	Seek a specific answer from a specific person.
Find out views from a large group of people who meet certain criteria.	To seek a response with some detail.
Usually closed questions.	Could be a closed question that just needs a yes or no answer.
Examine carefully, measure and count.	Something you do to one person or a small group.

SURVEYS

As we have suggested, there are some common misunderstandings about surveys and questionnaires; for example, Mukherji and Albon (2018) comment that often people believe they are the same thing whereas in reality, surveys are a research approach that may or may not include questionnaires as one of the data collection methods. However, it is true to say that the way people use the term 'survey' in research has changed over the years. Originally, a survey was the whole process of collecting data which could include different methods, such as interviews, questionnaires, or focus groups; for example, The Millennium Cohort Study 'surveyed' lots of different aspects of children's lives like their GCSE results, height, weight, parental smoking status (Hansen, Joshi and Dex, 2010). It collected numerical information from a large sample of the population which could then be used to measure and describe numerically. However, at the same time it also used questionnaires as a specific tool to collect qualitative responses from parents about their children. More recently, the terms survey and questionnaire have become muddled. Very often a research survey will only use a questionnaire making the two words appear synonymous.

Josephidou, Kemp and Durrant (2021) used the term survey in its second and more recent meaning when they wanted to find out what outdoor provision looks like for under-2s in English ECEC settings. They sent an online survey to all the settings they knew had provision for children from birth to 2 years in a certain area of England. They decided which questions to ask based on a literature review they had carried out before designing the survey. In one of the papers reviewed (Moser and Martinsen, 2010) they found a useful questionnaire that had been used with Norwegian settings; this helped them develop their thinking, although they knew that they could not copy the questions word for word because the settings in England were operating in an entirely different cultural and economic context to those in Norway. They consulted with practitioners in their professional networks to ensure that they would be able to capture all elements of practice and pedagogy. The audit was then piloted with a small group of practitioners and revised in the light of this.

The final draft of the survey contained both closed and open-ended questions. You can read the full set of questions if you are interested in their report: *Making connections with their world: Outdoor provision for under twos in early childhood settings in Kent* (Kemp, Durrant and Josephidou, 2020). None of the settings or individuals who completed the survey were identifiable, however they were asked to leave details if they wanted to be included in the next stage of data collection which was to be setting case studies. The survey was sent to 133 settings, and there was an overall response rate of 40%. This data collection method is notorious for having a lower rate of responses than other forms of data collection (Saleh and Bista, 2017). For example, they draw on others' work to claim 'Nulty (2008) cites 33% ... while Baruch and Holtom's (2008) analysis of surveys ... suggests 35.7%' (Josephidou et al., 2021, p. 929).

They recognised some limitations with their survey, including that those settings that responded were more likely to be found 'in less deprived, more rural locations' (p. 929) so that their sample was not particularly representative. They also raised the issue about participants' understanding what was inferred in the questions asked because although the survey had been piloted there was a misunderstanding around some of the questions.

Furthermore, because the researchers knew they had to be clear about the aims of the survey, they knew that the respondents may have responded in ways to meet these aims and be seen, or their setting be seen, favourably, even though, ironically, they were anonymised! Given these limitations, you may wonder if surveys, in this sense of the word, are worth doing and if Josephidou et al. (2021) were disappointed with the result. On the contrary, although they foreground the fact that 'these potential limitations need to be considered when interpreting the findings and their implications' (p. 930), they achieved the aim of their research which was to identify practices and pedagogies related to babies' and toddlers' engagement with the outdoor environment in settings in England. Because this is a neglected area, they believed their survey was important because it could offer new knowledge.

Activity 11.1   Using a Survey in a Small-Scale Project

In this activity you are going to consider how you might use a survey, in either sense of the word, in your small-scale research project. For example, think about how you might incorporate a survey in your research design to answer the main research question:

- How do children choose what to watch on the television?

You will need to think about who you would ask and why? Also think about any issues that you would need to consider.

(Continued)

Reflection

One student decided they wanted to survey parents to answer this research question. They decided to ask all the parents of children aged 7 and under in the school they worked in, which had the potential to be a sample size of 150. The questions mainly involved numbers such as asking parents to provided frequency and duration of programme watching, ranking criteria etc. but at the end was one open-ended question which the parents/carers were asked to complete with their child, i.e. the parent/carer posed the question and then wrote down the child's response. This question was 'Which is your favourite television programme and why?'

QUESTIONNAIRES

We are going to focus specifically here in this section on the questionnaire; this is a research tool you will be familiar with as we often come across it in our everyday life. For example, if we consider the questionnaires we have filled in this week, there has been one about furniture delivery, one about the local medical practice and another about a supermarket food delivery. Let's consider here how we might use questionnaires in our research projects.

What Is the Definition of a Questionnaire?

Questionnaires are a useful tool in research, however like all methods they have their own strengths and weaknesses. One strength is that they are an effective way to collect data, particularly if you have a large group of research participants. This is because they can be cost effective and quick to administer.

When thinking about how to define the term questionnaire, we draw on the useful definition by Ranganathan and Caduff (2023). Although they are writing from the perspective of clinical research, they make an important distinction between paradigms which is useful to us here:

> A research questionnaire can be ... a series of questions or items that are used to collect information from respondents and thus learn about their knowledge, opinions, attitudes, beliefs, and behavior and informed by a positivist philosophy of the natural sciences that consider methods mainly as a set of rules for the production of knowledge... Outside of such a positivist philosophy, questionnaires can be seen as an encounter between the researcher and the researched, where knowledge is not simply gathered but negotiated through a distinct form of communication that is the questionnaire. (pp. 152–3)

It is interesting to consider, alongside this definition, whether questionnaires can address one of our key concerns in this book, i.e. power imbalances in research. At first glance it would appear the answer is no. The researcher 'invites' participants (Clough and Nutbrown, 2012, p. 87), distributes and collects the questionnaire and then makes a judgement on the responses. Neither do questionnaires offer the opportunity to the participant to change their responses or consider them in the light of others as a group interview would do. On the other hand, it could be argued that questionnaires can increase the opportunity to express your own authentic thoughts as a participant because no-one can interrupt you, disagree with you or make you feel you should police your response to make it acceptable to others who are listening. They also potentially allow the respondent time to consider and revise their responses, even translate if necessary. Therefore, we might argue that the respondent might have increased power in the data that is being collected as opposed to an interview where their 'first thoughts' would be captured.

When considering the strengths and weaknesses of a questionnaire, it is useful to reflect on Mukherji and Albon's observation (2018) as they draw on Anderson's work (1998) to suggest that the questionnaire is one of the most 'used and abused' (p. 260) research tools. This may be because some researchers don't know how to use them properly and/or that the information revealed may lack in validity.

Some Important Considerations

One of the difficulties in using questionnaires is getting participants to fill them in. Many times students have said to us, 'Oh the teacher I had asked to participate just put it on their desk under a pile of papers to sort out later.' It can be very frustrating, especially when you have a limited timeframe in which to collect your data. One thing you may like to consider is what would encourage a participant to complete it. We have had our challenges here when looking to gather parental perceptions of spending time outdoors with their babies; eventually we decided to offer a prize for one randomly selected participant. This certainly encouraged participation but left us wondering about the ethical issues around introducing an incentive along with how this might impact on power imbalances.

We stress here, as we do throughout the book, the key issue is to ensure that the research is designed in the most effective way to answer the research question; you need to make sure that the questions you ask your participants will help you answer your main research question and sub-questions. It would not be usual to ask the participants your research questions. Bear in mind that you will never be able to design the perfect questionnaire, and this is why when you write up your research you will include an acknowledgement of its limitations and what you might do differently if you were to design it again. We like the way that Clough and Nutbrown (2012, p. 90) draw on

Walker (1985) to describe choosing your methods as 'an act of faith rather than a rational response to a clearly formulated problem' because you never really know if they truly will answer your research question.

If you have decided to design a questionnaire as part of your methods, how do you begin to go about it? Gourd (2023, p. 79) offers some useful questions to ask yourself before you begin: we list these here and hope you will find them useful.

Have I considered…

- who I want to answer the questionnaire?
- if the questionnaire is accessible?
- how I will distribute my questionnaires?
- any permissions I need?
- the number of responses I need and can manage?
- what my deadlines are?

Mixing It Up!

It is unlikely that you will only use questionnaires as a standalone data collection tool because they will provide only a limited response to your research question. Instead look for an accompanying method which encourages a different kind of response, such as interviews.

A good example of research in Early Childhood which uses questionnaires alongside other data collection tools to build up a rich and detailed understanding is the paper by Ceballos and Susinos (2022) that we looked at in Chapter 2 (*Issues of power in Early Childhood Research*). In their paper, they report on two case studies in settings in Spain as part of a project which focused on how to listen to the voices of very young children in research. Alongside questionnaires they used a 'wide variety of participative methodologies that provided a significant volume of multimodal data' (p. 84). This included 'elicitation tours [that] generated audio recordings … photographs and field notes … photographs and field diaries completed by the teacher. Informal conversation[s] … Observations' (p. 84). We are certainly not suggesting that as a new researcher you look to employ such a wide range of methods; however, it is useful to reflect on how they gained so much more information to support their understanding and to lead to their findings about the 'need to diversify the research "listening strategies" and to pay attention to the power imbalance between different children and between children and adults in the research process' (Abstract). Such findings could only have been superficially informed if they had merely chosen to give questionnaires to the practitioners in the setting.

So, if you decide to use a questionnaire, which many student researchers do, and for very good reasons, do consider how adding another approach alongside will provide a more rounded response to your research question.

Activity 11.2   A Questionnaire About Children's Technology Use

Why don't you have a go now at putting into practice what you have learnt in this chapter so far? Think about your main research question and try to come up with five open-ended questions you could add to a questionnaire. Then think about who you would ask to complete the questionnaire and why. Would there be any issues you would need to consider, what would they be and how would you address them? Finally, how could you encourage busy people to complete it. For example, Ncuti completed this activity based on her research question: 'What strategies do parents use to navigate technology use with 7-year-olds?' You can read her response below.

Reflection

Ncuti is a teaching assistant in a primary school and is in the third year of her ECS degree. She has come up with a draft research question 'What strategies do parents use to navigate technology use with 7-year-olds?' She thinks she will ask the parents of the children in the class she works in. This is because both the class teacher and the headteacher are supportive of her work and have given her permission if she has ethical approval in place, and they have signed off the questionnaire. There are 34 children in the class and her tutor thinks this is a big enough sample for an under-graduate dissertation even though she knows not all parents will choose to complete the questionnaire; if she only got half this number back, she could get some useful data. She does realise that there may be issues around parents feeling obliged to be involved, and that their responses may be aspirational rather than what really hap-pens in practice. As she thinks about these issues, and how at the same time she could encourage people to complete it, she decides that she will let parents know that she is going to use the anonymous responses to put together an information pack so they can learn how other parents manage this problematic area of children's lives. These are the draft questions she comes up with to share with her tutor:

Main question: 'What strategies do parents use to navigate technology use with 7-year-olds?'

Questionnaire questions:

- What kind of technology does your child engage with over the course of a week?
- Do you limit this engagement and if so, how?
- What is the most problematic issue for you as a parent regarding your child's use of technology?
- What are the positive impacts of technology you can see in your child's life?
- What would you like to find out from other parents about how they navigate technology use with their children?

You can see the care she has taken to ensure that the questions are open rather than closed so she should receive some rich, interesting and useful responses rather than sim-ple yes, no answers.

Having read through this section, we hope you now have a clear understanding of why and how you could use questionnaires in your small-scale project. Don't forget to use Gourd's checklist (2023) as you have a go at putting together your own questionnaire.

SURVEYS, QUESTIONNAIRES AND YOUNG CHILDREN AS PARTICIPANTS

We really like the way that Clough and Nutbrown (2012, p. 91) emphasise the importance of the hunch in research when choosing your methodology. This may not be so easy for a new researcher who hasn't got a lot of experience to draw on, but we still think it is an important consideration to do what 'feels right' to you. Obviously, all your methodological decisions need to be informed by the research literature, but you need to also be attentive to avoiding research blueprints that can make you feel constrained; this may result in you failing to find out what you really wanted to, and result in a dry and uninspiring piece of research. Our advice to you would be to read the research methodology literature carefully, think creatively, and perhaps outside the box, but then make sure you have a good discussion with your supervisor who will be able to perhaps see some of the assumptions you are making and some of the challenges which may not immediately be apparent. So, with these thoughts in mind, how could the data tools of surveys and questionnaires be used with young children?

What Could Surveys Look Like for Young Children?

We are thinking here about surveys in the sense of gathering numerical data with a big enough sample to do some descriptive analysis on. We have already noted that young children should not be asked to complete any data collection task which requires reading and writing even if they can do this confidently – of course some children may enjoy this, but here is the point, think about how you could work with the children to design something that would be appropriate, would answer a question and that they would enjoy. Think about early maths in a primary school classroom – how much children enjoy making a class bar chart about favourite chocolate bars or using a clipboard and tally chart to find out about favourite pizza toppings. Certainly, these are two ideas that you could use in your research approach. You could even use tallies to observe babies' actions which indicate their preferences in a setting.

Vera et al. (2024) surveyed young children (3–8 years) to evaluate an interactive museum experience in Spain. They used the term survey in the more traditional sense in that they used both observations of the children and a child-friendly questionnaire. They felt it was an appropriate data collection method as it enabled them to see how much the children had enjoyed the experience and how they had engaged with it. They initially adopted a survey approach because they had struggled to find an appropriate methodology and they didn't want to go down what they considered to be the well-worn route of asking parents to evaluate children's affective responses to what they experienced but they truly wanted to capture the children's voices. They believed that children could respond well in surveys, drawing on the work of Bell (2007) to make this claim. However, although they did gain some useful and interesting data, they realised that the children had not understood some of the questions. They decided to develop this research work by adjusting the questions asked to support the children's understanding better.

What Could Questionnaires Look Like for Young Children?

The work of Bell cited in the previous section is a useful source when looking at using surveys and questionnaires with young children. Published in 2007, in the intervening years her work has been cited many times. She writes specifically about designing and testing questionnaires for children. Written questions can be problematic because, as already suggested, of children's confidence with literacy skills. Roberts-Holmes (2018, p. 143) suggests that the only way to use them with young children is for the researcher to read them out loud. It is important to remember that even if a child can decode the words, they may not have the comprehension level to understand the inferences, although we would add that the same could be true of adults, particularly if they have undiagnosed reading difficulties, unless of course the researchers sample a certain demographic of adults which of course brings its own problems of bias.

Although Bell's work (2007) is from a nursing background it has been used effectively across disciplines. For example, Toni et al. (2024) drew on Bell's work to find out children's views (8 years old) on wellbeing in four different countries (Croatia, France, Finland and Ireland). They used a process called 'cognitive interviewing' to support questionnaire design for young children:

> Cognitive interviewing (CI) is a methodological tool for pre-testing questionnaires that focuses on the mental processes respondents use to answer survey questions (Collins, 2015b). The aim of cognitive interviewing is to provide evidence that the survey questions meet measurement objectives, namely that respondents can provide meaningful answers (P. Beatty, 2004; Collins, 2003). It involves in-depth interviews by a trained interviewer who attempts to understand the participants' cognitive process when answering a certain item (G. B. Willis, 2005). This evidence helps the question designer to decide if the original item or its translation is problematic and how to revise it if necessary. The use of CIs improves questionnaire design (Berthelsen et al., 2014; G. B. Willis, 2005) and enhances measurement validity (P. C. Beatty & Willis, 2007; Collins, 2003; Drennan, 2002). (p. 164; see original publication for cited references)

This means that the way children approach questions is analysed to support researcher understanding about how they perceive the question and its context. They are encouraged to 'think aloud' and share their thought process with the researcher. Cognitive interviewing in various large research projects has led researchers to understand that as far as questionnaires for children are concerned, they should be 'short, use simple vocabulary and structure, and be as concrete as possible; that time references should be avoided, or should refer to shorter and specific recall periods; and that a limited number of response categories gives better results' (p. 165).

Activity 11.3   Adapting Questionnaires and Surveys for Different Age Groups

Let's think now about one research question and how you could adapt the use of surveys and questionnaires to help you answer it. In particular, we are going to explore how they might be used with a different age range of children. For the purposes of this activity we are going to think about the research question 'What is children's favourite thing to do in the outdoor area?', a question you may ask if you are working in a setting, but you may prefer to use your own research question – particularly if you are considering using surveys and questionnaires in your own project. For the purposes of this exercise, to support you in thinking about possibilities, we are suggesting that questionnaires should include smaller samples and be more word focused (i.e. qualitative in approach) whereas as surveys could have larger samples and be more number focused (i.e. more quantitative in approach). Now think about three different ages of children you would like to research with; for each of these consider how questionnaires and surveys could be adapted to use with each age group. We have chosen:

- 6 months to 12 months
- 5-year-olds
- 8-year-olds.

Reflection

You probably needed to be quite creative when thinking about this activity and it does remind us that if you are able to pilot a data collection method before you undertake your main study, this will really strengthen your project. Karim considered the research question we suggested above 'What is children's favourite thing to do in the outdoor area?' and made a table to respond to this activity (Table 11.2)

Table 11.2 Adapting questionnaires and surveys

	Questionnaires	Surveys
6 months to 12 months	I could undertake a 'Show me' type activity where I ask the children to either point or lead me to their favourite area. I think this would be difficult for someone to do if they weren't working with these children every day, but I understand them well and can use language they can engage with.	I could watch the children interacting with the practitioners, observing the areas and activities they engage with and record this by keeping a tally, perhaps for an hour a day over the course of a week.
5-year-olds	I could ask the children a question about their favourite area and let them take a photograph as a response; then they could talk to me about their photograph.	I could make some bar charts with a large group of children, or I could observe and tally through observation.
8-year-olds	I could ask the children to design their own questionnaire or at least come up with their own questions and then they could ask each other.	The children could keep their own tallies or make their own bar charts.

Case Study 11.1 Children of the 2020s Study

This study focuses on 'babies born in England at the start of the 2020s' (Centre for Longitudinal Studies, n.d.) which, of course, coincides with the Covid-19 pandemic and societal changes brought about by a global lockdown. The implications of this lockdown on young children are being continually documented in research and this ongoing study offers some useful evidence. It is a piece of work that has been commissioned by the Department for Education and led by UCL (University of London), so it is set within the English context and is a slightly smaller study than the Millennium Cohort Study Institute of Education (n.d.) mentioned at the beginning of this chapter, in that it has a sample of 8,500 children (DfE, 2023). A variety of data collection methods are being use, including a longitudinal survey with data being collected when the children are:

- 9 months
- 2 years
- 3 years
- 4 years
- 5 years.

The intention is that findings 'will be used to improve early education and childcare services' (p. 11).

KEY POINTS FROM THE CHAPTER

- Both questionnaires and surveys can be a useful method for answering research questions in small-scale studies; however, the researcher needs to explore the potential pitfalls and understand how to minimise them.
- The term survey can be understood in different ways in research.
- If you do decide to use a questionnaire or survey, it is good practice to consider what would motivate or encourage your potential participants to complete them.
- Both these approaches can be used creatively with young children, and they do have the potential to address power imbalances between researcher and researched.
- Practice and pedagogy with young children have been particularly impacted by these two research approaches, including through large scale, longitudinal pieces of research such as the Millennium Cohort Study and the Children of the 2020s study.

FURTHER READING

1   This interesting paper, referenced in the chapter, explores an instance of using surveys with children through museum work.

Vera, L., Coma, I., Pérez, M. et al. (2024) 'The Mediterranean forest in a science museum: engaging children through drawings that come to life in a virtual world', *Multimedia Tools and Applications*, 83, pp. 76851–72. DOI: https://doi.org/10.1007/s11042-024-18606-0.

2   Amani and Fussy's paper (2023) is from the context of Tanzania; it sets out how questionnaires were used, alongside observations and interviews, to investigate practitioner perceptions of child-centred and adult-led approaches in ECEC pedagogy.

Amani, J. and Fussy, D.S. (2023) Balancing child-centred and teacher-centred didactic approaches in early years learning. *Education 3–13*, *53*(3), pp. 353–65. DOI: https://doi.org/10.1080/03004279.2023.2189905.

3   Dip into Gourd's very useful book. Chapter 6 is entitled 'Data Collection' and you will be able to read the author's thoughts on surveys and questionnaires in the context of Early Childhood.

Gourd, J. (2023) *Educational Research for Early Childhood Studies Projects*. London; Routledge.

REFERENCES

Anderson, G. (1998) *Fundamentals of Educational Research*. 2nd Edition. Abingdon: Routledge.

Bell, A. (2007) 'Designing and testing questionnaires for children', *Journal of Research in Nursing*, *12*(5), pp. 461–9. https://doi.org/10.1177/1744987107079616.

Ceballos, N. and Susinos, T. (2022) '"Do my words convey what children are saying?" Researching school life with very young children: dilemmas for authentic listening', *European Early Childhood Education Research Journal*, 30(1), pp. 81–95. DOI: 10.1080/1350293X.2022.

Centre for Longitudinal Studies (n.d.) *Children of the 2020s study*. Available at: https://cls.ucl.ac.uk/cls-studies/children-of-the-2020s-study/ (accessed: 20 March 2025).

Clough, P. and Nutbrown, C. (2012) *A Student's Guide to Methodology*. 3rd Edition. London: Sage.

Department for Education (DfE) (2023) *Children of the 2020s: Wave 1*. Available at: https://assets.publishing.service.gov.uk/media/65671ebdd6ad75000d02fc89/Children_of_the_2020s_technical_report.pdf (accessed: 20 March 2025).

Gourd, J. (2023) *Educational Research for Early Childhood Studies Projects*. London: Routledge.

Hansen, K., Joshi, H. and Dex, S. (2010) *Children of the 21st Century: The First Five Years*. Bristol: The Policy Press.

Institute of Education (n.d.) *Millennium Cohort Study*. Available at: https://cls.ucl.ac.uk/cls-studies/millennium-cohort-study/ (accessed: 20 March 2025).

Josephidou, J., Kemp, N. and Durrant, I. (2021) 'Outdoor provision for babies and toddlers: exploring the practice/policy/research nexus in English ECEC settings', *European Early Childhood Education Research Journal*, 29(6), pp. 925–41. DOI: 10.1080/1350293X.2021.1985555.

Kemp, N., Durrant, I. and Josephidou, J. (2020) *Making Connections With Their World: Outdoor Provision for Under Twos in Early Childhood Settings in Kent*. Froebel Trust. Available at: www.froebel.org.uk/uploads/documents/Froebel-Trust-Research-Making-Connections-With-Their-World.pdf (accessed: 31 March 2025).

Moser, T. and Martinsen, M. (2010) 'The outdoor environment in Norwegian kindergartens as pedagogical space for toddlers' play, learning and development', *European Early Childhood Education Research Journal*, 18(4), pp. 457–71.

Mukherji. P. and Albon, D. (2018) *Research Methods in Early Childhood: An Introductory Guide*. 3rd Edition. London: Sage.

Ranganathan, P. and Caduff, C. (2023) 'Designing and validating a research questionnaire – Part 1', *Perspectives in Clinical Research*, 14(3), pp. 152–5.

Roberts-Holmes, R. (2018) *Doing Your Early Years Research Project: A Step-by-Step Guide*. 4th Edition. London: Sage.

Saleh, A. and Bista, K. (2017) 'Examining factors impacting online survey response rates in educational research: perceptions of graduate students', *Journal of Multidisciplinary Evaluation*, 13(29), pp. 63–74.

Toni, B., Krpanec, E., Blažev, M., Dević, I., Downey, S., Huttunen, I., … Pollock, G. (2024) 'Children's understanding of well-being related questions: results of cognitive interviews in four European countries', *International Journal of Social Research Methodology*, 28(2), pp. 163–78. DOI: https://doi.org/10.1080/13645579.2024.2312621.

UCL. *Children of the 2020s*. Centre for Longitudinal Studies. Available at: https://cls.ucl.ac.uk/cls-studies/children-of-the-2020s-study/ (accessed: 7 July 2025).

Vera, L., Coma, I., Pérez, M. et al. (2024) 'The Mediterranean forest in a science museum: engaging children through drawings that come to life in a virtual world', *Multimedia Tools and Applications, 83,* pp. 76851–72. DOI: https://doi.org/10.1007/s11042-024-18606-0.

Walker, R. (1985) *Doing Research: A Handbook for Teachers.* London: Methuen.

12

INTERVIEWING ADULTS AND CHILDREN

CHAPTER OBJECTIVES

By the end of this chapter, you will:

- Understand about the many kinds of interviews that are commonly used in research
- Understand the importance of an interview schedule
- Have a good understanding of how interviews can be used as a data collection tool in small-scale studies
- Consider how certain power imbalances may or may not be addressed using interviews as a data collection method.

INTRODUCTION

As is the case with a lot of the terminology we have already looked at in this book so far, the word 'interview' is part of our everyday parlance. For example, we see the term 'interviews' used in conjunction with a variety of people and contexts, and it would be good to consider if it always means the same thing, including what the aim of the interview would be in each context. Let's begin the chapter with a short task to help us think about this point. Look at the variety of people and instances below and think about what the aim of an interview in each context would be:

- Celebrity interview
- Interview with a politician
- Interview at border control
- Police interview
- Job interview.

We thought of the following ideas:

- Celebrity interview: this could be to entertain or to satisfy the public's curiosity
- Interview with a politician: this could be to help the electorate understand their views on important issues and make decisions about whether to trust them
- Interview at border control: this involves gatekeeping and a decision about who meets the criteria to be able to cross or not cross the border
- Police interview: this is to build up a picture of what has happened when a crime has been committed or to gather evidence to convict a criminal
- Job interview: to decide who meets certain criteria and who would be the best person for a job.

Some of these aims could align with how interviews are used in research, for example the idea of building up a picture, a picture that could help to answer a research question.

In this chapter we will explore what interviews are in Early Childhood Research and how they may be used effectively to 'build up a picture'. We will examine how this data collection method can be used when collecting data with both child and adult participants and think about the strengths and limitations of using interviews. We are particularly interested in exploring why and how power imbalances can be addressed while engaging participants in interviews.

DIFFERENT APPROACHES TO INTERVIEWING

As we have seen in the introduction, there are many different approaches to interviewing in everyday life; this is generally because different kinds of interviews have different aims. In research too, there are very many kinds of interviews although generally the aim would be the same, i.e. to build up a picture. In this section we are going to look at some of these different ways so that you can decide if you would like to use interviews in your research work and if so, which type will help you best answer your research question. The three different types we will look at here are formal and informal, group and individual, and interviewing children as opposed to working with adult participants. We will consider what these different types could look like in practice.

Formal and Informal Interviews

To begin with, let's look at the differences between formal and informal interviews, including how they might be defined, what they could look like in practice and their various strengths and limitations. We will also consider how props such as photographs could be used alongside to lead to richer data.

When we think about formal versus informal interviews, we are not particularly focused on the stance that the researcher takes when engaging with the participant. For example, you would still be as friendly, relaxed and personable in a formal interview as you would be in an informal one. The difference is really in the prep work you would do and how you would put together an interview schedule. You may think it would be much easier to carry out an informal interview but in fact, we would argue, it is the other way around. For a formal interview, you have a clear list of questions you intend to ask, you would ask the same questions to all interviewees, and you would not deviate from them. However, with an informal interview, you would have a very different approach. You would still have some prompt questions, but they would be much more open ended and you would look to build on responses rather than sticking rigidly to a question script.

In informal interviews you may also be a little more creative; for example, you could use props to support the discussion. A common prop is photographs used to stimulate ideas. This approach is often referred to as photo elicitation. Briggs et al. (2014) used photographs to understand children's ideas about place, and particularly their sense of place. They considered this important work because research suggests that children's attachment to outdoor spaces encourages them to have more pro-environmental behaviours. The authors decided to use this photo elicitation because, when they were writing, it had been used successfully with adults but seldom with children. However, since their paper was published, with ever emerging child friendly methodologies such as the Mosaic Approach (Clark and Moss, 2011) we would suggest it has become particularly popular; we have used it ourselves both with adults and children. Research guidance from the LSE (London School of Economics) suggests not just photographs, but any visual aids are a great idea to use when interviewing children and that the interviewer should focus on the question words of 'who/what/when/where/why' (LSE, n.d.). The study by Briggs et al. (2014) was quite small; they worked with fewer than 20 children (9 years old) as participants. We draw your attention to it here as we believe their methodology is certainly replicable with younger children and may be an interesting approach you would like to adopt.

Sometimes in photo elicitation the interviewer may provide the photographs, on other occasions the researcher may ask the participants to provide them. Briggs et al. (2014) asked the children to take the photographs. Each child was given a digital camera and asked to explore an outdoor area well known to them bearing in mind the following question:

'What is meaningful to you in your surroundings and/or community?' (p. 154)

This is not a particularly accessible question for younger children so you might want to tweak if you wanted to adopt this research design for an Early Childhood project. For example, you could take the children to a location and ask:

- What is important in this place? OR
- What do you like in this place?

The children would then take photos in response to the stated question. Briggs et al. (2014) tell us they gave the children a short period of time (about half an hour) to collect the images they wanted.

However, the data collection didn't finish there, although you could argue that the resulting photographs were the responses and the researchers could have analysed them. One danger here would have been that of making assumptions about why the children had chosen the images they had. Briggs et al. (2014) avoided this approach by conducting individual interviews with the children using their photographs as a stimulus.

Group and Individual Interviews

Interviews in research may involve the researcher interacting with one participant at a time or indeed with several participants. You will often see the latter approach called group interviews or sometimes focus groups. You may very well wish to use these approaches in your work so we will look at ways you could potentially do this as well as making you aware of any problematic issues they might involve.

Group interviews have the potential to generate a substantial amount of rich and interesting data. Participants can build on each other's comments adding detail, both agreeing with and contradicting each other as they share their experiences. However, it is inevitable that the more vocal or confident participants in a group will dominate so that not everyone may have the chance to contribute as much as they would like, however skilled the interviewer is at trying to facilitate everyone having a voice. In addition, some participants may feel slightly intimidated and not able to say what they really think in case they get it wrong. Something we have noticed with young children is that if one of them decides to go off at a tangent and discuss something totally unrelated to the interview focus but which makes a great deal of sense to them, then the others will follow like dominoes, and it can be really hard to pull the interview back. For example, if you are asking about their friendships and then one of them decides to tell you about their Power Rangers collection – you may end up with a lot of interview data about the Power Rangers!

Interviewing Children

Ponizovsky-Bergelson et al. (2019) were interested to find out what best supported children to engage in interviews so that the researcher can obtain the richest data. This will be a key consideration when you are collecting data, although, even though the authors state that this piece of work is underpinned by a desire to address power imbalances between adult researcher and child participant, we could argue that having a starting point of wanting to collect the richest data is all about the researcher's wants and needs and so consolidates the power imbalance rather than minimising it. They carried out their analysis by reviewing data from a reasonably large sample of 1339 children who were aged 3–6 years old. They discovered that the richest data was produced when the researcher used strategies such as 'encouragement, open-ended questions, and question request' (p. 1) whereas the poorest data was collected through 'Sequence of utterances and closed-ended questions' (p. 1). To help you understand what this means in practice, so that you can potentially refer to this in your own data collection, we have defined and illustrated these categories in Table 12.1.

Table 12.1 Strategies to use when interviewing children (adapted from Ponizovsky-Bergelson et al., 2019)

Strategy	Definition	Illustration	Type of data collected
Encouragement	Giving the child support and confidence by showing approval	Wow, well done! This is very interesting! Repeating the child's answer You are right. Nodding and saying ahhh, mmmm	Rich data
Open-ended questions	Cannot be answered with a 'yes' or 'no' or specific information	Why do you think...? How does...? What happened to...?	Rich data
Question request	Closed-ended question formalised as a request	Can you explain what is...? Can you tell me that again? Can you tell me about...?	Rich data
Sequence of utterances	Two or more different statements or questions that cannot be replied to with a single response	What can you tell me about this drawing? You say it is the most dangerous. Why is it the most dangerous thing for children?	Less rich data
Closed-ended questions	Have a single option for an answer, usually 'yes' or 'no' or that specifies the given information	Who fell? From where is he trying to jump?	Less rich data

The LSE guidance (n.d.) also recommends that the researcher accepts 'I don't know' as an appropriate response and doesn't try to encourage the child to have a go further at finding a response if this is their first answer. We like this advice because we can see how it addresses somewhat power imbalances by taking pressure off the child to come up with an acceptable response.

Vogl (2013) carried out an interesting piece of research with over 100 children in Germany to see if there were any differences noted in their response to face-to-face interviews and telephone interviews. Note the date of this paper as it was written before the mass move to online communications which happened during the Covid lockdown.

However, we can learn some interesting insights from her research and consider how we might use them in a world where children are much more familiar with using a mobile phone than perhaps they were in 2013. Vogl suggests that many researchers would not think about doing qualitative data gathering with young children using the phone; she stresses how they would look instead for 'personal contact' and the importance of body language to put a young child at ease. However, she would encourage the researcher not to reject telephone interviews with young children; the youngest age of her participants was 5. She found very little difference between the two approaches although there was some suggestion that using telephones could be a more relaxing experience for all involved.

When a child is interviewed by an adult lots of power issues come into play. One primary school teacher recounts working with a small group of children as part of data they were collecting for a book. They asked a group of children if they would come and do an activity with them which involved sharing and talking about a book. One of the children decided he didn't want to come; this was unusual for him as he usually really enjoyed this kind of activity but perhaps he had something else in mind that he wanted to do. The children were 4 and 5 years old and they were used to moving between having their own time to organise their learning and time when they would expect to work with an adult – either the class teacher or the class teaching assistant. Because of this, when he declined to go with the teacher they were taken aback. They normally had their own strategies as a teacher if this were to happen, but in this context, they were acting as a researcher and didn't want to collect data under duress. At that moment, the teaching assistant intervened and insisted that the child joined the teacher's group, probably trying to be helpful. As the teacher didn't want to undermine the teaching assistant, they carried on with the group activity and the reluctant child. Of course, they could not then ethically use any data collected so decided not to record the session.

As a discipline, Early Childhood Studies has a particular view of the child, i.e. they are seen to have a certain expertise as we have already stated. The challenge is how to best let them show this expertise through an interview. Olson's (2025) work in Norway demonstrates how children can contribute their expertise to a tool which will support their participation. If you read the article, you will see that the children that the author cite as 12 years old; however if we see young children as experts we could also involve them in this kind of participatory research. Olsen draws our attention to the difference between consultation and collaboration, with the latter being the one that we should aim for. They encourage us not to see 'child participation as fixed' (p. 401) but as an interactive process between adult and child.

But what about the interactions between an adult and a baby? Do you think it would be possible to interview such a very young child and what would that look like in practice? We suppose that whether you answer yes or no to this question will depend on how you answer the below sub-questions:

- Do you believe babies are experts in their own lives?
- Do you believe that babies can share this expertise in a variety of ways?
- Do you believe that adults can learn to listen to babies in a variety of ways?

Really you would have to answer yes to all three of these questions to be able to proceed any further with designing a research project involving babies' participation and that is why often, to find out what babies think, adults will ask other adults.

This begs the question as to whether we should be using the term 'interview' when talking about babies, or indeed any children. It sounds so formal, so acknowledging of a power dynamic which positions the adult as in control of events and the child as one who needs to respond. It would be good to perhaps think of other ways of framing this data collection interaction. After all you wouldn't say to a child 'Can I interview you?' Rather you would say something like 'Can I talk to you?' 'Can you help me with some questions?' 'Could we have a chat?' You would then need to think about a more formal term you could use when you write up your work, such as encounter, interaction or research chat, which would describe how you went about your data collection.

In this section we have reflected on the power dynamics in interviews which are even more enhanced when the researcher is an adult and the participant is a child. The discipline of Early Childhood positions the child as an expert so it is important to consider how we can best let them show this expertise through an interview. And what about a very young child – how can we demonstrate in our research actions that we consider a baby as an expert in their own life?

Activity 12.1   Asking Questions About the Local Area

In this activity we are going to think about how an interview, or research chat, or encounter, depending on how you decide to term this data collection method, could be adapted for an adult and a child. For example, an ECS student called Corinne wanted to find out about families in her local area and the green spaces they were able to spend time in. Through her Brownie group, she had access to five different families. Her thoughts were to conduct one group interview with the parents, of which there were six, and then a separate group interview with the children, of which there were 11 aged between 3 and 8. Her research question was: How do families engage with the green spaces in their local area? But of course she had to think how this might translate into a series of questions which she could ask both children and adults. Her supervisor suggested that she took some photos of the local area and shared them in the interview to support the discussion. Can you think about the different questions that she might like to ask and any other considerations she needs to think about? Have a go at completing the following list and try to think of three questions for the adults and four for the children.

(Continued)

Questions for adults

1

2

3

Questions for children

1

2

3

4

Reflection

Corinne found it easier to think of questions once she had taken the photographs which encouraged her that the parents and children too would find it easier to talk about places if they could visually engage with them. She also trialled the children's questions with her Brownie pack to make sure that they made sense to the children and that she would get some interesting data. These are the questions she came up with for the adults:

- I'd like to talk about green places in the local area; what does 'green' places mean to you?
- Have a look at the photos – which of them shows your favourite place to take your children?
- Why did you choose that place?
- Are there other 'green' places in the local area that you like to take your children?

For the children she tried something different:

- Can you have a look at the photos?
- Do you recognise them?
- Which is your favourite?
- Why have you chosen that one?

She also thought about other things she would need to consider in terms of when and where the interviews should take place and what could potentially go wrong. Doing this meant she was able to put strategies in place to ensure that the interviews went as smoothly as possible.

In this section of the chapter, we have looked at different approaches to interviewing. For example, we have thought about formal versus informal interviews, group versus individual and different considerations you will need to make if you have a research question which needs to be answered by asking both adults and children. You will now have a better understanding of the strengths and limitations of these different approaches, that informal interviewing is quite skilled and that as a novice researcher you may prefer to be more formal, yet at the same time need to consider how this approach works with young children. Lots to think about! We remind you here that it is important to think about the aim of your interview and how you want to capture the expertise of your participants whatever their age, including what kind of picture you are trying to build up.

USING INTERVIEWS IN YOUR OWN RESEARCH

In the previous section you were introduced to examples of how other researchers have used interviews in their projects. In this section let us consider how we can apply this learning to your own project. To do this, we will draw on real world examples of how students have used interviews in their university projects and show you some from our own work. As part of this discussion, we will look at ideas for putting together an interview schedule. This is an important document that will help you conduct your research effectively, show rigour in your processes and is something that you will need to submit to those who will give you ethical approval.

Questions and Examples

You have a good understanding by now of how interviews can be used in research so it would be good to think of your own research question and if you might want to use interviews. One question students often ask is – if I do interviews how many people do I need to interview? We would answer this by saying – remember it is a small-scale study, so you don't need to collect vast amounts of data. If you are using interviews along with another data collection method, you could probably carry out five one-to-one interviews or three group interviews; this should be more than enough.

Let's look at some examples here. As a student, Dani wanted to find out about children learning languages from a young age. His question was 'What are the benefits of language learning for young children in the primary school?' He decided to give a questionnaire to 14 teachers and teaching assistants (TAs) within a local school he had connections with and then interview five children aged between 5 and 8. He wasn't confident in working with the children altogether so decided to interview them one to one. The children were familiar with him as he often did voluntary work at the school so he thought they would probably be happy to come and talk to him – and he was right, they were. He listened carefully to teachers' advice about when and where to best do the interviews and decided to carry them out immediately after a language lesson. Dani ended up with some useful and interesting data from the three different perspectives of child/teacher/TA.

Bolshaw, Josephidou and O'Connor (2017) on the other hand wanted to explore children's understanding of gender in the primary school. They carried out informal group interviews with children aged between 6 and 11, but with the younger age group they tried a different approach. This involved introducing the children to a teddy bear who had some questions for them. It wasn't their original idea, but an approach well tested in research, see for example see O'Reilly and Dogra (2017) or Roberts-Holmes (2011). The premise was that the teddy was going to be starting nursery and wanted to find out about it from the children. The children were encouraged to talk about their nursery experiences and Teddy had a variety of photos to show them of practitioners working in nurseries to facilitate the children's thinking about the gender of these practitioners.

When Josephidou (2018) interviewed practitioners about how they believed their gender informed the way they interacted with young children in play she used interviews as part of the data collection. To support participant engagement in the interviews, photographs of children at play were used as a stimulus. The photographs had been taken by the practitioners of children at play and so provided useful visual clues of the issues being discussed; they became a 'coat hanger for [the] conversations exploring behaviour and viewpoints' (Arksey and Knight, 1999, p. 118). The photographs were not taken specifically for the research; rather they were collected as part of normal everyday practice in the setting. The questions prepared to accompany the discussion of these photographs in the interview were as follows:

- Can you talk to me about play in your setting? You can use the photos to describe what happens.
- Do you think your gender influences how you see your role in play?
- Can you think of any specific strengths that male and female practitioners bring to play?
- Do you think there are other factors, besides gender, that might affect how a practitioner views play?
- How much does policy and curriculum influence your approach to play?
- How do you feel about the lack of men in early years? Does it matter as far as play is concerned?
- Do you think that there are specific kinds of play where the practitioner gender does matter?
- Is there anything else you would like to say that you think might be helpful to the research? Are there any of the photographs we have not discussed that you would like to discuss?

So, you are no doubt now quite confident about using an interview for your data collection and will know whether you want an informal or more formal approach. The important thing regardless of the type of interview you go for is to be very well prepared by putting together an organised schedule. This isn't just a list of questions, as we gave you examples of in this section; rather it is the whole process of how you intend the interview to proceed. By putting together a detailed schedule, you will put your participants at ease by showing them that you are professional and acting ethically. We will have a look now at what such a schedule could look like.

Putting Together an Interview Schedule

An interview schedule is not merely a list of questions; it is also a setting out in detail of all the elements of the interview. Whoever signs off your ethical approval will need to see that you have thought about this carefully. In the 'Group interview question prompts' box you can see an example of a schedule that we put together for a project researching into the experience of the Early Childhood student. You can see that the questions are described as 'suggested'. This is because it was an informal interview, so the interviewer intended to ask questions which built on what the participants said.

Box 12.1   Group Interview Question Prompts

Interview 1: 60 mins (Date: xxxxxx)

Introduction

Thank participants for agreeing to participate, and for returning the consent form. Introduce the project including its aims and purposes. Remind participants that the interview will be recorded, transcribed and their contribution anonymised. Ask if anyone has any questions.

Main Part: Suggested Questions

- Would you like to introduce yourself to the other members of the group: Your name, if you work or would like to work in Early Years, why you are studying Early Childhood.
- How is your studying going so far?
- What do you find helpful in the approaches to teaching and learning?
- What do you think of the materials?
- Which aspects of this kind of study are more problematic for you?
- Anything else you would like to add?

To Conclude

Stop recording.

Thank everyone.

Remind them about storage of data, right to withdraw, and what to do if they want to be kept up to date with the project, or to see their data. Remind them that they will receive an individual email to respond to.

Fix the date for the second interview.

The Problem of Power Imbalances

Anyan (2013) suggests it is incorrect to consider an interview in research as a dialogue because of the problem of power imbalances. This is not only because the interviewer decides which questions will be asked but also because it is the interviewer who generally decides how the data is then analysed. However, Anyan does recognise that the power dynamics are very complex within an interviewer/interviewee situation. He draws on the work of Fairclough (1989) to suggest that these power dimensions involve a 'controlling' and a 'constraining' of the one with less power in the interview scenario. Interestingly, this may not necessarily be the interviewee. He suggests that power can be 'built up' in an interview because of issues of socio-economic status, gender, ethnicity etc. of those involved. The interviewee may position themselves as the more powerful participant by refusing to answer questions while the interviewer may attempt to 'take on a less powerful role' (p. 3).

Anyan illustrates nicely how the power can pass back and forth within the interview drawing on one he was involved in. One person he was interviewing felt tired and fed up with being asked questions (the interviewee here holds the power of refusal) so Anyan as interviewer began to encourage and persuade them to complete the interview (the power of persuasion).

Case Study 12.1 Interviewing Children About Their Baby Siblings' Perspectives

Priya wants to find out about how babies feel about being outdoors. She decides, alongside observing their reactions when it is time for them to go outside at the setting, that she would also interview practitioners for their thoughts. She wondered whether to interview parents also but then her fellow student shared that she was going to find out about babies from their siblings so Priya thought she would also give this a go. She knew the parents well through her work at the setting and the older siblings (between 3 and 5) had been cared for by her when they were younger. Priya arranged for three older siblings to join her when their sibling babies went outside. Although it was a little complicated arranging cover, so she didn't have to be counted in ratio, her manager was very supportive, and Priya succeeded in collecting some lovely insightful data from the children.

KEY POINTS FROM THE CHAPTER

- There are many kinds of interviews used in research and therefore be careful about adopting a one-size-fits-all approach, especially if power imbalances need to be addressed.
- Even if you are conducting an informal interview, you must show rigour in how you put together your interview schedule.

- Interviewing in research is skilled and time consuming but it can provide some rich interesting data if done well.

FURTHER READING

1   This interesting thesis by Sharon Colilles explores children's awareness of ethnic identities. We would encourage you to look at Chapter 4 (*Methodology*) to see how Sharon developed her work through the three phases of one-to-one interviews, observations and group interviews.

Colilles, S. (2020) *Exploring how play-based pedagogies support mixed ethnic identity formation*, PhD Bristol City University. Available at: www.open-access.bcu.ac. uk/11679/1/Sharon%20Colilles%20Thesis%20Rev1%20March%202021%20 print%20version.pdf (accessed: 9 July 2025).

2   Don't be put off by the date on this study by Briggs et al. (2014) that we have cited in the chapter. It is a great example of using photo elicitation with children in research and you may be able to adapt some of the ideas.

Briggs, L.P., Stedman, R.C. and Krasny, M.E. (2014) 'Photo-elicitation methods in studies of children's sense of place', *Children, Youth and Environments, 24*(3), pp. 153–72.

3   Of course, we had to include Alison Clark's seminal book here, *Listening to Young Children* (2017). Look in particular at page 37 where there is a section entitled 'Interviewing children'.

Clark, A. (2014) *Listening to Young Children: A Guide to Understanding and Using the Mosaic Approach.* London: Jessica Kingsley.

REFERENCES

Anyan, F. (2013) 'The influence of power shifts in data collection and analysis stages: a focus on qualitative research interview', *The Qualitative Report, 18*(36), pp. 1–9.

Arksey, H. and Knight, P. (1999) *Interviewing for Social Scientists.* London: Sage.

Bolshaw, P., Josephidou, J. and O'Connor, S. (2017) 'Exploring children's perceptions of the gendered nature of the early years workforce', 69th Annual OMPE World Conference. Conference Centre Tamaris, Opatija, 20–24 June.

Briggs, L.P., Stedman, R. and Krasny, M. (2014) 'Photo-elicitation methods in studies of children's sense of place', *Youth and Environments, 24*(3), pp. 153–72.

Clark, A. and Moss, P. (2011) *Listening to Children: The Mosaic Approach.* 2nd Edition. London: NCB.

Fairclough, N. (1989) *Language and Power.* London: Longman.

Josephidou, J. (2018) *Perceptions of ECEC (Early Childhood Education and Care) practitioners on how their gender influences their approaches to play.* PhD Thesis Lancaster University. Available at: https://eprints.lancs.ac.uk/id/eprint/125771/ (accessed: 9 July 2025).

LSE (n.d.) *When is it good to use focus group, in-depth interviews, and observations?* Available at: www.lse.ac.uk/media-and-communications/assets/documents/research/eu-kids-online/toolkit/frequently-asked-questions/FAQ-3.pdf (accessed: 7 July 2025).

Olsen, R. (2025) 'The value of child participation in research – a qualitative child-centered approach to the early development of an empowerment inventory for children', *Child & Youth Services, 46*(2), pp. 400–21. DOI: 10.1080/0145935X.2024.2336914.

O'Reilly, M. and Dogra, N. (2017) *Interviewing Children and Young People for Research.* London: Sage.

Ponizovsky-Bergelson, Y., Dayan, Y., Wahle, N. and Roer-Strier, D. (2019) 'A qualitative interview with young children: what encourages or inhibits young children's participation?', *International Journal of Qualitative Methods, 18*. DOI: https://doi.org/10.1177/1609406919840516.

Roberts-Holmes, G. (2011) *Doing Your Early Years Research Project: A Step-by-Step Guide.* London: Sage.

Vogl, S. (2013) 'Telephone versus face-to-face interviews: mode effect on semi structured interviews with children', *Sociological Methodology, 43*(1), pp. 133–77. DOI: https://doi.org/10.1177/0081175012465967.

13

ANALYSING YOUR DATA

CHAPTER OBJECTIVES

By the end of this chapter, you will:

- Understand how to analyse your qualitative data
- Understand how to analyse your quantitative data
- Recognise how to write up your findings.

INTRODUCTION

So, you've collected your data, now what? This chapter is going to explore how when you've got your data, you need to do something with it. We know that the scope of what your data could be is quite diverse: it might include questionnaire responses, interview transcripts, photographs or written observations. To make your data meaningful, you need to do something with it. This chapter will explore how students can undertake the process of transforming raw data into findings and then begin analysing those findings.

Before we go any further, we should explain what we mean by 'analysis'. To analyse something means to examine it in a methodical way. Mukherji and Albon (2018) suggest that different types of data are suited to different types of analysis; they argue that numerical data 'lend themselves to statistical analysis; that is, the application of techniques that can process large amounts of numerical data and reveal trends' (2018, p. 338) whereas in contrast data with words 'lend themselves to non-statistical techniques, aimed at revealing patterns in the information gathered, allowing you to understand the topic of study in greater depth' (p. 338).

In this chapter we will consider both of these techniques, using as an example an online questionnaire that we recently distributed to parents of children aged up to 2 about their attitudes to the outdoors and nature (Kemp et al., 2025). The questionnaire asked respondents:

- demographic questions about themselves and their child
- about their access to outdoor spaces

- about what they do outdoors with their child
- what their attitudes and beliefs were about the outdoors and nature
- if they would like to provide any further comments.

STARTING TO ANALYSE YOUR DATA

Before starting your analysis, you need to get your data in a format in which you can systematically and methodically make sense of it. The way that you do this will depend on the type of data you have got. Mukherji and Albon (2018) suggest that there are several things you might have to do to get your data organised before you start. Table 13.1 outlines what these are, as well as provide a rationale for why they are necessary.

Table 13.1 Getting your data organised (adapted from Mukherji and Albon, 2018)

What do Mukherji and Albon (2018) suggest?	Why is this important?
Type up any handwritten data	Having all your data electronically means that it is easier to keep track of and manipulate.
Transcribe your interviews	Being able to read through your interview data means it is possible to code it, which we will talk about later. Transcribing can be time consuming; Microsoft Word has a 'Transcribe' function which will convert audio files into text, which is a helpful start but you will have to manually check the accuracy afterwards.
Ensure you have got the information you need.	It might be the case that you've made a note to yourself to ask a participant a further question or can't read something you've hastily recorded in an observation. Check if you need to ask your participants or gatekeepers any follow up questions. The sooner you do this, the easier it will be.
Number each piece of data	Whether your data is questionnaires, photographs, interview transcripts or something else, numbering them will make it easier to keep track of which is which when you analyse.
Ensure your research journal is updated	Mukherji and Albon (2018, p. 391) define a research journal as 'an ongoing record of your research which documents the research process as it unfolds. In qualitative studies the research journal is used to record reflections, ideas and feelings about the research.' Keeping it updated means that, for instance, you can remember any initial thoughts you had on the data when you first came across it, which might be useful when you look at it later in a more systematic way.

Our questionnaire was shared to parents of children aged up to 2 via email by their nursery settings. We used an online survey tool developed by JISC (the Joint Information Systems Committee) to construct our questionnaire, which meant that our data was collected electronically and we could download it as an Excel spreadsheet. If you are using questionnaires as your data collection method, you might consider using software such as JISC online surveys, Google Forms, Microsoft Forms or Survey Monkey so that your responses are recorded electronically and you don't need to type anything up.

We distributed the questionnaire at three points in time between October 2024 and April 2025, which meant that our data set of 233 responses was split over three spreadsheets. We combined these into one and numbered each row so that we could keep track of each response. We also recorded in one column which responses were collected at which point in time so that we had all the information we needed. Some of our columns featured data using words, such as open-ended responses about what the respondent's child likes to do when spending time outdoors. Other questions collected data that could be interpreted numerically, such as closed questions about whether the respondent had access to particular private outdoor spaces at home such as a garden, yard or balcony. We will now begin to think about how to analyse the quantitative responses we gathered.

ANALYSING QUANTITATIVE DATA

If you have got data that is numerical, you will be considering how to analyse it using a quantitative approach. Mukherji and Albon (2018) outline four ways to conduct quantitative analysis: descriptive statistics, inferential statistics, investigation of simple relationships between two variables and multivariate analysis, which they define as 'the effects of two or more variables' (2018, p. 340). Often undergraduate Early Childhood Studies students focus on using descriptive statistics to analyse their data, which are a way of 'describing the data in terms of frequencies, averages and ranges' (Mukherji and Albon, 2018, p. 340).

The term 'descriptive statistics' might not be familiar to you, but we would hazard a guess that you've been introduced to them during maths lessons at school. For instance, do you remember being introduced to how to calculate averages, ratios, frequencies and percentages? These are all types of descriptive statistics which can help us to understand a data set. In fact, Denscombe (2017) argues that more complex mathematical analysis is often not necessary as descriptive statistics are sufficient to 'summarize the profile of the data ... explore connections between parts of the data ... present the data and portray the findings' (2017, p. 265). Let's consider each of these three elements in turn.

Summarising the Profile of the Data

What Denscombe (2017, p. 265) means by 'summarising the profile of the data' is giving an overall snapshot of what the data tells us. Denscombe (2017) suggests that this can take the form of calculating frequencies, mid-points and spreads. Table 13.2 gives more detail about what each of these terms means and how they can be calculated.

Table 13.2 Techniques to summarise the profile of the data

Techniques to summarise the profile of the data	Definition	How can it be calculated?	Example from our questionnaire
Frequencies	Frequencies tell the researcher how often something occurs.	You add up how many times a response is recorded to find out its frequency.	We asked respondents whether they had access to a private balcony, garden or yard and counted how many said that they did. We then used these frequencies to calculate the percentage of respondents who had access to those spaces.
Mid-points	The mid-point of a data set tells the researcher what the average is or what is most common.	You can work out the average by calculating the mean (the arithmetic average), the median (the middle value) or the mode (the most frequent value).	We asked respondents the age of their youngest child that attends nursery. The mean age was 16.7 months.
Spreads	The spread of a data set tells the researcher what range the data covers.	You can work out the spread of a data set by subtracting the minimum value from the maximum value.	We asked respondents how much time they spent outdoors with their child per week. Some reported spending more than 11 hours outdoors and some reported spending no time at all. The spread is, therefore, at least 11 hours per week.

Exploring Connections Between Parts of the Data

When Denscombe (2017, p. 265) talks about 'exploring connections between parts of the data', what he means is the ways that more than one variable can be considered to assess the correlations and associations between them. One way that you might be familiar with doing this is through scatter graphs (also called scatter plots), which allow you to calculate 'the strength of the relationship between variables' (Denscombe, 2017, p. 284), where traditionally the variable on the horizontal (x) axis is independent, and the variable on the vertical (y) axis is dependent (Smith, 2022, p. 85). Mukherji and Albon (2018, p. 76) explain that independent variables are those that are 'not under the control of (independent of) the participant' whereas dependent variables are 'what is being measured'.

A strong relationship between two variables is called a *correlation*. If one variable increases as the other increases, this is known as *positive correlation*. If one variable decreases as the other increases, this is known as *negative correlation*. Figures 13.1 and 13.2 give an illustration of what positive and negative correlation looks like on a scatter graph.

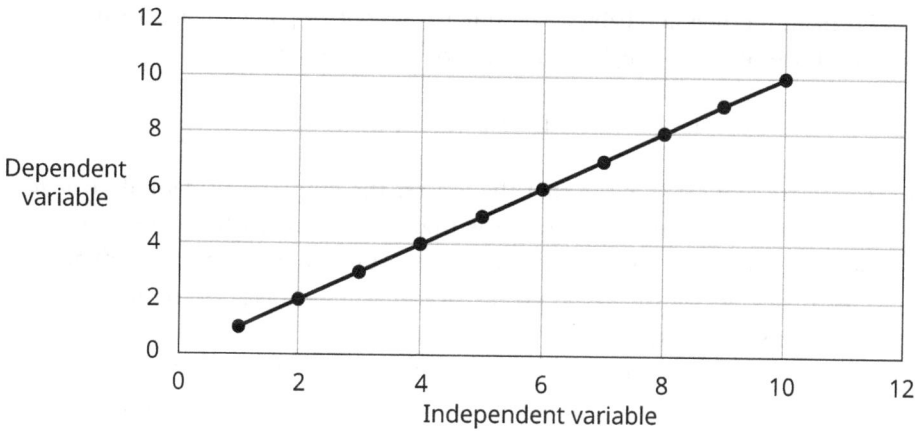

Figure 13.1 Scatter graph showing positive correlation

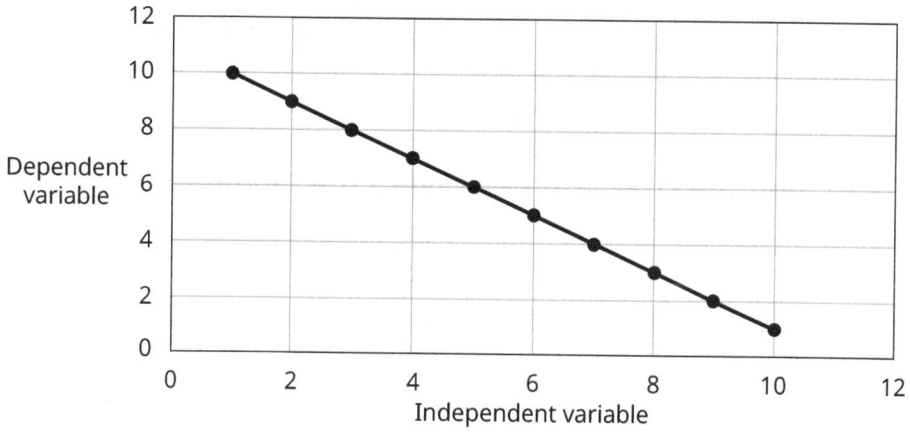

Figure 13.2 Scatter graph showing negative correlation

We didn't attempt to calculate the relationship between two variables from our data about the importance of the outdoors and nature to babyroom parents. But from our reading of literature about babies' experiences outdoors, we do know of some relationships that exist between the amount of time babies, or pregnant women, spend outdoors and babies' health outcomes. Have a look at the following pairs of variables. Make a note about whether you think a positive or a negative correlation exists:

1 How close pregnant mothers live to greenspace and how heavy their babies are when they are born.

2 Babies' exposure to greenspace and their likelihood of dying during infancy.

3   Pregnant mothers and babies' exposure to outdoor air pollution and their likelihood of developing lower respiratory tract infections.

Have you come to some thoughts? Here is what has been found:

1   Cusack et al. (2018) found that the greater the mother's residential proximity to greenspace during pregnancy, the higher the term birth weight. This demonstrates a *positive* correlation between birth weight and residential greenspace proximity (i.e. as greenspace proximity increases, term birth weight also increases).
2   Schinasi et al. (2019) found that higher levels of greenness are associated with lower levels of infant mortality. That means there is a *negative* correlation between babies' exposure to greenspace and infant mortality (i.e. as the rate of greenspace exposure increases, the rate of infant mortality decreases).
3   Aguilera et al. (2013) found that the more outdoor air pollution that pregnant mothers and babies were exposed to, the greater the likelihood of being diagnosed with a lower respiratory tract infection. That means there is a *positive* correlation between outdoor air pollution exposure and lower respiratory tract infection diagnoses.

Presenting the Data and Portraying the Findings

If you are reading a report that has taken a quantitative approach to data collection, you might notice that the Findings section often contains charts or graphs. This is because, as Denscombe (2017, p. 291) explains, charts and graphs 'provide a succinct and effective way of organising quantitative data and communicating the findings to others'. We would recommend using software such as Microsoft Excel to help you create tables or charts. Inputting your numerical data into an Excel spreadsheet can help you calculate frequencies and averages, and the software provides shortcuts and guidance to creating effective tables and a range of different types of charts. But do remember, as Roberts-Holmes, Levy and Harmey (2023) stress, that although software like Excel can be a useful tool to help you present your data, it won't do your analysis for you.

Whichever way you choose to present your data, it's important that any tables or charts are clearly labelled and contain enough detail that your reader can understand them. Using colour can be an effective way of drawing distinctions between your data, but make sure you use colour in a purposeful way so that it helps the reader interpret your data rather than distract them.

You are probably familiar with different types of graphs already, even if you don't know the names of them. Some of the most common are:

- **Bar charts:** these are useful if you want to present frequencies or amounts. They are typically presented vertically but can be presented horizontally if it makes it easier to be able to read the label for each bar.
- **Stacked bar charts:** are like bar charts but show proportions of a total.
- **Histograms:** these are like bar charts but, whereas bar charts have a space between each bar, histograms don't because they present continuous data. These are also useful for showing frequencies or amounts.
- **Pie charts:** these present proportions of a total, typically presented as percentages.
- **Line graphs:** these are commonly used for 'showing trends in data' (Denscombe, 2017, p. 298), such as identifying changes over time.
- **Scatter graphs:** as we've spoken about already, scatter graphs are used to show the extent of a relationship between two variables.

Activity 13.1   Thinking About Appropriate Charts

We used a variety of different types of charts when presenting the quantitative data about the importance of the outdoors and nature to babyroom parents (Kemp et al., 2025). Have a look at the following list which gives some examples of the graphs and tables we included in our report. Can you identify which type of chart would be appropriate for each example?

- A chart showing the breakdown of ethnicity of the respondents.
- A chart showing the number of respondents who stated they had visited a variety of outdoor locations in the last month, including woods, coast, fields and allotments.
- A chart showing how often respondents said that they spent time outdoors with their child (either never, once a week, several times a week, every day or more than once a day).
- A chart showing the number of parents that engaged their child in different sensory opportunities outdoors (touching, looking, listening, smelling and tasting).

Reflection

You can see from Table 13.3 which types of charts we used to present our data. There are some examples where more than one type of chart would have been appropriate. Different authors have different opinions on what to do in these instances; you might want to use a variety in the write-up to your study to demonstrate the breadth of your ability to present quantitative data, or you might want to stick to one type for consistency.

(Continued)

Table 13.3   Examples of charts featured in Kemp et al.'s (2025) report

Example of chart	Type of chart
Showing the breakdown of ethnicity of the respondents.	We included this as a table, but it would also have been appropriate as a pie chart.
Showing the number of respondents who stated they had visited a variety of outdoor locations in the last month, including woods, coast, fields and allotments.	We included this as a bar chart. We broke down the data further to differentiate between babies and toddlers, so had two bars in different colours for each of the locations visited.
Showing how often respondents said that they spent time outdoors at home and out of the home with their baby or toddler (responses limited to: never, once a week, several times a week, every day or more than once a day).	We included this as a stacked bar chart, with bars for: at home (baby), at home (toddler), out of home (baby) and out of home (toddler). Alternatively, we could have presented this as four pie charts.
Showing the number of parents that engaged their child in different sensory opportunities outdoors (touching, looking, listening, smelling and tasting).	We included this as a bar chart. We broke down the data to differentiate between babies and toddlers, so had two bars in different colours for each of the senses listed.

ANALYSING QUALITATIVE DATA

While you may use descriptive statistics to analyse quantitative data, if you have qualitative data to analyse then you will probably need to take a different approach, because words can't be made sense of in the same way as numbers. In this section we are going to consider the process for qualitative data analysis that Davies and Hughes (2014) outline. They talk about analysing interview transcripts specifically, but their steps hold true for all kinds of qualitative data. They argue that first you prepare your qualitative data by creating a two-column table and splitting the data into chunks in rows in the left-hand column and leaving the right-hand column for your commentary and annotations. Then, you need to complete the three steps of 'thinking, creating structures, and identifying themes' (2014, p. 225). We will now consider each of these three steps in more detail.

Thinking

The first step that Davies and Hughes (2014) outline is thinking about your qualitative data. They suggest that you should read through your data and make notes in your right-hand column commenting on the data. They describe this as 'a thinking process, an opportunity for you to react to your interviewee's material' (p. 222). Even if the data seems uncomplicated, this process should still be completed to give you a full overview of all your data.

There are other steps that you can follow to analyse qualitative data, and many of these start with the same advice to do your thinking first. For instance, back in

Chapter 6 (*Taking an autoethnographic approach*) we introduced you to Braun and Clarke's (2021) method of thematic analysis. They outline six phases to their approach, the first of which is 'familiarizing yourself with the data' (p. 87) which comprises of 'reading and re-reading the data, noting down initial ideas' (p. 87).

In the questionnaire that we distributed to babyroom parents about the importance of the outdoors and nature, we asked some open-ended questions. These questions included:

- Does your child have a favourite place? If so, where?
- When spending time outdoors with your child, what do they like to do?
- Is there anything else you would like to share with us about your outdoor experiences with your child? For example, you could tell us the last time you visited an outdoor space and made a memory with your child.

Because these questions were open-ended, they generated rich qualitative responses that we couldn't analyse using descriptive statistics as we had done with our quantitative data. Instead, we created a two-columned table, as Davies and Hughes (2014) suggested, and began by reading through the data and noting things that stood out. We took into consideration the four characteristics that Rapley (2011) suggests it is worth noting when examining qualitative data – elements that are 'essential, striking, odd [or] interesting' (pp. 277–8). Table 13.4 gives some examples from our raw data alongside our initial commentary.

Table 13.4 Thinking about our qualitative data

Response to 'What do you notice, if anything, about how your child reacts to being outdoors?'	Commentary
Their [sic] much happier and confident than indoors. They're more likely to explore and try new things. It helps improve their motor skills.	Response is detailed. Considers emotions of happiness and confidence. Compares indoors with outdoors. Notes exploration and physical motor development.
He goes from play mode to watch mode.	I am inferring they are referring to a difference between the child's behaviour indoors to outdoors in that outdoors the child is more observant and less active.
He loves having the freedom to run around.	Respondent suggests that the outdoors provides freedom. Refers to being physically active (i.e. running).

Creating Structures

After you've thought about the data, Davies and Hughes (2014) suggest that the next step is 'creating structures'. By this they mean you need to 'identify the principle emergent ideas in each piece of transcribed data' (p. 222) through 'creating a coding frame, into which (most of) your accumulated data will gradually fit' (p. 222).

Coding is something that students can struggle to get their heads around. Essentially it is a technique in which the researcher assigns codes to parts of their data to describe what that part of their data is talking about so that as a whole, the data is more digestible. It is 'essentially indexing or mapping data, to provide an overview of disparate data that allows the researcher to make sense of them in relation to their research questions' (Elliott, 2018, p. 2851). Elliott talks about how coding is a way of 'tagging data' (p. 2851); in the past students have found it helpful when we've mentioned the parallels between coding qualitative data and adding hashtags to social media posts, which is often done to categorise and label the posts so that others can find content that's relevant to them. In fact, people like Rapley (2011) prefer the term 'labels' to 'codes'.

So, to complete Davies and Hughes' (2014) second stage of 'creating structures', it's necessary to go back through the data and assign codes (or labels) which summarise sections of the text. Elliott (2018) sets out some useful guidance for doing this:

- You don't need to code every single part of your data; you might find that after close consideration, some data doesn't need a code.
- There's no hard and fast rules on how many codes you should assign your text, but Elliot draws attention to Creswell (2015, cited in Elliott, 2018) who aims for 30 to 50 codes, regardless of the length of his text.
- You can assign data to more than one code, although if you have too many codes then your data will be harder to interpret, when the purpose of coding is to condense it.

Table 13.5 shares some more examples of raw data that we collected via our parental questionnaire, alongside the codes we attributed to each response.

Table 13.5 Creating structures in our qualitative data

Response to 'What do you notice, if anything, about how your child reacts to being outdoors?'	code/s
Their [sic] much happier and confident than indoors. They're more likely to explore and try new things. It helps improve their motor skills.	• Curious • Confident • Happy
He goes from play mode to watch mode.	• Observant
He loves having the freedom to run around.	• Free • Active • Pleasure

Identifying Themes

The last step that Davies and Hughes (2014, p. 225) outline is of 'identifying themes'. They define this as 'the stage when you begin to identify and reduce to manageable proportions the central themes that will drive your report' (p. 222). This is something that Braun and Clarke (2021) talk about too when explaining how to take a thematic approach. They suggest that once a researcher has generated their initial codes, they must then:

1   **Search for themes:** 'Collating codes into potential themes, gathering all data relevant to each potential theme'
2   **Review themes:** 'Checking if the themes work in relation to the coded extracts (Level 1) and the entire data set (Level 2), generating a thematic "map" of the analysis'
3   **Define and name the themes:** 'Ongoing analysis to refine the specifics of each theme, and the overall story the analysis tells, generating clear definitions and names for each theme' (2011, p. 87)

In Table 13.5 we shared some extracts from our data about what respondents said that their child liked to do outdoors and noted which codes we'd assigned to them. Overall, for that question, we identified 314 codes from 175 responses. Table 13.6 outlines some of the final themes that were settled on from coding the complete data set of responses for that question.

Table 13.6   Identifying themes in our qualitative data

Quality	Example from the qualitative responses
Happy	*Their [sic] much happier and confident than indoors. They're more likely to explore and try new things. It helps improve their motor skills.*
Observant	*He goes from play mode to watch mode.*
Calm	*She is more calm and can regulate emotions better.*
Active	*He loves having the freedom to run around.*

Activity 13.2   Analysing Qualitative Data

In Chapter 10 (*Conducting observations*) we shared an observation of Asad sitting on a picnic blanket. Initially we shared the observation in a traditional narrative style and then re-wrote it to take an In-the-Picture approach which was written from Asad's point of view. Have a look at the observation again and see if you can apply the process of 'thinking, creating structures, and identifying themes' (Davies and Hughes, 2014, p. 225) to attempt to analyse the observation.

Daddy and I are sitting on a picnic blanket. I can see some tree branches swaying above me. I notice the grass beyond the picnic blanket and move onto all-fours so that I can crawl towards it. I stop when I get to the edge of the picnic blanket. I can reach the grass there. I touch the grass to see what it feels like. I wonder what it tastes like. I grasp the grass in my palm and try to pull it up but I don't manage it. I try again but it slips

(Continued)

through my fingers. I try again and finally manage to pull some grass up. This makes me smile. I put it to my mouth but suddenly I hear my Daddy behind me say 'no, thank you'. He immediately puts his hands under my armpits and picks me. He puts me on his lap and uncurls my fingers. My grass falls away.

Reflection

When you completed the three stages of 'thinking, creating structures, and identifying themes' (Davies and Hughes, 2014, p. 225) you might have initially noted how Asad is using his senses to explore his environment through touching (and attempting to taste) the grass, or have been surprised that Asad's dad appears to stop his engagement with nature prematurely. When making notes of codes, you might have recorded codes such as *nature, movement, tasting, touching* and *parent*. It is hard to draw out themes from such a small excerpt of data, but you may have some initial thoughts that one theme may be around the opportunities the natural environment offers for sensory engagement.

WRITING UP YOUR FINDINGS

Once you've analysed your data, you need to think about how you are going to translate what your data is telling you into *findings*, which you will then need to write up. How you write up your findings will depend on what they look like; but if you have a look at journal articles you might notice some commonalities. If you have quantitative data, your findings section is where you will include any graphs or tables that you have produced. If you have qualitative data, it can be useful to use a table to set out the themes you have identified, an explanation of the theme and an example from the data of that theme. Table 13.7 shares an example of what this might look like.

Table 13.7 Parents' observations about what they notice about how their child reacts to being outdoors

Theme	Description of theme	Example from data
Happy	Parents noted that their child displayed happiness when outdoors.	*If she's having a hard day, we know taking her to the garden or play park is a total reset and she is instantly happier.*
Observant	Parents noted that their child became more observant when outdoors.	*Our child loves to observe and stays very quiet but restful.*
Calm	Parents noted that the outdoor environment calmed their child.	*She is more calm and can regulate emotions better.*
Active	Parents noted that the outdoors was a place where their child was active.	*My toddler is very active and would rather climb or run exploring her surroundings.*

Typically, when a researcher reports their findings, they don't link to external literature as this is saved for the *Discussion*, in which you discuss how your findings relate to the wider body of literature and how they answer your research question.

Sometimes we find that this is when students start to panic and say things such as 'but what if my findings don't tell me what I thought they would?' But here's the thing – you can only find what you can find. And if you find something unexpected, or realise that your findings reflect a methodological flaw such as data collection tools that it would have been useful to revise, or a sample that would have benefited from being larger or more representative, then that is something you can reflect upon when you acknowledge the limitations of your study.

Case Study 13.1   Analysing Qualitative Data

Rose has carried out her small-scale undergraduate research project in which she has asked reception-aged children how they feel when they spend time with nature. She collected the data by doing group interviews with small groups of children in which she predominantly asked them open-ended questions about what they understood by the term 'nature', what types of natural places they visit and how they feel when they are there. She recorded the group interviews using a Dictaphone. She now begins to think about how she will analyse her data.

She decides to follow Davies and Hughes's (2014, p. 225) three steps of 'thinking, creating structures, and identifying themes'. She creates a table with two columns and copies her interview transcripts into the left-hand side in chunks. She then begins by reading through the data and making an initial commentary in the right-hand column to help her think about the data. She then reads through again but this time notes codes (which she refers to as labels) to summarise sections of her data to help her create structure. Finally, she looks at the codes she has generated across all her interview transcripts in order to group them into the main themes that her participants have stated in relation to their perspectives of spending time in nature. Overall, she identifies three themes: that nature is a place for exploring, nature is a place to take risks and nature is a place to have freedom.

KEY POINTS FROM THE CHAPTER

- The way in which you analyse your data will depend on what type of data you have; there are different techniques for analysing qualitative data and quantitative data.
- It can be useful to use descriptive statistics to make sense of quantitative data.
- It can be useful to approach qualitative data by 'thinking, creating structures, and identifying themes' (Davies and Hughes, 2014, p. 225).

FURTHER READING

1   Denscombe's (2017) *The Good Research Guide* is a really useful text for considering both quantitative and qualitative data analysis.

   Denscombe, M. (2017) *The Good Research Guide: For Small-Scale Social Research Projects.* 6th Edition. London: Open University Press.

2   Part 5 of Mukherji and Albon's (2018) *Research Methods in Early Childhood* is all about analysing and sharing your findings.

   Mukherji, P. and Albon, D. (2018) *Research Methods in Early Childhood: An Introductory Guide.* London: Sage.

REFERENCES

Aguilera, I., Pedersen, M., Garcia-Esteban, R., Ballester, F., Basterrechea, M., Esplugues, A., Fernandez-Somoano, A., Lertxundi, A., Tardon, A. and Sunyer, J. (2013) 'Early-life exposure to outdoor air pollution and respiratory health, ear infections, and eczema in infants from the INMA study', *Environmental Health Perspectives*, *121*(3), pp. 387–92. DOI: https://doi.org/10.1289/ehp.1205281.

Braun, V. and Clarke, V. (2021) *Thematic Analysis: A Practical Guide.* London: Sage.

Cusack, L., Sbihi, H., Larkin, A., Chow, A., Brook, J., Moraes, T., Mandhane, P., Becker, A., Azad, M., Subbarao, P., Kozyrskyj, A., Takaro, T., Sears, M., Turvey, S. and Hystad, P. (2018) 'Residential green space and pathways to term birth weight in the Canadian Healthy Infant Longitudinal Development (CHILD) Study', *International Journal of Health Geographics*, *17*(1), p. 43. DOI: https://doi.org/10.1186/s12942-018-0160-x.

Davies, M. and Hughes, N. (2014) *Doing a Successful Research Project Using Qualitative or Quantitative Methods.* London: Bloomsbury Publishing.

Denscombe, M. (2017) *The Good Research Guide: For Small-Scale Social Research Projects.* 6th Edition. London: Open University Press.

Elliott, V. (2018) 'Thinking about the coding process in qualitative data analysis', *The Qualitative Report*, *23*(11), pp. 2850–61. DOI: https://doi.org/10.46743/2160-3715/2018.3560.

Kemp, N., Josephidou, J., Durrant, I. and Bolshaw, P. (2025) *Making Memories Together… The Importance of the Outdoors and Nature to Babyroom Parents.* The Froebel Trust.

Mukherji, P. and Albon, D. (2018) *Research Methods in Early Childhood: An Introductory Guide.* London: Sage.

Rapley, T. (2011) 'Some pragmatics of data analysis', in D. Silverman (ed.), *Qualitative Research*, London: Sage, pp. 273–90.

Roberts-Holmes, G., Levy, R. and Harmey, S. (2023) *Doing Your Early Years Research Project: A Step by Step Guide.* 5th Edition. London: Sage.

Schinasi, L.H., Quick, H., Clougherty, J. and De Ross, A. (2019) 'Greenspace and infant mortality in Philadelphia, PA', *Journal of Urban Health: Bulletin of the New York Academy of Medicine*, *96*(3), pp. 497–506. DOI: https://doi.org/10.1007/s11524-018-00335-z.

Smith, A. (2022) *How Charts Work: Understand and Explain Data with Confidence*. Harlow: Pearson Education Ltd.

14

FORMING YOUR ARGUMENT

CHAPTER OBJECTIVES

By the end of this chapter, you will:

*   Understand how to pull all your work together to report on your research findings
*   Know how to move forward to complete your project successfully
*   Understand how your Findings and Discussion and your argument are linked.

INTRODUCTION

Well done for getting to this point with your work. By now you have probably gathered some data, analysed it and feel you have something important to share with the world. But everything is probably still looking quite messy. You may have accumulated various Word documents, an assortment of sticky notes and some colourful diagrams temporarily attached to your wall. How can you now turn these items into something useful to contribute to research conversations about Early Childhood? The aim of this chapter is to help you bring structure to this research messiness, including developing a strong argument to thread through your writing up. This argument will tell your audience why the work is important and what you are able to contribute. Therefore, we will consider what we mean by the term argument in this context and why it is helpful to have one when writing up your project.

PULLING EVERYTHING TOGETHER

It can be a daunting prospect to arrive at the point of pulling everything together. It is important that you are strategic and organised as you do this work so that you don't become overwhelmed and lost in the landscape of an extended piece of written work (perhaps longer than you are used to up to this point) and the more complicated layers a research report has; it may be one of the most complex pieces of assessed writing you have undertaken so far, especially if you are an undergraduate. It is also important that you can reflect not just on your findings but also on the whole process of your project so you can address any limitations when you write up your concluding thoughts. There are certain set down ways of setting out your research report, so we will have a look at those as well as thinking about the importance of being able to sum up your project in a few sentences. With this in mind, we will begin this section with a reflective exercise.

Reflecting on the Journey of Your Project

Pause for a moment and reflect on your research activity up to this point. We imagine that if you are reading this, you have already attempted your Literature Review (although you may need to return to it), your Methodology, you have already collected your data and analysed it to set out your findings. Or indeed you may be one of those students who like to get the bigger picture and have read most of this book before these tasks are completed. This is no problem, as you can reflect forwards, however you might have to engage with the useful activities in this chapter in a slightly different way.

The first thing it will be useful for you to look at is your review of the literature. As you engaged with peer-reviewed journal articles, did you notice that they often set out a particular argument? For example, if we look at some of our own, you will see that we try to set out an argument clearly:

- 'We *argue* that, given the rise in babies and toddlers attending ECEC settings globally, these may offer potential sites for developing counter-hegemonic practices that challenge the marginalisation of tiny humans and those that care for them' (Kemp, Josephidou and Bolshaw, 2025).
- 'The article *argues* there is a need to re-conceive of the ways in which the youngest children engage with the outdoors and to move beyond possible narratives of exclusion' (Kemp and Josephidou, 2021).
- 'We *argue* that the creation of such spaces requires explicit acts of resistance and disruption to neoliberal understandings about the place of infants and toddlers outdoors' (Kemp and Josephidou, 2023).

Some authors may not always use the word *argue* so you may need to dig a little deeper for the key message of the article. The abstract is a good place to start your digging, and the conclusion can also be helpful for this. As you explore the arguments in the work you have cited, think about the argument you may want to suggest in your own work; we will return to this later on in the chapter.

By focusing back on the beginning of your research journey, revisiting the literature you reviewed, reflecting on your data collection and then what you believe the findings have revealed, you are in a strong position to write up your work. For example, were your findings akin to those discovered in the literature review, or did you find something surprising, different or noteworthy? If so, remember to look at them critically – is this to do with your sample size or have things moved on in children's lives (we are thinking, for example, about the impact of Covid and how children's lives changed irreversibly). If you were to carry out such a piece of research again, would you use the same data collection methods or would you prefer to try something different and why would this be? All this thinking and reflecting is exactly what you need to write up in your research report.

The Importance of Clear Reporting

So, you are ready to begin writing up. There are accepted ways of doing this which we will discuss in this section as well as considering some of the most frequently asked questions from students that we have come across in our considerable years as dissertation supervisors. Setting out a research report, dissertation or thesis is done in a similar way to the structure you have seen in peer-reviewed articles; it is important to recognise at this point that there is something problematic about this accepted structure in that it privileges certain voices over others. Some, at doctoral level, have tried to address this issue by writing up their work in much more creative ways, e.g. through poetry, art, even song for example. However, we would recommend that you always check with your supervisor if you decide to stray from the conventional structure. Generally, a dissertation would contain the following elements in the following order:

1 *Abstract*

A standalone paragraph which sums up what you did, what you found out and your argument (we will have a go at doing this later in the chapter).

2 *Introduction*

To introduce the context of your research, your research question(s), perhaps any terminology or concepts you are going to use extensively. And to set out your argument.

3 *Literature review*

Look back at Chapter 4 (*Joining a research conversation*) for a reminder about how to do this. This section often needs to be rewritten or at least amended after the data has been analysed. Remember you will restate your research question(s) at the end of this section.

4 *Methodology and methods*

Remember to include a discussion of not just what you did (Methods) but why (Methodology). The latter will include some discussion of your ontological and epistemological stance, showing how this relates to the data collection methods, sample, ethics etc.

5   *Findings*

What you found out. Here you will include extracts from your data to support your statements. We wouldn't expect to find many references to literature in this section, which is sometimes called Results (usually if it is a quantitative study). Some people prefer to combine Findings and Discussion together.

6   *Discussion*

The implications of what you have found out (see Activity 14.3 to help you with this).

7   *Conclusion*

Remind the reader how all the above work answers your research question(s) and supports your argument. You can also include any recommendations and limitations in this section.

8   *References*

Your reader will expect to see an extensive reference list, with accurate referencing. There should be a selection of peer-reviewed journal articles, methodology texts, books, chapters, policy documents and reports. Don't forget Chapter 4's recommendations on finding quality sources.

9   *Appendices*

Good to include your ethical approval documentation, examples of data collection tools and perhaps a snapshot of your data.

We have noted that over the years we have been asked very similar questions by students so we will set out those questions here along with our responses. As we have said above – do please check with your supervisor or course documentation so that we are not contradicting any other advice you have been given. Let's tackle each of these questions one at a time.

Do I Put All My Data in the Appendices?

It is useful for your reader to have access to some of your raw data because then they can see your process and thinking. This links with our previous discussions around rigour. However, your reader doesn't want to have to scroll through pages and pages of data. So, think carefully about what you want to share and remember to anonymise. For example, when one student carried out some research for their MA, they asked the participants to each do one drawing. They collected 39 drawings all together but only selected three quite different ones to share with the reader in the appendices.

What Tense Do I Write In?

This is a good question which at first might seem to have an obvious answer, but it is one that continually trips up students and has sometimes confused us also in our own work. It is important to get it right to demonstrate rigour and trustworthiness. One of the issues is that students can base their chapters on their proposal or they can write certain chapters before they have carried out their research. For example, a mistake we have often come across is that students will write their methodology chapter before they carry out their research, so they quite rightly write in the future tense, i.e. 'I will collect data by...' Yet they then neglect to change to the past tenses and so write about what they did, i.e. 'I collected data by...'. It may seem such a small thing – but it really jars for the reader and can confuse. Another layer of complexity is that you may need to use the present tense elsewhere when you are describing the context of your research – be sensitive to your use of tenses and you will find that your work is much more polished, accessible, and trustworthy.

Can I Use I?

Also, a question that is frequently asked and like the 'tense' question may differ depending on which section of the report you are referring to. For example, it is generally acceptable to use the first person in the Methodology/Methods chapter as you are talking about what you have done, particularly in a small-scale qualitative study where your impact as researcher is important to recognise. When you describe your positionality, it matters that you use 'I'; some students refer to themselves as 'the researcher' which leaves the reader wondering who they are talking about. Elsewhere try to avoid phrases like 'I think...' 'I believe...' 'In my opinion...'. Such phrases are suggestive of an opinion piece and may lead your reader to question your rigour. However, it is perfectly acceptable to use phrases such as 'I argue...' 'I suggest...'.

We hope by now that you are confident in setting out your report. As you have been working on your project over several months you will probably have written up each of the sections detailed above as almost mini essays, you may even be encouraged to name them 'chapters'. The key thing now is to ensure that these sections/chapters link well, so that your narrative flows and makes sense as a whole.

Having an Overview

Having a clear overview of your work and knowing what your key message and your key argument are, will make dissemination much easier. After all, if you have some interesting findings, you want to let as many people know as possible. We will talk more about these opportunities in Chapter 17 (*Taking other opportunities for publication*) so if you have distilled your work down to these two items (i.e. message and argument) you will be good to go by then. We remember a tutor who used to say, imagine you are telling your friend/granny/dog about your work, what would you say in simple English to get the key ideas over. We think this is something that works well – why don't you give it a try!

In fact, there is also an academic approach to carrying out this activity called The Three Minute Thesis which you may be interested to hear about. As part of a competition, students are given just 180 seconds to present their work to an audience who are unfamiliar with their discipline (University of Oxford, n.d.). It is a competition aimed at PhD students, but we think that the principles are also useful for undergraduate students or MA students to consider, i.e. how could you simply and briefly explain your study including why it is important.

Activity 14.1 Explaining Your Project

This activity will support you in putting together a clear overview of your work which you could explain to a non-specialist. Have a go here at putting a short paragraph together in plain English – we have included some questions to help you.

- What is your research question about? (You might want to paraphrase it and make it into a statement to support a non-specialist to understand.)
- What do you know about this topic so far? (This is where you will give a short explanation of the literature.)
- What did you do? (A short description in simple English of your data collection.)
- What have you found out? (Try to sum up in one sentence – we know it is hard!)
- Why is this important? (Let your listener know one or two implications of your findings.)
- What next? (This may be harder to think about but certainly if you work in practice you might think about changes you would like to make.)

Reflection

Dmitri had a go at answering these questions as they came to the end of their project but before they began to write it up. Table 14.1 shows Dmitri's responses.

Table 14.1 Answers about my project

Question	Dmitri's responses
What was my research question about?	My research question was about why some children find school enjoyable, and others don't. This is how I phrased it: How do 5-year-olds understand and talk about enjoyment of school?
What do I know about this topic?	I know from my reading that there are issues around • Social/emotional development • Poverty • Expectations on young children – neoliberalism etc.
What did I do?	I had a research chat with three groups of children (all 5 years old with five children in each group)

Question	Dmitri's responses
What did I find out?	I found out that children:
	• focused on the level of their reading book a lot – and were worried about it.
	• talked about their friends and falling out a lot
	• talked about work and play with play being seen as not important in the school context.
Why is this important?	• This is the transition year into formal education for children, they are developing their identity as a learner.
What's next?	• I am going to do a PGCE when I graduate with my ECS degree so I would like to take what I have learnt into the Reception class.

WRITING AN ABSTRACT

Having a clear overview of your project will be useful if you need to include an abstract in your report. As part of this section of your dissertation you may like to include your argument which you will then thread through your work. We will think about the argument aspect shortly but before that let's see if we have achieved one of the aims of this book which was to support you in putting together a small-scale Early Childhood Research project. We hope that we have managed to scaffold your learning so that now you have arrived at this chapter, you feel confident that this is indeed something that you could do. Before we go any further, let's remind ourselves here of the important steps in this process and how this links to the idea of developing an argument. You will note in Table 14.2 the table of steps you were introduced to in Chapter 1 (*What is research in Early Childhood and why does it matter?*); check off everything you have achieved so far and note what you need to address next.

Table 14.2 Completing the steps in your small-scale Early Childhood Research project

Step	Chapter
1 Decide on an area of focus	3
2 Read about this area	4
3 Decide on a potential research question	3
4 Read some more!	4
5 Decide on your methodology	3
6 Decide on your data collection methods and approach	6–12

(Continued)

Table 14.2 (Continued)

Step	Chapter
7 Get ethical approval	2 and 5
8 Collect your data	6–12
9 Analyse your data	13
10 Write up findings	13
11 Analyse findings	14
12 Decide on your argument	14
13 Disseminate your findings	15–17

Activity 14.2   The Abstract

Your report or dissertation will need a standalone paragraph at the beginning of your work, as you have seen in peer-reviewed journal articles. This paragraph, or abstract as it is called, gives the overview of what you did, what you found out, the implications, possible argument and possible recommendations, although it is not necessary to always include all these elements. Have a look at some peer-reviewed articles to see how others have set their abstracts out, then have a go at writing your own. A useful structure would be to write one sentence for each of these numbered points:

1   A bold statement to introduce the context of your work.
2   Say why the above statement might be a problem.
3   Therefore, what did you set out to do in your research to explore this problem?
4   How did you gather your data?
5   Sum up your findings.
6   What are the implications of your findings?
7   Add a final statement to either sum up your argument, make a recommendation or both.

Now put the individual sentences together to form a paragraph, making sure it flows coherently and could read as a standalone abstract for your report.

Reflection

Nazaneen works in an Early Childhood setting and is very aware of tensions between parents who don't want their children to nap while attending the setting because then they will not sleep at home, and practitioners who noticed that some children still need to sleep in the day. Her question was: How can practitioners and parents best negotiate sleep routines for the child attending an ECEC setting? You can see her responses to each numbered point below:

1   A bold statement to introduce the context of your work.

An increasing number of very young children (birth to 2) are attending ECEC settings in England.

2   Say why the above statement might be a problem.

There are potential tensions between meeting the needs of the child, parent and setting around sleep routines.

3   Therefore, what did you set out to do in your research to explore this problem?

This project aimed to find ways that parents and practitioners could work together to support young children with their sleep routines.

4   How did you gather your data?

Five practitioners were interviewed and 30 parents from one ECEC setting in the north of England were surveyed.

5   Sum up your findings.

Findings showed that parents and practitioners had very different perspectives about the sleep needs of the child during the day.

6   What are the implications of your findings?

It may have a negative impact on the child if there is a lack of shared understanding between the important adults in their life.

7   Add a final statement to either sum up your argument, make a recommendation or both.

The setting needs to find a space for collaborative conversations with busy parents so that there is a sense of working together rather than against each other.

Nazaneen then put the sentences together and as you can see tweaked a little so that the paragraphed text flowed:

> An increasing number of very young children (birth to 2) are attending ECEC settings in England. There are potential tensions between meeting the needs of the child, parent and setting around sleep routines. This project aimed to find ways that parents and practitioners could work together to support young children with their sleep routines. Five practitioners were interviewed and 30 parents from one ECEC setting in the north of England were surveyed. Findings revealed that parents and practitioners had very different perspectives about the sleep needs of the child during the day. I argue that settings need to find a space for collaborative conversations with busy parents to support a sense of working together for the benefit of each child.

LOOKING FOR THE LINKS AND MAKING AN ARGUMENT

Sometimes students can be unclear about setting out their findings and how this is different from the discussion part of the report. There is not one specific way to do this, but people generally follow one of two options; either they will have a separate findings and discussion section, or they will present the two elements together.

What, So What, Now What

One useful way to think about these two elements is to see the findings as the 'What', i.e. this is what I found out, this is what I discovered, this is what people said, whereas the discussion is more about the 'So What', i.e. what are the implications of these findings, why does it matter that I have discovered this point, why does it matter that people said this?

The What/So What/Now What reflective model was designed by Driscoll (1994) building on the work of Borton (1970), according to the University of Edinburgh (n.d.). Although it may appear to be a very simple framework, please don't be fooled by this simplicity. It is particularly powerful in supporting you to reflect on your findings, the implications of these findings and the recommendations you can make from them (this is the 'Now What' bit). It is certainly a model we have used, and still do, extensively throughout our careers and studies. We really like its simplicity, which ironically can lead to a deep and reflective level of thinking about our work. It is also helpful in thinking about the structure of your research report – although it was not necessarily designed for this task. So how can you apply this framework to your own project? First think about the What. These are the messages you consider your data is revealing.

For example, our most recent research report based on practitioners taking babies outdoors tells us:

- There are significant differences in the types of outdoor spaces provided for babies and toddlers although they tend to be artificial, flat and bounded.
- The urban context of the settings demands a creative approach to garden design and use.
- There is a shared desire to understand how to create more natural garden environments (Kemp et al., 2025).

We arrived at these findings through our analysis of the data, collected through interviews, photographs, observations and reflections, and in the report, we used quotations from the data to evidence these findings, just as you will do when you write up your project. However, if your report ended with what you had found out, it would be incomplete. You then need a section to tell your reader the implications of what you have found out, i.e. in this reflection model, the So What. You can see what this could look like by noting Table 14.3; we have set out the three findings mentioned above and then considered the So What (implications) on the right. We want to stress here that, when you are writing up your own work, there are no right answers in terms of your So What. It really is your own reflections on what you have found out, although you will use some of the reading you have included in the literature review to help you do this.

Table 14.3 The 'What' and the 'So What' of babies outdoors

What	So What
There are significant differences in the types of outdoor spaces provided for babies and toddlers although they tend to be artificial, flat and bounded.	Babies do not have equal access to outdoor provision. More could be done to develop outdoor spaces to support babies' holistic learning and development.
The urban context of the settings demands a creative approach to garden design and use.	Practitioners may benefit from targeted training to support them with this.
There is a shared desire to understand how to create more natural garden environments.	Practitioners already have a lot of expertise and enthusiasm that could be tapped into.

Activity 14.3 Reflecting on the Use of 'Reading Dogs' in Primary School

Olga wanted to find out about dogs who went into school so that children could read to them; she sent a questionnaire to parents, interviewed three teachers and had a group interview with five children. When she analysed her data, these were her key findings:

- Some parents felt it was a novelty that distracted from teaching children to read properly.
- Some teachers were nervous about dogs because they had had bad experiences in the past.
- Some teachers weren't sure it was hygienic to have dogs in the classroom.
- Some children said they hated reading before this initiative had started.
- Not all the children got a turn with the dog, especially if they were doing well at reading.

So, this is the data; if we follow the advice given above in terms of What/So What/Now What, we now need to reflect on these findings and think about implications and recommendations (either of which might contain your argument). See if you can help Olga by thinking about these elements.

(Continued)

Reflection

How did you get on? This is quite a tricky exercise, firstly because you may not have done something like this before and secondly because it is not your own research that you are thinking about. When you come to your own findings, it will be much more intuitive for you because you will have a good understanding of some of the literature around your area of focus and this is what you will use to help you reflect and consider some of the implications. Neither have we any research expertise in this area, although we note it is a popular one with students; however, we have had a go at thinking about this – as usual, these are not the 'correct' answers, they are our interpretation. At times we have set out our reflection as a question because this is where we can see it would be important to engage with the literature. Questions would be a great starting point for your own reflections as you revisit the literature following your analysis.

Table 14.4 Considering implications and recommendations on research into reading dogs in primary school

Finding (What?)	Implication or reflection (So What?)	Recommendation (Now What?)
Some parents felt it was a novelty that distracted from teaching children to read properly.	Is this something about how schools communicate and work effectively with parents?	The school could look to see if they could get the parents onboard by having a parent champion for this initiative.
Some teachers were nervous about dogs because they had had bad experiences in the past.	This really made me think about how initiatives can be just dumped on teachers without them having a say. We talk about the unique child in the early years but what about the unique teacher?!	More consultation perhaps with teachers, a member of staff to lead on this who really likes dogs, and a special place which is not in individual classrooms.
Some teachers weren't sure it was hygienic to have dogs in the classroom.	There could also be some cultural issues it is important to explore here.	This is about the space allocated for this activity.
Some children said they hated reading before this initiative.	This begs the question why? Once the novelty of the dog has worn off, will some children go back to disliking reading?	I would suggest some further research to include the children's voice about learning to read at school and what they like and don't like about it.
Not all the children got a turn with the dog, especially if they were doing well at reading.	This is really interesting – so the children were punished for being good readers?	This initiative needs to be open to all children who would like to take part.

> ### Case Study 14.1   Forming an Argument for a Non-Specialist Audience
>
> We reflect here on our own work and some of the arguments we made in the section above. We thought about how we could translate an argument made for a peer-reviewed article into one that would be useful for practitioners in their work. For example, when we stated:
>
>> We *argue* that, given the rise in babies and toddlers attending ECEC settings globally, these may offer potential sites for developing counter hegemonic practices that challenge the marginalisation of tiny humans and those that care for them. (Kemp et al. 2025)
>
> We then had to consider what this argument should look like in the resources we provided for, and the conversations we had, with practitioners, and this is the argument we came up with:
>
>> It is important for practitioners to question, and also be given the opportunity to question, normal practice with babies in the setting.

KEY POINTS FROM THE CHAPTER

- There are agreed ways of how to set out a research report so that all the important components are included.
- It is useful to have an overview of your research that can be easily shared with a variety of audiences.
- Having a clear argument shows that your research has a contribution.
- You can arrive at this argument by considering the 'So What' question of your findings.
- There are no right answers to arrive at as you consider the implications of your findings but do use your literature review to help you reflect on them.

FURTHER READING

1   The book *How to Do Your Research Project* by Gary Thomas is now in its fifth edition and quite rightly. We really appreciate the way that Gary structures the whole approach to a research project and then journeys along with you as an encouraging friend. Look in particular at Chapter 10, 'Concluding and Writing Up'.

Thomas, G. (2025) *How to Do Your Research Project*. 5th Edition. London: Sage.

2   The University of Oxford has a website about the Three Minute Thesis including interesting videos of what it looks like in practice.

    University of Oxford (n.d.) *Three Minute Thesis competition*. Available at: www.mpls. ox.ac.uk/public-engagement/three-minute-thesis#:~:text=THE%20 BENEFITS&text=You%20will%20be%20able%20to,network%20with%20 like%2Dminded%20researchers (accessed: 12 July 2025).

3   If you would like to learn more about the 'What? So What? Now What?' reflective framework there is some useful information on this University of Edinburgh website.

    University of Edinburgh (n.d.) *What? So what? Now what?* Available at: https:// reflection.ed.ac.uk/reflectors-toolkit/reflecting-on-experience/what-so-what-now-what (accessed: 13 July 2025).

REFERENCES

Borton. T. (1970) *Reach Touch and Teach: Student Concerns and Process Education*. New York: McGraw-Hill.

Driscoll J. (1994) 'Reflective practice for practise – a framework of structured reflection for clinical areas', *Senior Nurse*, *14*(1), pp. 47–50.

Josephidou, J. and Kemp, N. (2024) 'Developing nature engaging/nature enhancing pedagogies for babies and toddlers', *New Zealand Journal of Infant and Toddler Education*, *26*(1), pp. 23–8.

Kemp, N. and Josephidou, J. (2021) 'Babies and toddlers outdoors: a narrative review of the literature on provision for under twos in ECEC settings', *Early Years*, *43*(1), pp. 137–50. DOI: https://doi.org/10.1080/09575146.2021.1915962.

Kemp, N. and Josephidou, J. (2023) 'Creating spaces called hope: the critical leadership role of owner/managers in developing outdoor pedagogies for infants and toddlers', *Early Years*, *43*(3), pp. 641–55. DOI: https://doi.org/10.1080/09575146.2023.2235913.

Kemp, N., Josephidou, J. and Bolshaw, P. (2025) '"Tiny humans" outdoors: understanding the factors that mediate opportunities for babies and toddlers', *Children's Geographies*, *23*(2), pp. 219–36. DOI: https://doi.org/10.1080/14733285.2025.2479683.

Kemp, N., Josephidou, J., Bolshaw, P. and Plowright-Pepper. L. (forthcoming) *Looking for the Wow and the Wonder; Supporting Babies to Be Outdoors in Urban ECEC Settings*. The Froebel Trust.

University of Edinburgh (n.d.) *What? So what? Now what?* Available at: https://reflection. ed.ac.uk/reflectors-toolkit/reflecting-on-experience/what-so-what-now-what (accessed: 11 July 2025).

University of Oxford (n.d.) *Three Minute Thesis competition*. Available at: www.mpls.ox.ac. uk/public-engagement/three-minute-thesis#:~:text=THE%20BENEFITS&text=You%20 will%20be%20able%20to,network%20with%20like%2Dminded%20researchers (accessed: 11 July 2025).

PART IV

TELLING THE WORLD ABOUT YOUR EARLY CHILDHOOD RESEARCH

15

DISSEMINATING YOUR RESEARCH THROUGH A PRESENTATION

CHAPTER OBJECTIVES

By the end of this chapter, you will:

- Recognise why oral presentations can be an effective way of disseminating your research study
- Appreciate why presentations can be used to challenge power imbalances
- Understand some effective presentation structures
- Identify some techniques that can help you think about how to deliver an effective presentation.

INTRODUCTION

If somebody asked you to do a presentation, how would you react? The thought of presenting fills a lot of people with dread. When we have broached the idea with students before, they've often told us how nervous presentations can make them feel, how they worry that their minds will go blank or that they will say the wrong thing. However, sometimes you may be required to complete a presentation as part of your university assessments, and other times you may be invited to disseminate your research through a presentation, which is a great opportunity to take. So, in this chapter we are going to consider how you should go about planning presentations, as well as some hints and tips that can make both individual and group presentations successful.

WHY PRESENT ORALLY?

If you are given the chance to present your research, we think it is a good opportunity you should take. There are many reasons for this but some of the most important reasons are because it can help to challenge power imbalances, it is a chance for you to continue the research conversation and because it can support you to showcase and develop your skillset.

It Can Challenge Power Imbalances

Throughout this book you have seen our commitment to thinking about power issues within Early Childhood Research, like in Chapter 2 (*Issues of power in Early Childhood Research*). In Chapter 2 we asked two big questions: *Who holds the power?* and *Whose voice counts?*

When you present, the presenter holds power in the sense that they have the chance to share their research findings with an audience who typically implicitly understands that their role is to listen. But because the audience are physically present and listening to what they presenter has to say, they cannot be seen in the abstract sense in which the reader of a written text may be perceived. Instead, they hold some power, because the presenter knows they are immediately accountable to them and that they have an instant opportunity to respond.

Presentations typically invite comments and questions from the audience, so this may be the audience's opportunity to reply to and reflect on the study, to respectfully critique, ask for clarification or offer suggestions or further food for thought. In this way, not only the presenter's voice counts, but the audience's voice counts too. We have spoken previously about how sometimes language in research is used as a gatekeeper (Bolshaw and Josephidou, 2018); the audience's ability to ask for clarification or explanations on the language you have used, to ensure they have full understanding of what you are presenting, can also lessen the power imbalance that can exist between the researcher and their audience. That is not to say, however, that all audience members will feel comfortable asking questions; the ethical researcher will think about how they present themselves in an approachable and welcoming manner so that the audience feel like they can interact via questions. It is also wise to offer details of how the audience can respond in other ways, for instance through offering your email address at the end of the presentation or giving the opportunity for individual questions at a later point in time.

Thus, by disseminating your research study through a presentation, you are giving your audience an opportunity to hold some power in how they react to and critique your research, ensuring that any power imbalances that may exist due to inaccessible language can be countered, as well as giving your audience the chance to have their voice counted in relation to how others perceive the study.

You Can Continue the Research Conversation

Earlier in this book we thought about how one of the first things you do when approaching your research study is look at what literature has already been published in your field and how, by publishing your own research, you are joining the research conversation about that topic (Chapter 4: *Joining a research conversation*). Presenting your research to an audience allows for a literal research conversation as your audience have the opportunity to respond to your study. They might tell you about other related studies that you've not come across yet, tell you how their own experiences or research aligns to what you have done or help you think about where to take your research next. When we've presented our research in the past we've had some very fruitful encounters with audience members, such as somebody offering their setting as a place where we could conduct further research and somebody else offering a meeting to chat about how they see our work progressing.

It's for this reason that Wallwork (2020) argues that it's important that, if you are using slides, you think carefully about your final slide as part of its aim is to let the audience know how to contact you and give them reasons to want to contact you, as well as to encourage them to read anything you have already published. In this way you will be continuing the research conversation beyond the presentation and may develop useful collaborations that can drive your research forward.

You Can Demonstrate a Different Skillset

Through carrying out your research you will have built up a lot of valuable graduate transferable skills, such as in project management, time management, problem solving and flexibility. Presenting your research allows you to foster and demonstrate different graduate skills, such as oral communication, confidence and active listening. Table 15.1 outlines the ways in which presenting can help you develop these skills.

Table 15.1 Developing your graduate skills through a presentation

Graduate skill	How a presentation can help
Oral communication	Presentations give you the opportunity to refine your skills in both verbal communication, which Theobald (2022) defines as power, pitch, passion and pace, and non-verbal communication like body language and eye contact.
Confidence	Presentations give you the chance to build your confidence in talking in front of groups of people and give a sense of satisfaction and accomplishment once you've finished.
Active listening	Presentations give you the opportunity to practise active listening when your audience members respond with questions, so that you can respond appropriately.

While some students might feel nervous about presenting, for others they recognise that presentations play to their skillset strengths and, in this way, presentations can be an inclusive form of assessment that challenge power imbalances in prioritising written work. Some students find articulating their ideas and thoughts in a written format difficult and presenting can allow them a more natural way to express their ideas without getting hung up on getting words down on paper and give them the opportunity to respond to questions to clarify what they mean, which is not possible in written work. A growing number of universities, too, are requiring students to present their work orally as part of their assessments, to mitigate against the risks that students have over-relied on GenAI to produce their written work.

Activity 15.1   Your Feelings About Presentations

We know that the thought of doing a presentation can illicit strong feelings in people; while some people look forward to them, to many others they feel daunting and make them feel anxious. Take some time to think about presenting. Ask yourself questions such as:

- Have you had experience presenting before? How did it go?
- How do you feel about presentations? Why do you feel this way?
- What advice would you give to a friend who told you they had a presentation to prepare for?

Reflection

If presentations do make you feel worried, we hope that by the end of this chapter, they make you feel slightly less nervous about them. Reading on to think about how to plan your presentation, as well as top tips for presenting, should help you to feel confident. Also remember that your audience are willing you to do well – nobody wants to sit through a presentation feeling awkward – sometimes presenters can forget that the audience are on their side, interested to hear what you have to share.

HOW SHOULD YOU GO ABOUT PLANNING YOUR PRESENTATION?

When thinking about how to plan your presentation, there are three key elements to bear in mind. Consider the story you are telling, your audience and (if appropriate) your co-presenters.

Think About the Story You Are Telling

It can be helpful to think about a presentation as a story you are telling. That doesn't mean that you should begin with 'once upon a time...' but it does mean that you should think about how your presentation, just like a story, has a beginning, a middle and an end. Hall (2013) suggests that it's important to think about presentations as stories rather than 'a deck of disconnected slides' (p. 39). He also argues that, rather than start at the beginning, instead start at the end with what you would like your final point to be, and then work backwards to plan how you are going to lead up to it. Your final point might be your argument, as we considered in Chapter 14 (*Forming your argument*).

Whereas in written work you may have a vast amount of words to get your point, or argument, across, and you also know that your reader can take breaks to digest what you are saying, in a presentation you have a much more limited amount of words and time; a 10-minute presentation is likely to be around 1200–1500 words. That means if you are converting a longer written piece into an oral presentation, you need to be very mindful of the key elements of your research story. Be prepared to cut out content that is superfluous and to repeat the key messages that you don't want the audience to miss.

And although your story won't end with 'and they all lived happily ever after', it is important that your presentation has a strong ending. Moore (2010, p. 165) reminds presenters to 'take control of the ending by ending with something memorable, like 'a powerful visual or convincing conclusion'. Similarly, your presentation should start with conviction and reassure your audience that you are in control; that means ignoring any latecomers and starting with a positive, affirming greeting and remembering to introduce yourself and the title of your presentation.

Think About Your Audience

When you are planning your presentation, it's important to think about who your audience are. Smale and Fowlie (2006) argue that doing this can help you pitch your presentation by ensuring that you are 'neither insulting their intelligence nor assuming too much prior knowledge' (p. 169). They suggest spending a few minutes thinking who your audience are, what they need to know (i.e. the ending of your story) and what you expect them to know already. It can also be helpful to think about how long you think you can capture their attention for. If you are presenting to children, the time you have got to get your main messages across while still holding their attention is likely to be much less than that of an adult audience.

Also think about your audience in terms of how you ensure it is inclusive. This means asking yourself questions such as:

- If you have images on your slide deck, are they representative of people of different ethnicities, races, ages and other protected characteristics?
- Have you thought about how accessible the visual presentation of your slide deck is for people who may benefit from a large font size or clear, contrasting colours?
- Have you considered facilitating subtitles on your presentation software, so that audience members who may benefit from reading what you are saying can follow along?

Think About Your Co-Presenters

Sometimes you might be presenting individually, but other times you might be presenting as a group. If this is the case, preparing together is absolutely key. While it is natural that you may want to divide up who has responsibility for which section of the presentation (or slides, if you are using a slide deck as a visual aid), preparing together ensures that there is consistency across your presentation. It also ensures that, if one person in the group is unexpectedly unwell or simply loses their train of thought, another member of the group can seamlessly step in and the audience is none the wiser that things haven't gone exactly to plan.

When thinking about your audience, what they want to see in group presentations is that the group truly are presenting as a group, rather than a series of individuals with little continuity or consistency. Here is a checklist that you can complete with your group to ensure that you are fully prepared for presenting in a coherent and seamless manner.

Do you know…

- Where each person is going to sit or stand to deliver, so that the group are in a logical order for the audience to follow?
- Who will be responsible for any visual aids, such as changing the slide changing the slide, if you are using a slide deck?
- Who is going to deliver what content?
- How will each group member know when it's their turn to start talking?
- Who is going to be responsible for ensuring all group members have a complete set of cue cards, so they can be ready to step in if necessary?
- Who is going to take the lead on fielding questions?
- (If your presentation is online) Who is going to take responsibility for sharing their screen?

While some people prefer group presentations because they've got 'back up' if need be, others find them difficult because it can be hard to organise times to rehearse together. Van Emden and Becker (2016) suggest that *at least* three full rehearsals are necessary, to ensure timings are correct and that each presenter's sections flow. The advantage of a group presentation is that in rehearsals group members can offer feedback on voice volume, pace and clarity. If you are doing an individual presentation, find a test audience to practise in front of so they can give advice on these elements. Cottrell (2024, p. 196) suggests asking your test audience to reflect on questions such as:

- What worked best?
- Did the main message come across clearly?
- Did anything sound confused or hard to understand?
- Was anything annoying or irritating for the audience?
- Was the material presented at about the right pace?
- What, if anything, could be better about the style of presenting?

If you don't have a willing audience you can practise in front of, try video recording yourself on your phone instead. Listening back can help you identify if you need to slow down, if you need to be mindful of using filler words like 'um' or 'err' or if you need to take care that your body language remains approachable through your use of eye contact and maintaining an open posture.

Activity 15.2   Presentation Rehearsal Checklist

As well as responding to Cottrell's (2024) questions, it can be useful to give your test audience a checklist of things to look out for. Have a think back to the presentations that you've seen that didn't quite hit the mark. These might have been presentations you've seen in person or watched online. Think about the behaviours that you observed that you don't want to replicate and have a go at creating a checklist for your test audience to assess your presentation rehearsal against.

Reflection

Sometimes we've watched presentations in the past where we've become disengaged because the presenter only read from their notes, or the slides were too cluttered, or didn't make eye contact with the audience. We would add these elements to a presentation rehearsal checklist, so that our test audience could let us know if they observed any behaviours we think are best avoided. Here is an example of what a presentation rehearsal checklist might look like.

Did you feel that…

- The presenter spent too much time looking down at their notes?
- The slides were too cluttered/unclear?
- The presenter didn't give enough eye contact?
- The presenter's body language could be more approachable?

PRESENTING TOP TIPS

There are several steps you can take to ensure that your presentation is as strong as it can be. These include making sure you practise, considering your visual aids and reflecting on good presentations you've seen before.

Practice Makes Permanent

The best way to ensure your presentation is successful is to make sure you have practised extensively throughout. We have already considered having rehearsals with a test audience, but before you get to that point it is important to practise by yourself, too.

Although it can be tempting to practise in your head, you need to do it out loud to ensure your timings are accurate and so that you can refine your pace, pitch and passion. If you are planning on presenting standing up, then stand up to practise, too. If you are using a slide deck and have the opportunity to practise somewhere that has an electronic whiteboard or projector, take advantage of trialling your slides on a big screen to check that the text is big enough and easy to read and that images don't appear pixelated.

Part of practising also means considering your 'Plan B's. If you are feeling worried, doing this can be particularly useful to think about what exactly it might be that you are worried about and what you would do if you encountered that scenario. Often students tell us that they are worried about things such as:

- A technical issue on their computer
- Losing their train of thought or their mind going blank
- Being asked a question they can't answer
- Missing some information out.

Take a moment to have a think about what 'Plan B' you would advise a student to put in place if they encountered one of the above scenarios. You might suggest something along the lines of:

- Having the presentation saved in more than one location, such as on an email as well as on a USB stick. Also have a hard copy printed out so the presenter can refer to it even if the audience isn't able to see it.
- Having cue cards with brief bullet points of the key elements that the presenter wants to remember to refer to. Ideally make these small (i.e. not much bigger than a credit card) and made of card rather than paper, so that if your hands get a bit shaky the distraction of your notes wobbling is minimised for the audience. Use colour to distinguish your points if you find that helpful and write any difficult pronunciations phonetically so you can say them with confidence.
- Responding to tricky questions with something along the lines of 'That's a good question' and pausing to allow yourself some time (perhaps up to ten seconds) to think about your response. If your presentation is being assessed then, as in any form of examination, you will need to respond with your best answer even if you don't feel 100% confident about it. If your presentation is not for assessment purposes then it is acceptable to acknowledge that you will need to give the question some thought and you could invite the audience member to contact you via email for a follow up conversation when you've considered your response. McMillan and Weyers (2006) suggest that when you are preparing, you spend some time anticipating what questions people might ask. They also suggest it is good practice to repeat the question for the benefit of other audience members who may not have heard it (which also gives you some extra

thinking time) and they say it is fine to ask for clarification if you didn't understand the question.

- Not dwelling on it too much if you miss information out. It is really easy to miss information out, either because nerves get the better of you or because the presentation topic is so familiar to you that you forget that the audience are not as well informed about your study as you are. If you realise you have missed out something important, it might be appropriate to say something like 'And to clarify, I must mention that...' But if you have missed out something fairly inconsequential, just keep going and perhaps make a mental note that it is something you might want to refer to if you are asked any questions afterwards. It will make the audience feel more relaxed and more confident with your presentation if they have the sense that everything is going to plan, even if it is not.

You might have other things that you are worried about, or other Plan B strategies to counter the problems we have suggested. Writing these down, perhaps as a table, can be a concrete way of addressing any worries you have and can provide reassurance that if something doesn't go as planned, you have thought about what steps you can take. If you are taking part in a group presentation then do this as a group – you might find that some members have other strategies or feel more confident at overcoming some problems than others. But something we would really like to reiterate is that the audience doesn't know what they don't know – if you don't highlight to them that something hasn't gone to plan, most of the time they will be none the wiser. So, although it can be natural to say something like 'Oh, I've forgotten to say...' or 'Oh that wasn't supposed to happen', keep it to yourself. In that way your audience will have more confidence about what you are delivering and can feel more relaxed as they listen to your presentation. (You can always tell them afterwards if you need to get it off your chest!)

Consider Your Visual Aids

Visual aids are a great way to support both you as the presenter and the audience as well to engage in oral presentations. We've seen them take both traditional and less traditional forms:

- A slide deck, such as a PowerPoint presentation
- A poster (you'll consider how to share your research through a poster in Chapter 16: *Using posters to share your research*)
- A cereal box (!) filled with cards with key points on, which the audience were invited to pick out for the presenter to elaborate on
- Online polling tools such as Mentimeter, which allow the audience to interact through responding to your questions
- Pre-prepared flipcharts

When thinking about how to use visual aids effectively, the important thing to remember is that they are intended to *aid* (i.e. help or assist) you, rather than replace you or dominate. This is something echoed by Van Emden and Becker (2016), who argue that 'visual aid fatigue is a recognised modern phenomenon: too many speakers either think they can get away with lots of well-prepared visuals and not much real content or they want to "entertain" their audience ... by showing all the many clever things that PowerPoint can do' (p. 35). Alternatively, you might have heard of people refer to 'death by PowerPoint', which is the idea that lengthy, unengaging PowerPoint presentations can cause one's untimely demise. So, to ensure that visual aids help rather than hinder, here are some strategies to bear in mind:

- Ensure that your visual aids don't do your talking for you. There's no point repeating in-depth the information that your aids already share; use them as signposts, to reiterate key points or provide links to literature instead.
- Make sure that your audience's attention isn't constantly being split between you and your visual aids. That means making sure they aren't too wordy and giving them time to take in information on them before diverting their attention back to you.
- Provide handouts or reassure your audience at the start if the visual aids will be made available to them electronically, so that the audience can take in what you are saying without having to focus on making copious notes.
- Ensure that they don't distract the audience by containing errors or typos that take the audience's focus away from what you are saying or contradict the points you are making.
- Use them to showcase things that you want to highlight without saying out loud, such as how what you are saying links to literature or by including models, images or photographs that are difficult to explain in words.

Think Back to Presentations You've Seen Before

One exercise we like to do with students when talking about presentations is to encourage them to make a list of some of the best presentations they have ever been in the audience for and note down what made them memorable. Doing this can help you identify strategies for successful presentations that you may be able to adopt but also help you think about what it was about those strategies that you may be able to replicate. We've had a think about some of the features of the best presentations we've seen, and why we liked them, whether they were at conferences, online seminars or as assessed student work. Table 15.2 illustrates some of our top presentation moments.

Table 15.2 Top presentation techniques we've observed

What was the presentation strategy?	Why was it effective?
The presenter took off his watch and held it, glancing at it very occasionally to ensure that he kept to time.	It put the audience at ease that the presenter was in control and understood the importance of timekeeping.
The presenter asked the audience to put their hand up if she said something that wasn't clear or needed further expansion.	It demonstrated that the presenter had the audience's needs in mind and was prepared and able to elaborate on the points she was making.
The presenter had one small cue card per slide with key words on to prompt their memory, which they looked at occasionally.	It ensured that the presenter remembered the key points but did not enable them to 'read from a script' and encouraged them to look up and engage with their audience.
The presenter referred to seminal authors using their first name, i.e. 'As Chris Athey's work on schemas illustrates...'	It reassured the audience that the presenter had an in-depth level of knowledge and implied a respectful tone to the people she was citing.
The presenter had prepared a slide deck which looked professional, was attractive, accurate and contained citations.	The strong visual presentation helped keep the audience on track and engaged and demonstrated to them the effort that the presenter had devoted to preparation.
The presenter carried on presenting despite the fact that the computer froze and she was unable to use her visual aids.	It made the audience feel reassured that the presenter had sufficiently prepared and thus could weather things not going to plan.

Do you notice anything in particular from why the presentation strategies we've noted in Table 15.2 were effective? They all take the audience into account. The strategies that you put in place for your presentation will depend on who your audience are, but whoever your audience, it is important to think about what they might want from your presentation and how you can provide that.

Activity 15.3 Thinking About the Best Presentations You've Seen

Think about the best presentations you've seen in the past. They can have been in an academic or non-academic environment, either face-to-face or online. Have a go at identifying what the presentation strategies were that you enjoyed, and what it was about them that made the presentation successful.

Reflection

The strategies you've identified will depend on the presentations that you've seen in the past. If you haven't had much experience in watching other people's presentations before, looking online, perhaps at TED Talks, is a good way to observe other people's presentation techniques.

Case Study 15.1 Disseminating Research to a Wider Audience

Ade has finished his undergraduate dissertation, which explored how childminders perceive the role of a key person. He has begun thinking about how he can share his study as an oral presentation to disseminate his main messages and a local childminder hub offers for him to do a 10-minute presentation plus questions at their next meeting.

Ade thinks carefully about who his audience are, what they will already know and what he would like them to know by the end of his presentation. He decides to create a PowerPoint as a visual aid to help scaffold him through the presentation and act as signposts for his audience to follow what he is saying. In advance he rehearses in front of a trusted friend several times and asks for constructive feedback, comes up with a list of questions he thinks he might get asked afterwards as well as a list of things he is nervous about and what his Plan B would be for different scenarios.

On the day he feels a little bit anxious, but he takes some big deep breaths before-hand and speaks to his audience with confidence and clarity. His presentation is well-received and most of the audience's questions he has already prepared for. He leaves feeling a sense of accomplishment and proud to have disseminated his research to more people.

KEY POINTS FROM THE CHAPTER

- Oral presentations can be an effective way to share your research findings, particularly because they can help challenge the power imbalance between those disseminating knowledge and those listening to it, because it can help you to have an active role in continuing a research conversation and because you can demonstrate a different skillset to that utilised within a written report.
- It is key to think about who your audience are when presenting. Bear in mind what you think they might know, what you think they might want to know and how you can ensure you are meeting their needs in terms of accessibility. Offer them the opportunity to ask questions to ensure you are valuing their comments and contributions and providing any clarification they may need.
- It can be useful to reflect upon presentations that you've seen before that you found impactful; think about what it was that made them effective and how you could bear that in mind when planning your own presentations.

FURTHER READING

1   Van Emden and Becker's (2016) book for students about presenting gives some really useful guidance on delivering presentations, including thinking about your voice and non-verbal communication as well as developing and using visual aids:

Van Emden, J. and Becker, L. (2016) *Presentation Skills for Students*. London: Bloomsbury.

2   Theobald's (2022) book about presenting skills goes into a lot of helpful depth about delivering an effective presentation:

Theobald, T. (2022) *Develop Your Presenting Skills: How to Inspire and Inform with Clarity and Confidence*. 5th Edition. London: Kogan Page.

REFERENCES

Bolshaw, P. and Josephidou, J. (2018) *Introducing Research in Early Childhood*. London: Sage.

Cottrell, S. (2024) *The Study Skills Handbook*. 6th Edition. London: Bloomsbury Publishing.

Hall, R. (2013) *Brilliant Presentation: What the Best Presenters Know, Do and Say*. 3rd Edition. Harlow: Prentice Hall.

McMillan, K. and Weyers, J. (2006) *The Smarter Student: Skills and Strategies for Success at University*. Harlow: Pearson Education Ltd.

Moore, S. (2010) *The Ultimate Study Skills Handbook*. Berkshire: Open University Press.

Smale, B. and Fowlie, J. (2006) *How to Succeed at University; An Essential Guide to Academic Skills and Personal Development*. London: Sage.

Theobald, T. (2022) *Develop Your Presenting Skills: How to Inspire and Inform with Clarity and Confidence*. 5th Edition. London: Kogan Page.

Van Emden, J. and Becker, L. (2016) *Presentation Skills for Students*. London: Bloomsbury.

Wallwork, A. (2020) *100 Tips to Avoid Mistakes in Academic Writing and Presenting*. Cham, Switzerland: Springer.

16

USING POSTERS TO SHARE YOUR RESEARCH

CHAPTER OBJECTIVES

By the end of this chapter, you will:

- Understand how posters can be used to disseminate research findings
- Understand how different posters can be used to reach a variety of audiences, including children
- Know how posters can address power issues in terms of research dissemination
- Know how to put a range of posters together.

INTRODUCTION

In Chapter 15 (*Disseminating your research through a presentation*) we thought about different ways you could share your research work through a presentation. We will build on this knowledge here and discuss how a research poster is a tried and tested way of sharing research findings, sometimes accompanied by a presentation although not always. We will consider different audiences and the ways that a poster can be tailored to meet their information and engagement needs in an accessible way, whether that be at academic conferences, in the workplace, in the home as a parent and, importantly, as a child. The chapter will explore how posters may be one of the most inclusive ways to disseminate research findings to mitigate against power issues that exist in terms of who has access to knowledge.

ACADEMIC RESEARCH POSTERS

Melchiori, Upadhyay and Blankenship, (2024) suggest that there are many advantages for a student in learning to put together a conference poster, including developing 'technological expertise' (p. 1). This section of the chapter will set out exactly what academic research conference posters are, the types of features they include, how they differ from a written report, and why they are particularly effective in disseminating research findings.

The Academic Poster

Attend any conference and there will be at least one session that contains posters. Attendees are invited to submit a poster of their research in the same way that they are invited to submit an application to present. As part of your studies, you may also have been required to submit an academic poster as one of your assessments – sometimes this might not be to give a full overview of your project but rather to set out your proposal or your literature review either before the project begins or is completed. In essence, the research poster builds on the idea of the Three Minute Thesis that we discussed in Chapter 14 (*Forming your argument*); it is a way of quickly, clearly and effectively getting over your ideas to an audience, non-specialist or otherwise. In much the same way as the Three Minute Thesis model, it is also an effective way for you to gain clarity on what you are trying to do with your project. Clarity is the key word here – it is not about your work being fancy, or eye catching. Yes, there is an element of aesthetics, but this is only one element. The overall look of the poster shouldn't distract from the clear message it is trying to communicate.

If you put the term 'academic posters' into a search engine, you will find lots of results most often linked to university academic skills pages, so we can see that designing a poster is a key academic skill, and we would argue a transferable graduate skill, which universities feel it is important to teach. For example, Newcastle University, on their page dedicated to this form of research presentation, explain:

> Academic posters are a visual form of communicating academic research, projects or literature reviews that often combine elements of text, diagrams and other media to convey ideas as effectively as possible… Academic posters are usually presented at conferences, exhibitions or networking events and you may be expected to accompany the poster to discuss your work, answer questions and provide additional information. (Newcastle University, n.d.)

Key Features

The key features that should be included on an academic poster will depend on its purpose and type. We will discuss here the kinds of features you would expect to see on a conventional academic poster viewed at a conference and then also posters that you may be asked to put together as a piece of assessment.

Conventional

A conventional academic poster of the type you will see presented at conferences will include all the elements of your dissertation or research report although in a much more condensed form so that you have picked out the key elements that you want to convey. This means it will include something about:

- The context of your work
- The problem you are trying to address, including the research question
- A very brief overview of the relevant literature, i.e. so you may just include the key themes
- A brief overview of the data collection methods
- A summing up of the findings
- A summing up of the discussion with one or two implications; the latter could even be added as questions to show what needs to happen next in research
- Use of different fonts and colour to guide the reader's eye around the poster
- Some images to illustrate the points made or as provocations for the reader.

In essence, if you submit a poster to a research conference you are doing an informal presentation using a poster instead of a slide deck. We have seen this is an effective way to communicate your work. What usually happens is that all posters are set up in one large room; at indicated times, the author of the poster will be there to answer questions or interact with their strolling audience. This is done in a relaxed manner and can lead to rich conversations and important networking opportunities.

Assessed Piece of Work

If, on the other hand, your academic poster is for an assessed piece of work, there will be specific criteria and assignment guidelines you will need to address. However, we can discuss here examples we have seen which we hope are helpful: (1) the literature review and (2) the research proposal.

1   Literature review

Often students can be required to submit for assessment a poster which sets out the relevant background literature to their work. This is seen as a useful introductory step in the intended research project. This can be quite a daunting prospect as it requires doing a lot of reading and then condensing that reading into something that will fit on a poster. It is such a useful activity to undertake though as not only does it mean you end up with effectively what is an essay plan for the literature review of your report, with many of your useful literature sources collected in one place, but this activity is part of the important work of refining your research question. In terms of thinking about where to start, we would suggest looking at the key words you have used here and then they can be your search terms – but do look back at the advice we gave in Chapter 4 (*Joining a research conversation*).

You may want to begin by just using the abstracts for finding the key messages and/or arguments of the papers you have found in your literature search. There is no need at this point, we would suggest, to read all the paper unless you need further clarification or if you end up with very few papers due to the focus you are interested in. You may like to draw out three key ideas from the literature to form the foundations of your poster. Our advice would be don't try to do too much or your clarity will be lost, and it will be very difficult to add lots of information to a poster. There is nothing worse than a poster with far too much text on – especially if the author of the poster has reduced the font size to make sure that they can fit everything on. In the same way, you don't want to include lots of quotations as they will take up valuable space and might show a lack of criticality in that you are demonstrating you have nothing to say so must use the work of others; perhaps you might use one powerful quotation at the centre to foreground the problem or why the proposed research is important.

Of course, just as in an academic piece of writing, it is important that all sources are referenced properly. An extensive reference list, although to be commended, can use up valuable space on the poster so check with your tutor and the specific guidance about how this should be included, for example, we have seen it attached to the back of the poster or even included as a separate handout. As you consider the layout of your poster, this is a good opportunity for you to see what kinds of sources you are drawing on and to check you don't have too many webpages. For some reason, we have noted in the past that students can include these much more frequently on an academic poster than they would in an essay or report. Such easily accessible webpages would be appropriate if the poster was for a lay audience, i.e. parents or practitioners; however, for an academic poster it is important to show how you are joining a research conversation by drawing on peer-reviewed journal articles.

2   *Research proposal*

Another common type of assessment is the requirement to set out the research proposal in the form of a poster. This should include sections on all the important elements:

- The context
- The problem
- The research question
- Brief overview of the literature
- Proposed methodology/methods
- Ethical issues

How Are Posters Different From a Written Report?

Let's return here to the conventional academic poster seen at conferences where the researcher is usually setting out a completed piece of work. You may be wondering why a researcher would choose to do this rather than presenting to a group of people with a slide deck. In fact, we would say it achieves a very different purpose such as:

- A poster supports the researcher's own understanding; we talked about the stage of messiness in Chapter 14 (*Forming your argument*), putting together a poster is a way of pulling all your thinking together and distilling your thoughts into something important that you can easily share.

- A poster supports much richer conversations with those who have sought your work out because they want to talk to you about it.
- A poster supports the development of ideas; we have all been in presentations that have not necessarily been supportive of audience interaction and therefore extending thinking, i.e. the presenter is against the clock trying to get over as much information as possible.
- The poster allows much deeper, targeted conversations.

So, we can see from the above bullet points why a poster presentation can be particularly effective.

Activity 16.1   A Literature Review Poster

Priya is required to put together an academic poster for the end of her level 5 studies, in preparation for carrying out her dissertation work the following year. Along with some student colleagues, they decide to get together to discuss how they might go about this most effectively. They all share their draft research question and then help each other refine it. Priya's question is developed into the following: 'What are reception teachers' perspectives on working with parents to support young children's (aged 4 to 5 years) social and emotional development?' The group decide that they will underline the key words in their question and organise their poster around these. What advice would you give Priya in terms of organising the layout of her poster if you were in this peer group?

Reflection

Priya found this activity helpful in deciding how to set out her poster and the reading she needed to do to prepare for it. She underlined the key terms in her question: What are reception teachers' perspectives on *working with parents* to support young children's (aged 4 to 5 years) *social and emotional development*? She knew that often social development and emotional development can be lumped together but decided to first look at them separately before looking at the connections. For these three key areas, she noted that certain themes were appearing regularly in the articles she reviewed. These were:

- Social development: the role of the media; importance of animals; issues of social withdrawal
- Emotional development: the important role of creativity; developing empathy; emotion regulation
- Working with parents: listening to parents; parents as educators; the unique parent.

(Continued)

She then considered how she wanted to reference the context of her research at the top of her poster, including how the Covid lockdown had had a negative impact on children's social and emotional development. At the bottom of her poster she added her research question, so it was clear that her reading of the literature had informed it. Her draft poster design looked something like this:

Title: Working with parents to support social and emotional development		
Social	Working with parents	Emotional development
Add an image here	*Add an image here*	*Add an image here*
• Role of media • Animals • Social withdrawal	• Listening to parents • Parents as educators • The unique parent	• Creativity • Empathy • Emotion regulation
Research Question: What are reception teachers' perspectives on working with parents to support young children's (4 to 5 years) social and emotional development?		

Figure 16.1 Priya's poster design

OTHER KINDS OF POSTERS FOR DISSEMINATING RESEARCH

In the above section, we looked at putting together an academic poster whether that be for a conference or an assessment. However, as we discussed in Chapter 15 (*Disseminating your research through a presentation*) there are many audiences you might like to share your findings with such as children, parents, participants or other stakeholders. Also discussed in Chapter 15 is the importance of doing it in a way that is meaningful and useful to them. So, in this section of the chapter, we are going to think about these different audiences and the diverse ways in which posters can be tailored to meet their needs in an inclusive way, including in the workplace. As we have suggested, posters may be one of the most inclusive ways to disseminate research findings to overcome the power issues that exist in terms of who has access to knowledge, so here, we will look at:

- Who (is the audience)
- What (is useful to them)
- Where (is this information best shared)

Who

If we think about Priya's work in Activity 16.1, and imagine that her project is now complete and she has some interesting findings, who might she like to share them with? She has an opportunity to share at her university student research conference, but she is also concerned to share with as wide an audience as possible. She makes a list and comes up with the following:

- Children
- Parents
- Teachers and teaching assistants in her school

What

Thinking about what to share was a little more complicated and depended on Priya being able to translate her findings into a non-specialist language for an audience of a range of ages. She also realised that she didn't need to tell all the findings to everyone, just the specific findings that would be useful to each type of audience. She began by focusing on who her audience is and what she wanted to share with them. She also considered her reasons for doing so and collected her thoughts in Table 16.1.

Table 16.1 Considering which findings to share

Who	What	Reason
Children	How to support children who may be shy Empathy Emotion regulation	To enable children to support their peers and have strategies to regulate their own emotions.
Parents	Role of media Creativity Empathy Emotion regulation	To make parents aware of the impact of the media on their child's socio-emotional development, to make parents aware of the importance of creative activity in developing both socially and emotionally, to support parents in developing empathy and emotion regulation in their children.
Teachers and teaching assistants	Animals Supporting children who are shy Listening to parents Parents as educators The unique parent Creativity Empathy Emotion regulation	To make teachers and teaching staff aware of the role of animals in supporting very shy children, to make educators aware of other strategies to use with these children, to offer teachers and teaching staff strategies for active listening with parents, to encourage teachers to plan for creativity to support socio-emotional development, to give teachers strategies to support children with developing empathy and emotional regulation.

Where

The third consideration was where Priya should share these findings.

Children

Priya made a poster which would appeal to children using characters from their favourite television programme. The poster contained just a few key statements and each point was illustrated. The poster was shared with the children during circle time and then it was put up in the classroom for both children and adults to refer to. Two unexpected consequences were that the children became part of the dissemination process because (a) they brought their parents in to see the poster and tell them about it and (b) they extended the message of the original poster by making their own and sticking them up around the classroom.

Parents

The parents' poster had a clear title 'How can I support my child socially and emotionally?' and then was organised around three key questions that parents often asked the teachers:

- Why does my child still have tantrums?
- Why is my child so shy?
- I am worried my child doesn't have many friends, what should I do?

Each key question then had a structured response with three key points. Priya was careful not to include too much text but there was a section at the bottom that had some useful follow up reading and websites if parents wanted to find out more. There were also contact details of who the parents could talk to if they were concerned. The poster was shared at the annual parents' association who gave Priya a small pot of funding so that she could have them printed professionally and then put up in key areas around the school where parents often congregated.

Teachers/Teaching Assistants

Priya presented her academic poster to colleagues at a staff meeting to get their feedback. They thought it was useful but gave her the feedback to remove the section at the bottom where she had included the research question because this just focused on the reception class whereas they saw that these findings were of relevance regardless of age group. They suggested she use this space instead to list lots of easy access resources such as webpages. They liked the fact that in the main section of the poster she had linked the three key ideas to literature; however, they reminded her that they could not easily access peer-reviewed journal articles if they wanted to follow up. When Priya reworked the poster, she ensured that all sources cited were open access. The finished poster was put up in the staff room for the academic year, and over the year Priya noted that people continued to refer to it and ask her about it or recount some successes in their own classroom. The sharing of the poster set in motion an agreement to use this spot in the staffroom for a year's focus on what the staff agreed was a particular issue.

Activity 16.2   A Poster for Parents

You may recall Olga's project (Activity 14.3) in Chapter 14 (*Forming your argument*) about reflecting on the use of 'reading dogs' in primary school. Olga wanted to find out about dogs who went into school so that children could read to them; she sent a questionnaire to parents, interviewed three teachers and had a group interview with five children. As she thought about her findings, their implications and any recommendations she would like to make, she considered designing a poster so that she could share these with parents. She had to decide which of the findings were relevant to parents and which were not particularly important to share in this way. Remind yourself of her findings now (they are in Table 16.2) and then have a go at designing the overview poster. You could use the draft structure in Figure 16.2 if it is helpful but of course there are many ways the poster could be organised.

Table 16.2   Olga's findings, reflections and recommendations

Finding (What?)	Implication or reflection (So What?)	Recommendation (Now What?)
Some parents felt dogs were a novelty that distracted from teaching children to read properly.	Is this something about how schools communicate and work effectively with parents?	The school could look to see if they could get parents onboard by having a parent champion for this initiative.
Some teachers were nervous about dogs because they had had bad experiences in the past.	This really made me think about how initiatives can be just dumped on teachers without them having a say. We talk about the unique child in the early years but what about the unique teacher?!	More consultation perhaps with teachers, a member of staff to lead on this who really likes dogs, and a special place which is not in individual classrooms.
Some teachers weren't sure it was hygienic to have dogs in the classroom.	There could also be some cultural issues it is important to explore here.	This is about the space allocated for this activity.
Some children said they hated reading before this initiative had started.	This begs the question why? Once the novelty of the dog has worn off, will some children go back to disliking reading?	I would suggest some further research to include the children's voice about learning to read at school and what they like and don't like about it.
Not all the children got a turn with the dog, especially if they were doing well at reading.	This is interesting – so the children were punished for being good readers?	This initiative needs to be open to all children who would like to take part.

Reflection

The first thing that Olga did was to highlight all the findings that she believed parents would want to know about. For example, she felt that teachers' concerns were not relevant to share. So, she designed her poster around four distinct areas as you can see in her draft design (see Figure 16.3):

(Continued)

Section 1:		
Section 2	Section 3	Section 4
Section 5:		

Figure 16.2 Draft poster design

Section 1: An eye-catching title, e.g. Everything you want to know about reading dogs in school		
Section 2 The benefits for children (This was based on her findings and also some of the literature)	Section 3 How to get involved (This section contained information about being a champion, creating a space, organising the initiative)	Section 4 Children's thoughts (This section included anonymised quotations from the children involved)
Section 5: If you want to find out more…. (Lots of sources listed here so that parents could do some follow up reading)		

Figure 16.3 Olga's draft design

One unexpected consequence was that a parent, on reading the poster and finding out more about the initiative, contacted the local paper who further disseminated the work by writing up an article on it. Other schools in the local area read the article and then contacted Olga to find out more about the initiative.

THE PRACTICALITIES

We have looked at poster content but what about the practicalities of putting together a poster; where should you begin? As we have already mentioned, most universities have online guidance so let's have a look here at some from the University of Staffordshire (n.d.).

They suggest that the following steps need to be taken:

1   First identify the poster content: What is the main message you want to get over and what are the key points that come from this main message? Who is your audience and what do they need to know? Perhaps not all your findings will be relevant to them.
2   Next, design the poster layout: Think about if and how you are going to use images, diagrams, figures and text. Consider also where you want your reader to begin reading and where your poster should 'end' and if that matters. Make sure that the 'story' of your research flows. Think carefully about font style, size and the colours that will best get your key message over,
3   Produce the poster: We will have a look at how you can do this a little further on in this section. You will need to think about which online tools you would like to use to help you.
4   Polish your poster: You need to make sure that you have proofread carefully and that the layout you have chosen will support your reader's engagement.

(Adapted from University of Staffordshire, n.d.)

What Online Tools Can I Use?

There are many online resources that can help you with both designing and producing your poster. Long gone are the days of cutting and sticking – you can have a polished poster without it costing too much money. For example, often people will use PowerPoint to design their poster and there are numerous videos and guides online of how to do this. You will also see various AI options online to help you design your poster – if you decide to go down this route, make sure you are allowed if it is for an assessed piece or if there are conference guidelines. For example, conference guidelines will often insist that any use of AI throughout the research process is transparent. As a poster is often part of the dissemination stage then the author would need to be transparent about this. We pick up this discussion further in Chapter 18 (*Conclusion*).

Where Should I Have My Poster Printed?

There are lots of services online where you can upload your poster and then they will print for you and post back. There are a variety of prices to select from; ones we noticed were the equivalent of two cups of coffee. Most universities will also have print services on campus who will very probably offer reduced rates for their own students. The most important thing is not to leave the printing until too late so that you become rushed and make mistakes.

Where Can I Present My Poster?

You may at this point feel quite enthusiastic about putting together a poster but at the same time are wondering that if you did so where you would have opportunity to share it. Many universities now have student conferences where you can display a poster even online. Then there are a variety of undergraduate conferences such as the BCUR (British Conference of Undergraduate Research). This conference 'is the biggest conference in the UK dedicated to celebrating undergraduate research' (BCUR25, n.d.) and is open to all. One criticism of academic conferences is the cost to attend, which is paid both by attendees and those presenting. The BCUR tries to keep its price at an affordable level for students and some universities will offer funding to allow selected students to attend although this can be very competitive.

Then there are the one-day conferences such as the BECERA (British Early Childhood Education Research Association) conference, established over 15 years ago, which attracts both academics and professionals who work with young children and offers excellent networking opportunities. There are also online conferences where you are able to submit an electronic copy of your poster which will then be included in a gallery which is presented over the course of the day. Often these conferences can be free to attend and of course require no travel so they can be a good option for students.

Case Study 16.1 Designing a Poster for a Conference

Nina is an Early Childhood student who was studying a module which focused on listening to children. She decided to adapt one of her assignments and turn it into an academic poster to present at the BECERA (British Early Childhood Education Research Association) conference. She felt it was important to share her work as 'regardless of where we are on the academic journey, whether undergraduate, postgraduate or beyond, we are all researchers and thus should be willing to share our findings with others as long as they are valid' (Taylor, 2025). Her poster explored the use of the 'Magic Carpet' (Clark and Moss, 2001) to listen to children and involved two young children and photographs of the local area. Nina enjoyed the process of putting together the poster because it allowed her to tell the story of her research using both text and visuals in a concise and engaging way to highlight key points that she wanted to emphasise. The thing she found more problematic was trying to get a balance between text and photos and ensuring that the layout was organised effectively so that the photos used married up with the information presented. As she reflected on the process, she noted that in comparison to a research paper or PowerPoint presentation, a poster is limited as far as the amount of information it can convey; thus, it was important to ensure that the information included did indeed support the key findings and that, as with any research presentation, it must contain evidence for the claims it was making. When Nina presented her poster at the conference, she greatly enjoyed the opportunity to talk about her project with other people in a more informal but extremely supportive context. All the posters at the conference were displayed in a room that participants could explore at their leisure and thus it provided the ideal platform for sharing knowledge and engaging in discussions with peers but without the pressure of addressing a whole roomful of people, as in the case of formal presentations. As such, she felt that it allowed less experienced and less confident researchers the opportunity to disseminate their work, alongside other highly respected academics, thus promoting a more inclusive environment.

KEY POINTS FROM THE CHAPTER

- Posters are a method often used to disseminate research findings including at academic conferences.
- Posters can be adapted to disseminate findings to a variety of audiences.
- Using posters can be supportive in terms of addressing power imbalances in research and who has access to knowledge.
- They allow the researcher's 'story' to be told in a way that includes both text and images.
- There are a variety of spaces both physical and online where undergraduate students can disseminate their work.

FURTHER READING

1   As we have mentioned there are many university webpages that offer good advice on how to put together an academic poster. If you are still not sure where to begin, check two of our favourites, one from Newcastle University and the other from Sheffield Hallam University.

Newcastle University (n.d.) *Academic Posters*. Academic Skills Kit, Newcastle University. Available at: www.ncl.ac.uk/academic-skills-kit/assessment/assignment-types/academic-posters/ (accessed 21 July 2025).

Sheffield Hallam University (n.d.) *Research Posters*. Library Skills Centre guide, Sheffield Hallam University. Available at: https://libguides.shu.ac.uk/researchposters (accessed 21 July 2025).

2   If you would like to read a blog post by Nina whose poster was the focus of Case Study 16.1, you can read it on the BECERA website. Here she discusses the content of her poster.

Taylor, N. (2025) *Participatory action research with young children*. Available at: www.crec.co.uk/becera-posts/participatory-action-research-with-young-children (accessed 17 July 2025).

3   Another superb resource is this one from the University of York. It has a great
     section on the use of different fonts on academic posters and some useful videos.

> University of York (n.d.) *Posters with a powerful point: A practical guide to designing
> academic posters*. Available at: https://subjectguides.york.ac.uk/posters/home
> (accessed 23 July 2025).

REFERENCES

BCUR25 (n.d.) *The British Conference of Undergraduate Research*. Available at: https://
conferences.ncl.ac.uk/bcur25/ (accessed: 29 July 2025).

Clark, A. and Moss, P. (2001) *Listening to Young Children: The Mosaic Approach*. London:
National Children's Bureau.

Melchiori, K.J., Upadhyay, S.S.N. and Blankenship, B.T. (2024) 'Mentoring undergraduate
collaborators through the academic conference experience', *Scholarship of Teaching
and Learning in Psychology*. DOI: https://dx.doi.org/10.1037/stl0000393.

Newcastle University (n.d.) *Academic posters*. Available at: www.ncl.ac.uk/academic-skills-
kit/assessment/assignment-types/academic-posters/ (accessed: 18 July 2025).

Taylor, N. (2025) *Participatory action research with young children*. Available at: www.crec.
co.uk/becera-posts/participatory-action-research-with-young-children (accessed: 17
July 2025).

University of Staffordshire (n.d.) *Academic poster; things you need to know*. Available at:
https://libguides.staffs.ac.uk/assignments/poster (accessed: 21 July 2025).

17

TAKING OTHER OPPORTUNITIES FOR PUBLICATION

CHAPTER OBJECTIVES

By the end of this chapter, you will:

- Understand why it is important that you take other opportunities for publication
- Recognise who some of your potential audiences and readers are
- Consider some creative approaches to disseminating your research.

INTRODUCTION

We've considered in Chapter 15 (*Disseminating your research through a presentation*) and Chapter 16 (*Using posters to share your research*) how presentations and posters are two common ways of sharing your research, particularly when thinking about an internal audience of your university tutors and peers. Now we are going to move on to thinking about how you can take opportunities for publication that widen the reach of your study beyond that of your home institution. Can you think of ways that you might be able to do that? And who do you think it might be important to do that with?

In this chapter we will focus on why it is important to take opportunities for publication, who your potential audiences are and the ways you might go about sharing your research. We will begin by discussing how three of the most important reasons to think about dissemination are because it is ethical to share your research findings, because it can promote good practice and because it can help you strengthen your graduate skills. We will then move on to consider who your audience might be, including your participants, parents, policymakers, professionals and, of course, children. Finally, we will think about some of the ways that you might want to think about publishing your research, for instance through blog posts, student journals or in other creative ways.

At this point we want to stress that although you might be thinking of 'publications' in the traditional sense of a written report, we will discuss the importance of thinking about how your work can be shared in ways that are accessible to a wide range of people, including those who would prefer alternatives to a text-heavy document.

WHY IS IT IMPORTANT TO TAKE OPPORTUNITIES FOR PUBLICATION?

It is natural that when you have finished your piece of research and, if it's part of a university assignment, submitted it for marking, you might feel like you never want to look at it again! But it is important that you think about how to share your findings with a wider audience. There are three big reasons why you might want to do this: because it demonstrates your ethical values, because it will promote good practice and it will also help you to develop your graduate skills.

To Act Ethically

One of the reasons why it is important to take opportunities for publication is because it is an ethical thing to do. It shows your ethical commitment towards your participants and also towards your field and those within it, such as children, families and practitioners.

We will talk in more detail about disseminating directly to an audience of participants a little bit later in this chapter, but sharing your research study more broadly is a way of acting ethically to your participants. By the time you finish your study, you will have put a great deal of blood, sweat and tears into what you have produced. But it's not only you who has made it a success, your participants have also given up their time and shared their knowledge with you, which has informed your findings. It is ethical, therefore, to think about how you value your participants' contribution to your study by thinking about how your findings can be disseminated more widely. Alderson and Morrow (2020, p. 169) argue that if research findings aren't shared then participants may feel disappointed that it wasn't worth helping with the research or disheartened that the research findings will not benefit other people in the future.

The idea that findings should benefit people in the future is another reason why Alderson and Morrow (2020) say it is ethically important to disseminate. If through your Early Childhood Research you have found something that could help develop good practice, it is key to share those findings with others so they too can develop their work with young children. This is something that the British Educational Research Association (BERA) say in their ethical guidelines. They state that 'researchers have a responsibility to make the results of their research available for the benefit of educational professionals, policymakers and the wider public' (2024, p. 30). Imagine how you might feel otherwise, if you knew someone had knowledge about how your work with young children could be developed but they'd chosen not to share it? However, there are some caveats outlined by BERA of disseminating research findings. For instance, if a study has findings that may reinforce stereotypes about a group of people, care should be taken when the findings are reported so it doesn't lead to discrimination, particularly of marginalised groups.

To Promote Good Practice

In Chapter 1 (*What is research in Early Childhood and why does it matter?*) we thought about why research in Early Childhood is carried out. One of the things that we spoke about was how research is conducted to have an impact on policy and practice. When you have read pieces of research you might have seen how authors talk about what potential impact they think their research might have, which is often referred to as 'implications'. We discussed this in Chapter 14 (*Forming your argument*) when we encouraged you to think about the 'So What?' of your research. These are typically presented after the researcher has shared and discussed their findings. They are not always explicitly referred to as 'implications', however. Powell and Goouch (2012, p. 124) instead talk about 'how things might be different' in their research study about the narratives of those who work in baby rooms in Early Childhood settings and how they are often disempowered and oppressed by the 'multiple voices [who] exert an influence over baby room practice' (p. 113). In their study specifically, the way in which things might be different is that if babyroom practitioners have opportunities to engage in critical professional dialogue, this may support them to feel empowered. By sharing your research, you are introducing to others 'how things might be different' in positive ways that may impact on the field.

To Develop Your Graduate Skills

Finally, it is important for you personally because disseminating your research can help you build your graduate skills. In particular, thinking about how you can translate your research findings from what might be a traditional dissertation-style report so that they are accessible and relevant to a wide range of audiences will help you develop your communication skills.

Publishing your research study findings can also be a valuable thing to do in terms of your employability. You can introduce potential graduate employers to your research publications via your CV, who may be eager to see that you are taking an active role in sharing your knowledge with the sector. Graduates should also think about taking opportunities to network with members of their sector through professional social media channels such as LinkedIn; sharing links to your research publications via your online platforms is another valuable way of showcasing your graduate skills and contribution to the sector to potential employers.

Activity 17.1   Responding to a Well-Meaning Friend

One of your friends has sent you the following message about why you are still focussing on your research project even though you've submitted your work for assessment. Write a response.

> Hi, how are you doing? Bethia mentioned that you are still focusing on your dissertation research even though you submitted last month. She said something about re-writing it!? For other people to read!? I know you've been stressing about finding a job – I mean this kindly, but I think it's time to put the dissertation to bed and focus on getting some work experience instead. Best wishes, Dominika

Reflection

You may have written something like this:

> Hi Dominika, good to hear from you. So you've been talking to Bethia! I understand your concern but it's important to me that I think about how I can share my research with a wider audience, because my Early Childhood practitioner participants spent a lot of time and energy sharing their perspectives and observations on children's sleeping routines in the Early Childhood settings and I want to make sure their effort doesn't go to waste. And I actually think this might help me get a job – employers want to see evidence of my transferable skills like written communication, creativity, taking the initiative and professionalism and the different ways that I'm planning to disseminate my findings to practitioners, parents and setting managers will be good evidence of this. Thanks for keeping an eye on me though – coffee catch-up soon?

You might want to extend this activity by making a list of graduate skills and thinking about how disseminating your study can support in building and evidencing these.

WHO IS YOUR AUDIENCE?

When thinking about taking opportunities for publication, it is important to bear in mind what audience you want to target, as this may inform the approach you take to sharing your findings. We think there are three key audiences you should consider: your participants, other interested adults (who we are referring to as the 3 Ps: parents, professionals and policymakers), and finally, of course, children.

Your Participants

It can be easy for researchers to spend a lot of time thinking about and interacting with their participants when they are seeking ethical approval, devising their data collection tools and collecting their data, but then once the participants have completed their surveys or taken part in their interviews, they no longer become the researcher's primary focus. In many cases, after the data collection the researcher no longer has any contact with the participants at all. And this is fine if the participants no longer want any ongoing contact. But in terms of your ethical values, it is important to think about how your relationship with your participants might continue.

As part of gaining ethical approval, it is likely that you will have set out how you will share your research findings with your participants and may have informed them of how you plan to do this when you sought their consent. Smith (2011, p. 22) talks about the ethical obligation to disseminate directly to your participants, and how 'an important and challenging part of ethical research is the fulfilment of an obligation to ensure that participants have the opportunity to hear about findings of research'. She also talks about how it is important to acknowledge the role that the participants have played in the study by giving them access to the research outputs. This is supported by the Ethical Guidelines for EECERA, which is the European Early Childhood Education Research Association, who state that 'all research participants, including young children, have a right to feedback on the research process and outcomes. Researchers should debrief participants at significant points in the research process and at the conclusion of the research, providing copies of any reports or publications arising from their participation' (Bertram et al., 2025, p. 15).

The BERA Ethical Guidelines (2024) also state that how studies are disseminated 'should take into account the needs and interests of the communities that were involved in the research. Researchers have a responsibility to share their findings with participants and their wider social groups as fully as possible, while maintaining confidentiality' (2024, p. 33). This means that researchers should continue to communicate with their participants, if they are willing, after data collection so that they can maintain an accurate picture of what their participants' interests are in relation to the findings.

You may also want to talk to your participants about what they think are the best ways to disseminate the findings more widely. We did this recently as part of a study about developing nature-engaging and nature-enhancing pedagogies in baby rooms in urban nursery settings. We asked the babyroom practitioners who had taken part what they thought the key messages from the research were that others ought to know, and what would be the best ways of sharing the information with them. They gave us some really valuable insights, for instance suggesting that short videos distributed via social media would be a good way to engage with practitioners, rather than lengthy documents for them to read.

Parents, Professionals and Policymakers

As well as disseminating to participants, it is important to think about how you can disseminate to other adults who may have a vested interest in your research. We refer to these as the 3 Ps: parents, professionals and policymakers. One group of researchers,

Marsh et al. (2015a, 2015b, 2015c, 2015d) considered this carefully in their study exploring the tablet use of children aged birth to 5 to investigate what preschool children's access to tablets is like, what they do on tablets and how particular apps can promote children's play and creativity. As well as publishing an overall report and articles in academic journals, they also published reports aimed at different audiences, namely early years practitioners, parents, media industry and policymakers.

All of the reports consider the background to the project and some of the main findings, but vary in length, style and content. For instance, the report for practitioners focuses on the implications of the research for those working with young children specifically, for instance how they should provide support and guidance to parents on choosing apps and includes principles for using tablets in Early Childhood settings (Marsh et al., 2015d). Meanwhile the report for parents gives guidance about the importance of setting up safe online habits for young children and also includes a page of 'top tips from parents to parents' (Marsh et al., 2015c, p. 8).

The report for the media industry is the longest and includes detailed information on which apps limit and which apps promote play and creativity for different age groups, so that the media industry can take this information into account when designing new apps for preschoolers (Marsh et al., 2015c). And finally the report for policymakers succinctly summarises the implications of the research for policy, for instance through highlighting how parents would benefit from further support and guidance from, for instance, health visitors on using tablets with under 3s, as well as family digital literacy programmes to be offered by schools and Early Childhood settings. It also highlights how policymakers should consider how Early Childhood settings ensure that children have access to tablets and how those working with young children have guidance on how to use tablets effectively (Marsh et al., 2015a).

By writing different reports for different audiences, Marsh and her colleagues were able to tailor the information they provided so that it focused on the most relevant elements and was written in the most accessible way. They didn't, however, produce a document specifically for children. Can you think about why this might be? We would suggest that it's because there are more appropriate ways to share the findings of your research with young children than writing them up into a report.

Children

We hope that throughout this book you have noticed how we have positioned children, whatever their age, as 'tiny humans' who are powerful and competent (Kemp, Josephidou and Bolshaw, 2025). Because we take this viewpoint, we also acknowledge that it is important to think about how research findings that could impact on them are shared with them. Earlier in this book (Chapter 8: *Centring the voice of the child*) we considered how the UNCRC (UN, 1989) has been instrumental in shifting how we view children in research and the need to take their voice into account, and alongside this has been instrumental in recognising that children have the right to receive information (e.g. as part of Articles 13 and 17).

This is why there is a growing move to disseminate research findings in ways that are appropriate and accessible to children. For instance, Blaisdell et al. conducted research about the experiences of Covid-19 for children of colour in Scotland, and as well as writing up their findings in traditional formats like a report (2022a) and journal article (2024), they also produced a comic (2022b), arguing that 'the use of a comic book to convey findings makes the research output accessible in a visual format' (2022a, p. 5) and also 'offers a different way to engage with the findings, going beyond the written word alone, and particularly highlights the emotionality of the project's findings' (2024, p. 404).

And even if you have conducted a study that hasn't recruited child participants, this doesn't mean that your findings are not relevant to them. For instance, the academic Tom Delahunt (2022) has translated the findings from research he is doing as part of his PhD about the impact of trauma on identity into a children's storybook that shares the message of acceptance and unconditional love, and he's also working on representing his research findings as a play.

Activity 17.2 Disseminating Findings About Digital Play to Children

We spoke earlier about how Marsh et al. (2015a, 2015b, 2015c, 2015d) disseminated their findings about children's digital play to a range of audiences. Take some time to draw up a list of how you think Marsh et al.'s findings could be shared with children. Bear in mind that their research focused on children aged birth to 5.

Reflection

Because the focus of Marsh et al.'s (2015a, 2015b, 2015c, 2015d) study was about digital play, you might have thought about digital ways of sharing their findings with children, such as through a video, online app or computer game. Or you might have thought about non-digital options, like how Blaisdell et al. (2024) disseminated their findings to children through a comic book, or Delahunt (2022) via a picture book. In the next section we will think about other ways to disseminate creatively, many of which are appropriate for child audiences.

HOW CAN YOU SHARE YOUR FINDINGS IN ACCESSIBLE WAYS?

Previously we have written about how in research, language can act as a gatekeeper to people accessing information (Bolshaw and Josephidou, 2018). This may be particularly true for marginalised groups, such as those who speak English as an additional language, who have SEND or are children. We agree with Gary Thomas, who talks of his dislike of 'people who try to make things sound more complicated than they are' (2025, p. 7) and are therefore advocates for writing in ways that are accessible and for using strategies that will help get key messages across. That means thinking about methods of dissemination that go beyond the traditional report, and that do not have financial barriers to access like being behind a paywall, as is often the case with academic journal articles. In this section we will think about how you might want to take opportunities to publish blog posts or in student journals or think about more creative ways to disseminate your research findings to ensure your means of communication meets your audience's needs.

Write a Blog Post

Translating your piece of research into a blog or social media (i.e. LinkedIn) post can be an effective way to have the crux of your study read and understood by a large audience. While there may be barriers to wider audiences reading academic texts published in journal articles because of log-in restrictions, which can create a power imbalance in terms of who has access to information, online blogs hold the advantage that anyone with internet access is able to read them, so in this way they challenge issues of power. You might have a professional blog already, or there's a good chance that your university department might. Alternatively, some Early Childhood professional organisations also seek guest authors for their blogs, such as the Early Childhood Studies Degrees Network's *The Curious Minds – Student Blog*. We have a blog called *Contemplating Childhoods* and welcome guest writers too.

The best advice we can give about writing a blog post is to read a range of other blog posts first, so you get a sense of what a typical style looks like. You might want to have a look at our blog, *Contemplating Childhoods*, or other blogs we author such as *Research Conversations: By and for Education Researchers* and the Open University's *EC@OU Early Childhood Blog*. You will often find that they are written in language that is more accessible than in a journal article and often cite sources that are freely available to access rather than are behind a paywall, which are hyperlinked to rather than cited in line with traditional referencing conventions. They are typically written in the first person and tend not to be overly long – perhaps between 500 to 1500 words – which means the researcher needs to think carefully and skilfully about the main points they want to include. The researcher will also think carefully about who their intended reader is, and tailor their language and focus accordingly.

Publish in a Student Journal

Do you remember how in Chapter 4 (*Joining a research conversation*) we spoke about how when you carry out a piece of research, you are joining a conversation about your area of interest? Before you carry out your data collection, you will have listened to others' voices (as evidenced in your literature review) and when you write up your study you will discuss how your findings link to the wider body of knowledge about your research topic. So, it is important that you think about how you continue the research conversation by publishing your own study, so that others in academia can learn from what you have found out and so the research conversation can continue.

One way that you might want to consider sharing your research so it can be read by other students and academics is through submitting it for publication in a student journal such as the *Early Childhood Studies Degree Network* student journal. We introduced you to this in Chapter 1 *(What is research and why does it matter?)* when we shared a study that an Early Childhood student and nursery practitioner had conducted about listening to babies' perspectives (Kirby, 2024). For instance, Buehring (2023), a recent ECS graduate, shares details of her small-scale study about how six young children aged between 2 and 5 perceive the natural environment. She shares valuable implications for practice, such as how young children can be given opportunities to share their perspectives and what outdoor experiences for children should look like, based on their perspectives, such as ensuring spaces afford both 'physical movement and somewhere to relax' (p. 11).

Find a Creative Way to Disseminate

Finally, you may wish to consider a more creative way to disseminate your research than a blog or student journal. Earlier we spoke about how Blaisdell et al. (2022b) created a comic book to share findings and their study with child participants. Similarly, Ma et al. (2023) developed a graphic novel to share their research findings on children's perspectives about their neighbourhoods during the Covid-19 lockdowns. They also give a comprehensive list of different creative dissemination methods (2023, pp. 3–6):

- Audio-enriched posters
- Cartoons, comics and graphic novels
- Exhibitions
- Infographics
- Leaflets
- Movies/videos
- Podcasts
- Research showcase
- Social media bots
- Storyboarding
- Storytelling
- Theatre
- Video podcasting

- Website creation
- Workshops

Different forms of dissemination will be appropriate for different audiences, participants and research findings. While many of the types outlined by Ma et al. (2023) may be more appropriate for adult audiences, Elgi et al. (2019) disseminated their findings about the role neighbourhoods play in children's health by an 'individual physical activity and food-purchasing behaviour summary, school physical activity and food-purchasing behaviour summary, colouring-in poster, a video, comic, results booklet, school summary report and school data' (p. 257). Had you considered that a colouring-in sheet, for instance, may count as a method of dissemination?

Activity 17.3   Assessing the Strengths and Weaknesses of Creative Approaches to Dissemination

When Ma et al. (2023) list different forms of dissemination, they also set out what the strengths and weaknesses of each type might be. When considering taking one of these creative approaches to sharing your research findings, you will need to consider which are the most important strengths and the most troubling weaknesses when deciding how to share your study. Take some time drawing up a table like Table 17.1 to help you identify what key strengths and weaknesses might be.

Table 17.1   Strengths and weaknesses of creative approaches to dissemination

Creative approach to dissemination	Strengths	Weaknesses
E.g. Cartoons, comics and graphic novels	E.g. Can support understanding of the research findings to those who benefit from pictures to supplement an understanding of written text	E.g. May be time-intensive and expensive to produce

Reflection

Every creative approach to dissemination has its own strengths and weaknesses and it is important to acknowledge that when you think about how to share your research findings. Based on their consideration of the literature, Ma et al. (2023) share the following strengths and weaknesses for cartoons, comics and graphic novels (Table 17.2).

Table 17.2 Strengths and weaknesses of creative approaches to dissemination (continued) (adapted from Ma et al., 2023)

Creative approach to dissemination	Strengths	Weaknesses
Cartoons, comics and graphic novels	• Cartoons are able to elicit strong reactions. • Provides a non-linguistic method for learning and is a visual experience. • Cartoons are widespread and are versatile in terms of topic. • Involves collaboration that can bring out different perspectives. • Gives a voice to those who are not normally portrayed in good light in mainstream media and people who are not talked about at all. • Helps with understanding lived experiences. • Many opportunities for distributing the comics. • Using words and images together could help with maximising the meaning wanted by the researcher. • Graphic novels provide an attractive medium for storytelling. • Graphic novels can be catered towards more mature audiences and can communicate concepts more thoroughly than comics. • Graphic novels involve high audience participation as the audience needs to use their imaginations to fill in the missing gaps from the story.	• Cartoons could be deemed as inappropriate as they tend to be humorous. • Requires a professional cartoonist/illustrator and is labour-intensive for the researcher, as they need to make sure the themes within the cartoon are conveyed properly. • Sacrifices academic detail for impact and accessibility.

Case Study 17.1 Disseminating in Accessible Ways

Radu has completed his undergraduate Early Childhood Studies dissertation about parents' experiences of attending free library groups such as *Stories and Songs* with their children aged birth to 4. He found some interesting things; parents were positive about how attending groups were a good way to meet other parents and how the groups encouraged them to borrow children's books from the library to read at home.

(Continued)

They also, however, spoke about how library staff in the children's section of the library were always welcoming, but they sometimes were made to feel unwelcome by other staff members or patrons of the library, believing this was because their children were noisy. He has already shared his findings with his participants. He thinks that it is important that he disseminates his study with parents more widely, so that they are aware of what other parents say the benefits of attending song and story time groups are, and with library staff so that they can consider whether they need to consider how parents can be made to feel more welcome.

He thinks about what the most effective ways of publishing his study might be. For parents, he decides to summarise his findings about what parents say are the benefits of attending children's library groups into a poster that his local children and family hubs agree to display on their notice boards. His university department publishes a weekly blog featuring student contributions so he decides to use the platform to write a post aimed at those working in public libraries about his findings and what they can do to ensure that everyone feels welcome, which he also shares on his LinkedIn page. He then begins to think about how he can share his findings with children, knowing how parents suggest they benefit too from attending the groups.

KEY POINTS FROM THE CHAPTER

- It is important that you think about taking opportunities for publication, because it will demonstrate your ethical values, it will promote good practice and it will develop your graduate skills.
- When considering publishing your research you need to bear in mind who your intended audience are; think about how to disseminate your study to your participants as well as parents, professionals, policymakers and children.
- There are many different approaches you can take to disseminating your research, including blogs and student journals alongside more creative approaches like posters, comics, colouring sheets, leaflets, online games, websites and workshops.

FURTHER READING

1   Alderson and Morrow (2020) dedicate a chapter, called 'Disseminating and Implementing the Findings', in their brilliant book *The Ethics of Research with Children and Young People* to thinking ethically when it comes to dissemination:

Alderson, P. and Morrow, V. (2020) *The Ethics of Research with Children and Young People*. London: Sage.

2   Ma et al.'s (2023) study about how they shared their research findings about children's perspectives of Covid-19 lockdowns through a graphic novel gives some good context about the importance of research dissemination and how they went about disseminating in a creative way. The graphic novel itself, by Smith et al. (2021), is also freely available to access online:

Ma, C., Green, C., Zhao, J., Egli, V., Clark, T., Donnellan, N. and Smith, M. (2023) 'Creative and visual communication of health research: development of a graphic novel to share children's neighbourhood perspectives of COVID-19 lockdowns in Aotearoa New Zealand', *Visual Communication*. DOI: https://doi.org/10.1177/14703572231157042.

Smith, M., Green, C., Ma, C., Clark, T., Zhao, J., Elgi, V and Donnellan, N. (2021) *Kidshare: Lockdown Perceptions in Aotearoa New Zealand*. DOI: 10.17608/k6.auckland.14073467.

REFERENCES

Alderson, P. and Morrow, V. (2020) *The Ethics of Research with Children and Young People*. London: Sage.

Bertram, T., Pascal, C., Lyndon, H., Formosinho, J., Gaywood, D., Gary, C., Koutoulas, J., Loizou, E., Vandenbroek, M. and Whalley, M. (2025) 'EECERA ethical code for Early Childhood Researchers', *European Early Childhood Education Research Journal*, *33*(1), pp. 4–18. DOI: doi.org/10.1080/1350293X.2024.2445361.

Blaisdell, C., Daramy, F., Sarma, P., McDonald, T., Iradukunda, B., Sarma, A. and Imran, J. (2022a) *The impact of the Covid-19 pandemic on children of colour in Scotland: Final project report*. Available at: www.qmu.ac.uk/media/ch0fysmy/combined-final-draft-of-report-ac.pdf (accessed: 8 July 2025).

Blaisdell, C., Daramy, F., Sarma, P., McDonald, T., Iradukunda, B., Sarma, A. and Imran, J. (2022b) *The Impact of the Covid-19 pandemic on children of colour in Scotland: Visions for change*. Available at: www.qmu.ac.uk/media/cpkogqqd/impact-of-covid-comic-compressed.pdf (accessed: 8 July 2025).

Blaisdell, C., Daramy, F.K. and Sarma, P. (2024) 'The impact of the Covid-19 pandemic on children of colour in Scotland: methodological and ethical reflections', *Amicus Curiae*, *5*(3), pp. 399–428.

Bolshaw, P. and Josephidou, J. (2018) *Introducing Research in Early Childhood*. London: Sage.

British Educational Research Association (2024) *Ethical guidelines for educational research*. 5th Edition. Available at: www.bera.ac.uk/publication/ethical-guidelines-for-educational-research-fifth-edition-2024-online (accessed: 15 June 2025).

Buehring, R. (2023) 'Outdoor voices: children's perception of the natural environment', *Early Childhood Studies Degrees Network Journal*, *1*, pp. 5–12.

Delahunt, T. (2022) *The Wandering Lamb*. Hertfordshire: Firesky Books.

Elgi, V., Carroll, P., Donnellan, N., Mackay, L., Anderson, B. and Smith, M. (2019) 'Disseminating research results to kids: practical tips from the Neighbourhoods for

Active Kids study', *Kōtuitui: New Zealand Journal of Social Sciences Online, 14*(2), pp. 257–75.

Kemp, N., Josephidou, J. and Bolshaw, P. (2025) "Tiny humans' outdoors: understanding the factors that mediate opportunities for babies and toddlers', *Children's Geographies, 23*(2), pp. 219–36.

Kirby, C. (2024) 'Listening to young children and babies', *Early Childhood Studies Degree Network Journal*, Volume 2. Available at: www.ecsdn.org/_files/ugd/c871c5_ a5138422af4240ecaffa1c72680cc4ff.pdf (accessed: 30 July 2025).

Ma, C., Green, C., Zhao, J., Egli, V., Clark, T., Donnellan, N. and Smith, M. (2023) 'Creative and visual communication of health research: development of a graphic novel to share children's neighbourhood perspectives of COVID-19 lockdowns in Aotearoa New Zealand', *Visual Communication*. DOI: https://doi.org/10.1177/14703572231157042.

Marsh, J., Plowman, L., Yamada-Rice, D., Bishop, J.C., Lahmar, J., Scott, F., Davenport, A., Davis, S., French, K., Piras, M., Thornhill, S., Robinson, P. and Winter, P. (2015a) *Exploring play and creativity in pre-schoolers' use of apps: Report for policy makers.* Available at: www.pure.ed.ac.uk/ws/portalfiles/portal/28932777/2015.play_creativity_ with_apps_report_for_policy_makers.pdf (accessed: 27 March 2025).

Marsh, J., Plowman, L., Yamada-Rice, D., Bishop, J.C., Lahmar, J., Scott, F., Davenport, A., Davis, S., French, K., Piras, M., Thornhill, S., Robinson, P. and Winter, P. (2015b) *Exploring play and creativity in pre-schoolers' use of apps: Media industry guide.* Available at: www.sheffield.ac.uk/media/28761/download?attachment (accessed: 27 March 2025).

Marsh, J., Plowman, L., Yamada-Rice, D., Bishop, J.C., Lahmar, J., Scott, F., Davenport, A., Davis, S., French, K., Piras, M., Thornhill, S., Robinson, P. and Winter, P. (2015c) *Exploring play and creativity in pre-schoolers' use of apps: A guide for parents.* Available at: www.researchgate.net/publication/282701609_Exploring_Play_and_Creativity_in_Pre-Schoolers'_Use_of_Apps_A_Guide_for_Parents (accessed: 27 March 2025).

Marsh, J., Plowman, L., Yamada-Rice, D., Bishop, J.C., Lahmar, J., Scott, F., Davenport, A., Davis, S., French, K., Piras, M., Thornhill, S., Robinson, P. and Winter, P. (2015d) *Exploring play and creativity in pre-schoolers' use of apps: Report for early years practitioners.* Available at: www.sheffield.ac.uk/media/28759/download?attachment (accessed: 27 March 2025).

Powell, S. and Goouch, C. (2012) 'Whose hand rocks the cradle? Parallel discourses in the baby room', *Early Years, 32*(2), pp. 113–27.

Smith, A.B. (2011) 'Respecting children's rights and agency', in D. Harcourt, B. Perry and T. Waller (eds), *Researching Young Children's Perspectives: Debating the Ethics and Dilemmas of Educational Research with Children.* Abingdon: Routledge, pp. 11–25.

Smith, M., Green, C., Ma, C., Clark, T., Zhao, J. and Egli, V. and Donnellan, N. (2021) *Kidshare: Lockdown perceptions in Aotearoa New Zealand.* The University of Auckland. DOI: https://doi.org/10.17608/k6.auckland.14073467.v1.

Thomas, G. (2025) *How to Do Your Literature Review.* London: Sage.

United Nations (UN) (1989) *United Nations Convention on the Rights of the Child.* Treaty no. 27541. Available at: www.unicef.org.uk/wp-content/uploads/2016/08/unicef-convention-rights-child-uncrc.pdf (accessed: 16 December 2025).

18

CONCLUSION: WHAT'S NEXT?

CHAPTER OBJECTIVES

By the end of this chapter, you will:

* Know how to think about power issues throughout your research project
* Understand what your next steps in research might be, following the completion of your study
* Know about options for further research and study.

INTRODUCTION

This chapter draws together the main messages of the book giving a recap of the skills and knowledge covered. It includes a checklist to consider power issues throughout the research process. We will think about how those working with young children might be encouraged to also reflect on, and challenge, similar power issues in their work. You may like to consider your next steps in either using your research findings in the workplace or building upon them in postgraduate study and we will help you to do this.

LOOKING BACK ON WHERE WE'VE COME FROM

In this section of the chapter, we will remind ourselves of the key messages of the book and include a brief recap of skills and knowledge covered. As we do so, we hope that you can chart your own progress and the development of your skills (you might like to audit these) and we will show you how you can do this. Such an audit will be useful to you as you put together a CV, apply for graduate jobs or for postgraduate study. But before we go any further, let's remind ourselves of the three key messages of the book.

Three Key Messages

The key messages of this book have been:

- You can carry out a successful research project which can have a meaningful impact however small.
- Your voice counts in research, however novice you may feel, however marginalised you consider yourself to be whether because of job title, education up to this point, ethnic group or socio-economic status.
- Never stop looking for issues of power in both your research activity and beyond in your practice with young children.

We hope that you have taken onboard these messages and that it is learning you can take forward in your career whether academic, personal or professional.

Having arrived at this final chapter, we hope you feel that you can carry out a successful research project. This includes confidence in undertaking all the different steps, understanding the terminology, dealing with the messiness, and knowing the parts which can never be messy and that you must get right, such as ethical approval. We have included a checklist as part of this discussion so that you can audit your skills. We also hope that you are thinking about the impact your research could have, even if it is just to share your findings in the workplace. We use the word 'just' tentatively here, as sharing your findings in the workplace can have great impact; just imagine if you shared something that made one child happy in the setting so able to engage in learning much more, or a colleague whose wellbeing is impacted. Don't forget that your small finding could be one domino in a whole positive chain of events.

This image of the line of dominoes leads us on to our second key message, the importance of your particular voice in research. If you consider for a moment that in a setting where research is never carried out, all the initiatives introduced to support children's learning and development, however well evidenced, are not based on the specific needs, of specific children, practitioners or parents of that specific setting. This is the unique contribution that a practitioner who engages in research can make.

What about those not in practice, who may be wondering if and how their research could ever have an impact. We would argue that there are several ways you could do this. The very fact that you are now sensitised to power issues, ethical considerations, and what is important to, and about young children, means that you are contributing to a society that may be able to see children in a different, less deficit way.

Which leads us to our third key message, the importance of continuing to look for power issues both in your research activity and your practice with, or contribution to discussions about, young children and the important adults in their lives. This can include disrupting discourses which you feel present children and those that care for them in a deficit way by being an ally, being a resistor (Kemp and Josephidou, 2023) and gently changing practices in your own personal sphere of influence.

So, these are the three key messages, let's now look back at each chapter and how they will have contributed to the development of your skills and knowledge.

Recap on Knowledge and Skills

In Table 18.1 we have set out very briefly the key knowledge (what you now know) that you will have gained from each chapter, accompanied by the key skill (what you now can do) each chapter focused on. We do not expect that you will be experts in these research skills, but you will have been introduced to them and will have sufficient understanding to carry out your own small-scale study in Early Childhood.

Table 18.1 Overview of knowledge and skills covered in each chapter

Chapter	Skills	Knowledge
Chapter 1	Baseline audit of research skills and knowledge	What research in Early Childhood is
Chapter 2	Consider power issues in research project	Power issues that exist in the field of ECEC research
Chapter 3	Collect data, choose a research question and method	Circumvent difficulties in collecting empirical data
Chapter 4	Conduct a literature review	Joining a research conversation
Chapter 5	Consider ethics in research project	How ethical approaches address power imbalances
Chapter 6	Autoethnographic approach in research	Importance of adding to breadth of voices that make up ECEC research
Chapter 7	Using creative approaches in Early Childhood research	What counts as data
Chapter 8	Design research which centres voice of child	Importance of including voice of child
Chapter 9	Listening to babies and toddlers	Ethical issues in listening to babies and toddlers
Chapter 10	Observations	Strengths and limitations of observations
Chapter 11	Using questionnaires and surveys	Strengths and limitations of using questionnaires and surveys
Chapter 12	Using interviews	Strengths and limitations of interviews
Chapter 13	Transform raw data into findings	Different ways of analysing data
Chapter 14	Form an argument	Why an argument is important
Chapter 15	Put together an oral research presentation	Structures of presentations and using visual aids
Chapter 16	Put together a poster for a range of audiences	Using posters to disseminate research findings
Chapter 17	Turn your research into a publication	Ways to publish your research
Chapter 18	Audit your research skills	Next steps in your research journey

Now you have reminded yourself of all the skills and knowledge you have acquired thus far on your research journey, you can undertake a simple audit of your skills which will be helpful in determining your next steps.

Audit Your Progress in Research Skills

We are going to focus on the skills element of research here. In Table 18.2, you will find all the skills covered in the book have been listed so that if you want to audit your skill development you could do so. We have completed the first three for an imaginary student so you can see what it might look like.

Table 18.2   Reflecting on your research skills

Skill: How to....	Reflection on how I have developed this skill	My next steps
Do a baseline audit of your research skills and knowledge.	*I have become more confident at carrying out an objective audit of my skills rather than feeling I am supposed to know everything all at once.*	*I can use what I have learnt from this to support other student practitioners.*
Consider power issues in a research project.	*I feel so finely tuned to this issue now that I think I am seeing power issues everywhere.*	*I would like to continue my reading around this – and also keep being mindful.*
Collect data, choose a research question and a method.	*I probably would do it very differently if I carried out my study again. In many ways, I think I have learnt what not to do – but I suppose that is the messiness of research and it was certainly a learning experience.*	*I am going to keep 'noticing' what is happening in my practice and hope I can build on my first project in Masters level work.*
Conduct a narrative and a systematic literature review.		
Consider ethics in a research project.		
Take an autoethnographic approach in research.		
Use creative approaches in Early Childhood research.		
Design research which centres the voice of the child.		
Listen to babies and toddlers in research.		

Skill: How to....	Reflection on how I have developed this skill	My next steps
Carry out different types of observation in Early Childhood research.		
Use questionnaires and surveys in Early Childhood research.		
Use interviews in Early Childhood research.		
Transform raw data into a set of findings, including presenting those findings.		
Form an argument.		
Put together an oral research presentation.		
Put together posters for a range of audiences.		
Turn your research into a publication.		
Audit your research skills.		

Don't forget if you have decided to audit your skills this is useful information which will help inform CVs, job applications or postgraduate study applications.

Activity 18.1   Transferable Skills

It is also useful to note how these gained research skills are transferable in terms of the graduate workplace. Select two skills and consider how you could use them in a wider, professional context. One effective way of doing this is to set them out as 'I can' statements and then consider what this would look like in the professional workplace.

Reflection

Ravi had just handed in their Level 6 dissertation when they carried out this audit; they decided it would help them put together a CV as they were applying for jobs. There was one job that took their eye as an education officer at the nearby football club. They chose two skills to reflect on which they were then able to feed into their CV and cover letter. You can see their reflection and 'I can' statements below:

(Continued)

Skill: How to Consider Power Issues in a Research Project

I can notice when others may be marginalised, not listened to or not given opportunities to contribute. In the professional workplace this means I will be sensitive to my colleagues, ensuring not only that I respect everyone's contribution but that I sensitively notice when others may not have equal opportunities to participate. I will also be perceptive in my work with children and ensure that everyone has the same opportunities to take part or make their views and needs known.

Skill: How to Collect Data, Choose a Research Question and a Method

I can 'notice' issues that it would be helpful to explore, come up with useful questions we need to answer in our professional practice and design approaches to find answers to these questions. In the professional workplace this means that I can use my initiative and will not be dependent on others telling me what needs doing. I will be able to enhance our professional practice because I will always be looking for ways to improve it.

Ravi found this exercise helpful when putting together the application and also to have concrete examples to confidently talk about when they got an interview.

KEEPING AN EYE ON ISSUES OF POWER

In this section of the chapter, we remind ourselves about real issues of power throughout the research process. We include a checklist for you to work through to record how you have addressed this issue throughout your project; you may like to draw on this as you write up your work. This is a discussion you could include as part of your ethics or perhaps even your limitations. We will then consider how this disposition to seek out issues of power and gaining knowledge about how power imbalances in research can occur will enable you to become a much more sensitive and effective practitioner as you use your research knowledge to address power imbalances in practice.

Power Issue Checklist

Throughout the book we have stressed the importance of being mindful of the power issues that exist in research at each stage of the process. Table 18.3 reminds you of the questions you could ask as you progress.

Table 18.3 Questions to ask at each stage

Step	Questions about power
1 Decide on an area of focus.	Did I choose an area of focus that favours voices already privileged in research or society? Am I contributing to harmful stereotypes by having chosen this area of focus?
2 Read about area of focus.	Did I ensure that I included a wide range of diverse voices in my reading?
3 Decide on a potential research question.	Does my question contain anything that would support my participants being seen in a deficit way?
4 Read some more.	Have I discussed with my peers, tutor, library support, ways of making the marginalised voice stronger in my work?
5 Decide on methodology.	Have I considered how my methodology may mitigate against issues of power or conversely reinforce power dynamics?
6 Decide on data collection methods.	How will my data collection methods and approach foreground more marginalised voices?
7 Obtain ethical approval.	In addition to ethical compliance have I considered how my ethical decisions will mitigate against issues of power or conversely foreground more marginalised voices?
8 Collect data.	Have I listened respectfully to my participants and questioned any tendency I have to make assumptions?
9 Analyse data.	Have I asked a critical friend to question me on my analysis to foreground any assumptions I may be making?
10 Write up findings.	Have I shared my findings with my participants so that I am including their voice?
11 Analyse findings.	Which literature, theoretical or conceptual frameworks am I using to consider the So What of my findings? And how might they reinforce issues of power?
12 Decide on an argument and write up full report.	Does my argument reinforce power dynamics or promote a deficit view of my participants or other members of society?
13 Disseminate findings.	Have I ensured I have disseminated to a variety of audiences in a way that is useful and accessible to them?

NEXT STEPS AND MOVING FORWARDS

In this section of the chapter we will think about what your next steps might be following the completion of your successful project. We will discuss how you might use your research findings in the workplace and options for further research and study.

Your Practice

Without a doubt, if you are working in practice, what you have learnt through undertaking a research project will have impacted on how you see both children and your pedagogy. Research can often contradict practice, which (ironically) is said, in turn, to be research informed, and this contradiction can be a key issue in Early Childhood. We think for example of all the research around play which continually stresses its importance in terms of children's holistic development (Children's Alliance, 2024). Yet, within practice there are ever increasing concerns that pedagogy is becoming more and more formal as very young children undergo a 'schoolification' (Murray, 2025) which squeezes out play in favour of less holistic teaching and learning approaches which are more in line with pedagogies appropriate for older children. To resolve this tension, practitioners working with young children are already skilled in asking themselves the key questions to bridge the gap which can exist between research and practice. These questions arise from their understanding of the unique child in front of them, as they ask: What are they doing? What are they learning? What do they need? Who do they need us to be? How are they feeling? As skilled practitioners, they have a knowledge that comes not from research but from experience; the question is: How does this experience knowledge compare with research knowledge?

This is a concern explored by Reinertsen and Aslanian (2025) in their powerful and provoking conceptual paper 'The real and the ridiculous of Early Childhood education and care research'. The authors suggest that not all knowledge about Early Childhood education and care is seen as valid and that this discrepancy means that there are 'blind spots' in our pedagogies with young children. These 'blind spots' occur because the importance of practitioner knowledge is not included in the research informed policies they are obliged to incorporate into their practice. We have used the phrase 'joining a research conversation' often in this book but we have also emphasised that some voices are silenced or perhaps even not welcomed into this conversation although, as is the case of the early years practitioner, they have a great deal to contribute. This situation arises from perceived hierarchies of knowledge which recognise that some people's knowledge is more important than others (Ratuva, n.d.) with practitioner knowledge being low down on the list. This is a 'ridiculous' situation, if we come back to Reinertsen and Aslanian's terminology (2025); as they argue, practitioners have a wealth of knowledge that they can contribute to key pedagogies with young children. They have their own ways of 'knowing' that Early Childhood Research would do well to recognise.

Reinertsen and Aslanian (2025) poignantly ask, 'What happens to the knowledge gained on the kindergarten floor?' And this might be a good question to ask yourself if you work with young children or are a parent or carer. What happens with all the knowledge you have gained? Is anyone interested? How is it captured? Does anyone ask you about it? Can you use it to rebut and push back on initiatives that you don't see working well for the children in your care? Can you use this knowledge to impact on practice or inform policy? We believe this is why it is so important for Early Childhood practitioners to undertake research as you have done in your small-scale study; working in this context, engaging in Early Childhood Research and being a knowledge contributor is a political act (Eacott, 2014).

Further Research and Study

If you want to think beyond practice and consider how you might continue to engage in further research opportunities, there are also various options open to you, including looking for alumni opportunities, free Early Childhood online conferences, further accredited study at Masters or doctoral level and free courses.

For example, the ECSDN (Early Childhood Studies Degree Network) holds a free online conference every year which is attended by academics, practitioners and students. Although online, it is a great networking event and provokes rich conversations about research and practice. Other organisations which offer free or low-price training are Early Education and The Froebel Trust.

You may decide on further study; for example, you could undertake a Masters degree. Many universities will have an online option, if it is more difficult for you to attend face to face. Many people who do a Masters in Education or Early Childhood complete this while working fulltime so the structure of the programme is usually built around this constraint. As part of a Masters you will usually undertake a piece of research, so this is a great opportunity to build on what you did at undergraduate level and/or to carry out research in your workplace.

Finally, if you would like to continue studying for your own interest, without completing any assignments, many universities have a range of free online learning opportunities. For example, the Open University has a range of courses offered to parents, practitioners, academics etc. on a range of subjects including Early Childhood and research subject knowledge (OpenLearn, n.d.).

Case Study 18.1   An Ongoing Research Journey

Mel Green is a Lecturer in Education Studies. She talks here about her ongoing research journey from undergraduate, through Masters to her current doctoral studies, including what motivates and inspires her in her research work. Mel has two boys, one of whom is autistic, and she has co-authored a book examining Black mothers' experiences of raising autistic children (Malcolm and Green, 2025).

> Someone described my research profile as being a bit like a magpie because I go for all the shiny things rather than have a sort of specialism. I think it was said in a negative way, but it really got me thinking. I realised I do go for things that I am passionate about when it comes to research. I consider myself to be interdisciplinary, and I think that's what my research reflects with my varied focus on the experience of black mothers raising autistic children, anti-racist work in higher education, working with online students, and identity work.

(Continued)

All the research skills that I've developed from each project have been transferable to the others.

When I think about my research journey, I remember a trekking trip I went on and the many experiences over the four days such as sleeping up high on the mountain, nearly getting altitude sickness, and having conversations in broken Spanish with my guides. All these experiences were evidence of me growing as a person. And then when we got to the destination, I was like, is this it? I see similarities here with my research journey. I often get told to just finish my thesis and hand it in because no one is going to read it anyway. That made me wonder about the point of a research thesis and why I am putting my heart and soul into something that no one's going to read.

So I'm not taking that advice; I hope my work is going to be transformative. As an undergraduate, I felt I just had to cite others, but not really have an opinion. The experience of going from undergraduate to postgraduate has made me see the importance of lived experience and how that is relevant, rigorous, and academic. So I have gone from being someone who's really focused on the words of white men who are long gone to looking at work that has been developed by Caribbean scholars, black women, auto ethnography, and critical ethnography.

When I started working in higher education, I had many assumptions about what it was like. As I began teaching online, I felt an identity shift and I began to question many things such as who am I if I'm not in the same room as my learners? How do I teach in an online space? Who do I want to be in this space? So it felt perfect to take these questions into a doctoral research project. So this is what motivates me in research, all my own lived experiences of teaching online, being a black mother raising autistic children and being the first of my family to go to university and my experiences there. All these areas of interest have made me question my own experiences and motivate me to making things better for others going through similar things by transforming practice.

If I think back to my research journey, I remember how I used to cry after every supervision. One thing that's happened to me is that I have developed a real confidence in my abilities and my research choices so that when my supervisors counter something that I'm saying or question why I'm doing something, I can confidently explain. You know, those people with doctorates and professorships had to start somewhere to get to where they are now. They've had to learn too. So I would encourage others who are starting out on their research journey to believe that your understanding of things is a valid understanding that can be built upon. I suppose it's revering less those who have gone before you in research. It's realising that we all started somewhere and this is your beginning.

KEY POINTS FROM THE CHAPTER

- Many of the skills you have learnt by undertaking research are transferable to the professional graduate context.
- Research projects, however small, are able to have an important impact.
- Understanding about power issues throughout the research process can also impact on the way you view your professional work with young children.
- There are lots of options open to you now you have finished your first research project, whether you would like to do further study, research or develop your practice.

FURTHER READING

1   If you would like to read Mel Green's co-authored book which we mentioned in the case study, this will give you further insights into how she has used her lived experiences to not only inform her research but also to support others who may be going through similar things to the ones she has experienced.

Malcolm, C. and Green, M. (2025) *Mothering at the Margins: Black Mothers Raising Autistic Children in the UK*. Lived Places Publishing.

2   This interesting, and provocative, paper which we have drawn on in this chapter challenges us to consider what counts as knowledge as far as practice with young children is concerned.

Reinertsen, A. and Aslanian, T. (2025) 'The real and the ridiculous of Early Childhood education and care research: A multi-ethnography of knowledge creation', *Contemporary Issues in Early Childhood*. Available at: https://journals. sagepub.com/doi/10.1177/14639491251352214 (accessed 2 January 2026).

3   This thought-provoking article by an academic at the University of Canterbury, New Zealand, invites us to consider which knowledge is considered to be the most important and why that is the case.

Ratuva, S. (n.d.) *Hierarchies of knowing*. Available at: www.acu.ac.uk/the-acu-review/ hierarchies-of-knowing/ (accessed 30 July 2025).

REFERENCES

Bolshaw and Josephidou, J. (2018) *Introducing Research in Early Childhood*. London: Sage.

Children's Alliance (2024) *The power of play: Building a creative Britain*. Available at: https://childrensalliance.org.uk/wp-content/uploads/2024/05/Play-Policy-18Apr2024-Childrens-Alliance.pdf (accessed 1 August 2025).

Costa, A. and Kallick, B. (1993) 'Through the lens of a critical friend', *Educational Leadership*, 51(2), pp. 49–52.

Eacott, S. (2014) 'Research as a political activity: the fallacy of data speaking for themselves', *Leadership and Policy Quarterly*, 2(4), pp. 223–35.

Flood, A. (2016) *'Post-truth' named word of the year by Oxford Dictionaries*. Available at: www.theguardian.com/books/2016/nov/15/post-truth-named-word-of-the-year-by-oxford-dictionaries (accessed: 31 July 2025).

Kemp, N. and Josephidou, J. (2023) 'Creating spaces called hope: the critical leadership role of owner/managers in developing outdoor pedagogies for infants and toddlers', *Early Years*, 43(3), pp. 641–55.

Malcolm, C. and Green, M. (2025) *Mothering at the Margins: Black Mothers Raising Autistic Children in the UK*. Lived Places Publishing.

Murray, J. (2025) 'Premature schoolification during Early Childhood hinders later academic success and productivity', *International Journal of Early Years Education*, 33(1), pp. 1–7. DOI: https://doi.org/10.1080/09669760.2025.2481759.

OpenLearn (n.d.) *Dive in and start learning*. Available at: www.open.edu/openlearn/ (accessed: 1 August 2025).

Ratuva, S. (n.d.) *Hierarchies of knowing*. Available at: www.acu.ac.uk/the-acu-review/hierarchies-of-knowing/ (accessed: 30 July 2025).

Reinertsen, A. and Aslanian, T. (2025) 'The real and the ridiculous of Early Childhood education and care research: a multi-ethnography of knowledge creation', *Contemporary Issues in Early Childhood*. Available at: https://journals.sagepub.com/doi/10.1177/14639491251352214 (accessed 2 January 2026).

INDEX

Page numbers followed by "f" indicate figures; those followed by "t" indicate tables.